ON TARGET

BART STARR HOLDS THE PRO RECORD IN PASSING EFFICIENCY— 56.8 %...

...AND IN NOT BEING INTERCEPTED —HIS N.FL. RECORD IS AT 277 !

I FEEL OUT OF TOUCH

ERRY YS, ANDING ENDER

75

WO

WITH ITS DOUBLE-HALFBACK THREAT, CITY MATCHES ANY PRO BALL FOR R YARDAGE AT ONE P

BERT COAN, HB

MIKE GARRETT, HB

A PURE CASE OF DOUBLE JEOPARDY

WHEN IT WAS JUST A GAME

WHEN IT WAS JUST A
GAME

REMEMBERING THE FIRST SUPER BOWL

HARVEY FROMMER
FOREWORD BY FRANK GIFFORD

TAYLOR TRADE PUBLISHING
Lanham • Boulder • New York • London

Published by Taylor Trade Publishing
An imprint of The Rowman & Littlefield Publishing Group, Inc.
4501 Forbes Boulevard, Suite 200, Lanham, Maryland 20706
www.rowman.com

Unit A, Whitacre Mews, 26-34 Stannary Street, London SE11 4AB

Distributed by NATIONAL BOOK NETWORK

British Library Cataloguing in Publication Information Available

Library of Congress Cataloging-in-Publication Data

Frommer, Harvey.
  When it was just a game : remembering the first Super Bowl / by Harvey Frommer.
      pages cm
  Summary: "Written by acclaimed sports author and oral historian Harvey Frommer and with an introduction by pro football Hall of Famer Frank Gifford, When It Was Just a Game tells the fascinating story of the ground-breaking AFL-NFL World Championship Football game played on January 15, 1967: Packers vs. Chiefs"— Provided by publisher.
  Includes bibliographical references and index.
  ISBN 978-1-58979-920-2 (hardback) — ISBN 978-1-58979-921-9 (electronic) 1. Football— United States—History. 2. National Football League—History. 3. American Football League— History. I. Title.
  GV954.F76 2015
  796.330973—dc23   2015005712

Printed in the United States of America

Incidentally, I hate that name—Super Bowl.
I wish you guys would change it to THE Bowl.

—Vince Lombardi, December 19, 1966

For Myrna.
Still the golden chance
I didn't let pass me by.

Contents

Foreword

IT WAS LONG AGO and far away that I was at the Los Angeles Memorial Coliseum, a field I had played football on as a college All-American. Now it was January 15, 1967, and I was in the beginning stages of what would become a long and highly successful television broadcasting career.

I was a member of the CBS team, which, along with NBC, was televising the game. That in itself was something new for this newest of football games, which pitted the Kansas City Chiefs of the American Football League against the Green Bay Packers of the National Football League.

No one really knew what to expect. No one expected the contest officially called the AFL–NFL World Championship Game to become what it became—the Super Bowl, the greatest sports event in history. No one perhaps except NFL commissioner Pete Rozelle, who wanted it to become bigger than the World Series.

I am one of the more than 60 oral history voices in this book talking about the game and the action, as well as remembering my experiences with the great Vince Lombardi pregame and postgame. As you will see, pregame was much more of a challenge than postgame, when I was there with Pete Rozelle and my former coach, "Vinny," as he was presented with the championship trophy made by Tiffany, an award that would be named after him just a few years later—the Lombardi Trophy.

With this detailed oral and narrative history, author Harvey Frommer has created a dramatic narrative arc that takes us back in time. It includes information on the merger of the American Football League and National Football League; the coaches, Vince Lombardi of Green Bay and Hank Stram of Kansas City; pregame preparations and struggles; the game itself on that sunny day in Los Angeles and the action on the field of play; and the postgame fallout. The book also features a special chapter on what happened to many of the participants afterward.

Through exclusive interviews with players, coaches, the media, and viewers of the game, this volume enables us to relive a special time in American sports and culture, making this the definitive book on the first Super Bowl.

Frank Gifford

NBC announcer Paul Christman and CBS announcer (and member of the Pro Football Hall of Fame) Frank Gifford discuss Super Bowl I, January 15, 1967. Since there were separate TV contracts for the old AFL and NFL, the game was broadcast by both networks.

AP Photo/NFL Photos

The Roster

BILL ADAMS was a close friend of Lamar Hunt, a college fraternity brother, and a well-known Dallas, Texas, area attorney.

FRED ARBANAS was a prototype tight end and member of the All-Time AFL Team. Number 84 was a Kansas City Chief standout from 1963 to 1970. He began his pro career with the Dallas Texans.

BOBBY BELL was a Pro Football Hall of Fame linebacker/defensive end who played for the Kansas City Chiefs. An AFL All-Star for six straight seasons and a three-time NFL Pro Bowler, he is also a member of the Chiefs Hall of Fame.

KEN BOWMAN is a member of the Green Bay Packers Hall of Fame. Born in Milam, Illinois, and graduating the University of Wisconsin, he was the starting center for the Pack from 1964 to 1973.

TOMMY BROOKER came into the AFL with the Dallas Texans after playing at the University of Alabama for "Bear" Bryant. Primarily a kicker, he also played tight end. A thigh injury prevented him from playing in the 1967 Super Bowl.

JOE BROWNE began working in the NFL office as a college intern in 1965. He is now senior advisor to the commissioner and spends a great deal of his time working on retired player issues. He is the longest-serving league office employee in NFL history.

ED BUDDE played in 177 games for the Chiefs from 1963 to 1976. An explosive 6-foot, 5-inch, 265-pound guard out of Michigan State, he made seven AFL All-Star/Pro Bowl appearances. President of the Kansas City Chiefs Alumni Association, the powerful Budde was named to the All-Time AFL Team by the Pro Football Hall of Fame.

CHRIS BURFORD is in the Chiefs Hall of Fame. An All-American selection at Stanford, the talented wide receiver played for Kansas City from 1963 to 1967.

ANN BUSSEL is a native of Florida, director of the Shepard Broad Foundation, and a woman who still remembers going with her husband to the NFL–AFL World Championship Game in 1967.

CLIFF CHRISTL is the Packers' official historian. He grew up in Green Bay during the Lombardi era and later spent 35 years as a sportswriter for papers in Green Bay and Milwaukee, writing about the Packers for much of that time. He has been a member of the Pro Football Hall of Fame Selection Committee since 2002 and authored or coauthored four books on the Packers or pro football.

PAT COCHRAN is the widow of Lombardi era Green Bay assistant coach Red Cochran.

HOWARD COSELL was a famed ABC sportscaster on *Monday Night Football*. In 1993, *TV Guide* named him All-Time Best Sportscaster. The aggressive Cosell was inducted into the Television Hall of Fame in 1994.

BILL CURRY was a first-year starter at center who later started in Super Bowl III and Super Bowl V for the Baltimore Colts. He also served as president of the National Football League Players Association and played in two Pro Bowls.

WILLIE DAVIS was a defensive end for the Packers from 1960 to 1969. A five-time Pro Bowl selection, he is a member of the Pro Football Hall of Fame.

LEN DAWSON was quarterback for the Kansas City Chiefs in three AFL Championship Games and Super Bowl I, and directed the Kansas City victory in Super Bowl IV, winning the MVP award. He was sports director of KMBC-TV in Kansas City for many years and longtime cohost of HBO's popular program *Inside the NFL*.

BOYD DOWLER was one of the sport's great wide receivers, who played 12 seasons for the Green Bay Packers and Washington Redskins. A two-time Pro Bowler and member of the Packers Hall of Fame, he is also a member of the 1960s NFL All-Decade Team.

STEVE FOLVEN is a Babe Ruth impersonator. He still has memories of watching the first Super Bowl.

JOHN FORTUNATO, Ph. D., is author of *Commissioner: The Legacy of Pete Rozelle*. He is also professor and area chair of communication and media management at Fordham University's Schools of Business.

FRANK GIFFORD is a Pro Football Hall of Famer, sportscaster, and commentator for the first Super Bowl.

MARTY GLICKMAN was a Jewish track and field competitor who went on to a career as sportscaster for more than half a century. He and his distinctive voice were behind the microphone for numerous types of games.

PETER GOLENBOCK is author of nine *New York Times* best sellers, including *The Bronx Zoo* (with Sparky Lyle), *Number 1* (with Billy Martin), *American Prince* (with Tony Curtis), and *Personal Fouls*. He lives in St. Petersburg, Florida.

CURT GOWDY was one of the greatest announcers in sports history. He was on the scene as one of the broadcasters for the first Super Bowl.

FORREST GREGG had a Hall of Fame career, starring for the Green Bay Packers at right tackle and winning five championships. He also played for the Dallas Cowboys and was head coach of three NFL and two Canadian Football League teams.

BILL GUTMAN is a longtime freelance writer of many sports books, including two on the Super Bowl.

MICKEY HERSKOWITZ is a Texas-based author of 60-plus books, Hall of Fame sports columnist, and former Warner Endowed Chair of Journalism at Sam Houston State University. A former pro football executive and an original partner in the Houston Rockets, he was one of the owners of the 1986 Breeders' Cup Classic winner Skywalker. At the first Super Bowl, he was assistant director of operations, reporting to Commissioner Rozelle in New York City.

DAVE HILL was starting right tackle for the Kansas City Chiefs in Super Bowl I and Super Bowl IV. Number 73 played from 1963 to 1974 and was an iron man, a starter in 149 games for the franchise. He is a member of the Chiefs Hall of Fame.

PAUL HORNUNG was a star running back for the Green Bay Packers from 1957 to 1966, winning four NFL titles and the first Super Bowl. The Hall of Famer was one of the most versatile players in team history. He was named NFL MVP for 1961.

SHARRON HUNT is the daughter of Lamar Hunt. She was at Super Bowl I as a seven-year-old.

LAMAR HUNT JR. is a son of Lamar Hunt and was at Super Bowl I. The founder of Loretto Properties and Loretto Charities, he is a member of the founding family of the Kansas City Chiefs. He was a flutist in the Kansas City Symphony for nine seasons.

JERRY IZENBERG is one of three daily newspaper columnists to have attended every Super Bowl. *Newark Star-Ledger* Columnist Emeritus and a sportswriter for almost 60 years, he is a member of the New Jersey Sports Hall of Fame.

WILLIAM O. JOHNSON was a longtime senior editor at *Sports Illustrated*. His groundbreaking sports and media book *Super Spectator and the Electric Lilliputians* was published in 1971.

DOUG KELLY was an assistant director of public relations for the Kansas City Chiefs from 1974 to 1982.

JERRY KRAMER had an illustrious 11-year career with the Green Bay Packers as an offensive lineman, a key component in the "Packers' Sweep." A five-time All-Pro and member of the NFL 50th Anniversary All-Time Team, he is a member of the Packers Hall of Fame but strangely not in the Pro Football Hall of Fame. Kramer is author of the best-selling *Instant Replay* and other football-related books.

CHUCK LANE was director of public relations for the Green Bay Packers intermittently from March 1966 to 1979.

BUD LEA was a longtime sportswriter for the *Milwaukee Sentinel*. He spent many decades covering the Green Bay Packers.

SUSAN LOMBARDI is the daughter of Marie and Vince Lombardi.

BOB LONG was a wide receiver for the Green Bay Packers from 1964 to 1967. He is the only player to have played for both the Packers and Washington Redskins under Vince Lombardi.

ED LOTHAMER was a defensive tackle who played eight seasons for the Kansas City Chiefs from 1964 to 1972.

MICHAEL MACCAMBRIDGE is one of the top authorities on professional and college football in the United States. His *America's Game: The Epic Story of How Pro Football Captured a Nation* was cited as one of the most distinguished works of nonfiction by the *Washington Post* in 2004. MacCambridge' s work has appeared in such publications as the *New York Times*, the *Wall Street Journal*, the *Washington Post*, *Sports Illustrated*, and *GQ*.

JERRY MAGEE was a sportswriter in San Diego for almost 52 years, retiring from the *San Diego Union-Tribune* in 2008. He has attended almost every Super Bowl.

CURTIS MCCLINTON was a powerful back for the Dallas Texans and Kansas City Chiefs from 1962 to 1969 and a three-time AFL All-Star. He was the first AFL player to catch a touchdown pass in the Super Bowl.

HOWARD MCHENRY was a multifaceted entrepreneur and an automobile dealer for more than three decades in Kansas City. He was a member of the "Red Coater" organization, founded to support the Chiefs.

BILL MCNUTT III was a ball boy at the Kansas City Chiefs training camp for the Super Bowl I and Super Bowl IV teams. For 50 years, he has been an owner of the Collin Street Bakery in Corsicana, Texas, which ships its famous Christmas cakes to more than 150 countries.

CURT MERZ played guard from 1962 to 1968 in the AFL. He was in the starting lineup for the Kansas City Chiefs in Super Bowl I and is a member of the Missouri Sports Hall of Fame.

GEORGE MITROVITCH is president of the City Club of San Diego and the Denver Forum, as well as chair of the Great Fenway Park Writers Series.

BOB MOORE is the longest tenured public relations director in Kansas City Chiefs history, having served from 1989 until he moved to the position of team historian and curator of the club's Hall of Honor in 2009.

MURRAY OLDERMAN is a Hall of Fame sportswriter and award-winning sports cartoonist who has followed pro football since 1952. He is also author of 14 books.

TOM OLEJNICZAK has been a member of the Executive Committee of the Board of Directors of the Green Bay Packers since 1986. His father Dominic, former president of the Packers, hired Vince Lombardi. Tom grew up with the teams of the glory years in Green Bay.

PAT PEPPLER was scouting and personnel director of the Green Bay Packers during the Lombardi era, from 1963 to 1971, serving in the same capacity with the Miami Dolphins. He also held front-office positions with the Houston Oilers, Atlanta Falcons, and New Orleans Saints.

MILT RICHMAN was sports editor at United Press International from 1972 to 1985. He spent 42 years with UPI. In 1981, the prolific Richman was inducted into the Writer's Wing of the Baseball Hall of Fame. He died five years later, at the age of 64, from a heart attack.

DAVE ROBINSON is a 2013 inductee into the Pro Football Hall of Fame and member of the Green Bay Packers Hall of Fame and College Football Hall of Fame. A three-time Pro Bowler, he was a big-time defender for a decade with Green Bay during the Lombardi years and after. Robinson was selected to the 1960s NFL All-Decade Team.

JOHNNY ROBINSON played a dozen years in the AFL, nine of them for the Chiefs. He is considered one of the great safeties of all time. Robinson is a member of the Pro Football Hall of Fame's AFL All-Time Team.

PETE ROZELLE was NFL commissioner from 1960 to 1989 and a driving force behind the creation of the Super Bowl, known in its first two contests as the AFL–NFL World Championship Game.

TOM SAHARSKY is a member of the Green Bay Packers shareholders group whose ancestors were part of the original group.

BOB SCHNELKER coached the Green Bay Packers from 1966 to 1971. His relationship with Vince Lombardi dated back to his time as a wide receiver with the New York Giants.

BART STARR is a Hall of Fame quarterback who played for the Green Bay Packers from 1956 to 1971 and was head coach from 1975 to 1983. Among many awards, he was selected as number 51 player of all-time by NFL.com and named to the 1960s NFL All-Decade Team.

WILL STEWART "SMOKEY" STOVER signed on to play during the 1960 AFL season as an original Dallas Texan. Converted into a top-flight linebacker by Coach Hank Stram, he played his entire seven-season AFL career with the Texans and Kansas City Chiefs.

DALE STRAM is the son of the late football coaching legend Hank Stram and actively involved in celebrating Hank'sheritage. He heads up Dale Stram & Associates, a real estate group.

PHYLLIS STRAM is the widow of Hank Stram.

JIM TAYLOR played from 1958 to 1967 as a bruising fullback for the Green Bay Packers. The Hall of Famer was the "power" in Lombardi's power sweep and retired as Green Bay's leading rusher. Number 31 is the author of *The Fire Within*.

LU VAUGHN attended the first Super Bowl game as a fan as part of a junket from Kansas City.

FRED WALLIN is a longtime sports radio talk show host presently at Sports Byline. As a youngster, he watched the first Super Bowl at his home in the Los Angeles area.

PAUL ZIMMERMAN was a sports columnist for the *New York Post* and author of several outstanding books on football.

Pete Rozelle, commissioner of the NFL from 1960–1989.

Photofest

Backstory

We'll start signing Negroes when the Harlem Globetrotters start signing whites.

> —George Preston Marshall, owner of the Washington Redskins

I come to you with clean hands.

> —Pete Rozelle

Pro football was nothing until he became commissioner.

> —Red Auerbach, legendary Boston Celtics coach and president

The merger started the most successful growth period in the NFL. We were able to create the Super Bowl, kind of the icing on the cake. Interest kept rolling until it was the most popular spectator sport in the United States.

> —Tex Schramm, Dallas Cowboys general manager

A LOT OF twists and turns, evolution and revolution, mistakes and major steps forward, colorful characters, dedicated idealists, and guys with an eye on making a quick buck—and much more—were part of the mix in the history of professional football before it finally found solid footing and great success in the sports landscape of the United States and became a global phenomenon.

It was not until August 20, 1920, at a meeting in Canton, Ohio, at the Jordan and Hupmobile Auto Showroom of the owner of the Canton Bulldogs, that a semblance of professional football as we know it came to be.

At the meeting were seven men, including the legendary Jim Thorpe, who would later become the organization's first president. There were delegates from the Bulldogs, Akron Pros, Cleveland Indians, and Dayton Triangles. They formed the new league—the American Professional Football Conference. One hundred dollars was the announced membership fee for that first season. It was reported that none of those original teams actually paid what was then considered a hefty fee.

The initial teams had a decidedly small-town, midwestern feel: Akron Professionals, Canton Bulldogs, Chicago Cardinals, Cleveland Tigers, Dayton Triangles, Decatur Staleys, Hammond Pros, Rochester (New York) Jeffersons, Rock Island (Illinois) Independents, and Muncie Flyers.

Teams came and went during the league's first years. The idea of organized football was appealing, but there was a lot of challenge, work, and money involved. Only four clubs survived that first season in 1920: Akron, Buffalo, Canton, and Decatur.

From the start, African Americans were playing pro football. In 1920, Fritz Pollard, standout halfback at Brown and an All-American, starred for the Akron Pros. He and Bobby Marshall were the NFL's first black players. The next year, Pollard became the league's first black head coach. He also maintained his position as one of the best players in pro football.

Approximately 13 African American players appeared on NFL rosters between 1920 and 1933. Paul Robeson, who later gained great fame as a singer, actor, and civil rights leader, was encouraged by Pollard to play for Akron in 1921. The following year, Robeson had a stint with Milwaukee. Playing football enabled the powerful athlete to pay his way through Columbia University Law School.

In 1920, the Decatur Staleys had a net profit of $1,800. All 22 members of the team shared in the profits. "[They] practiced every afternoon, six days a week, on a very well-kept baseball field owned by the Staley Company" (Frommer, 1974, 187).

The next year, the Decatur franchise moved to Chicago after being sold to player-coach George Halas, who went on to become one of the most important figures in the first half-century of pro football. Halas gave the Staleys a new name—the Chicago Bears.

On June 24, 1922, the American Professional Football Conference was renamed the National Football League, eliminating the organization's unwieldy name and evocation of a soccer league. By the mid-1920s, the struggling and cumbersome NFL included 25 teams, each experiencing varying degrees of success and hardship.

On April 23, 1927, in a season where professional baseball was king and the New York Yankees of Murderers' Row were the talk of the town, the NFL made some tough decisions. Weak and struggling franchises were dropped. The league shrank from 22 franchises to 12. It also moved away from its midwestern roots. The focus was now on placing teams in populous cities in the East to solidify the league and make it more financially solvent.

In 1932, the NFL recorded official statistics for the first time. It was a good thing. A bad thing was the behavior of racist George Preston Marshall, who made his money in the commercial laundry business. Using some of that cash, he became owner of the Boston football team. Marshall convinced other NFL owners to institute a policy of total racial segregation. They didn't have to heed the suggestions of a bigot, but they did. No blacks played in the NFL between 1933 and 1946.

Marshall moved his Boston Redskins to Washington in 1937. Born in segregated West Virginia, the Redskins owner opposed adding blacks to his team's roster, claiming it would alienate fans. "We'll start signing Negroes when the Harlem Globetrotters start signing whites," he snapped.

By 1962, the Globetrotters still did not have whites, and the Redskins still had not fielded a black player for decades. Change, however, loomed. The U.S. secretary of the interior, Stewart Udall, in President John F. Kennedy's cabinet, said he would evict the Redskins from publicly funded RFK Stadium if a black player was not signed. Marshall gave in.

Ernie Davis, the black Syracuse running back and Heisman Trophy winner, was the number-one draft pick by the Washington Redskins. A week later, Davis was traded to Cleveland for Bobby Mitchell and Leroy Jackson. John Nisby was also signed and Ron Hatcher drafted. The NFL (and the 'Skins, with four for a time) now had at least one African American player on each team. Sadly, Ernie Davis never played in the NFL. He died in 1963, of leukemia.

Although the NFL Draft started in 1939, no franchise selected an African American player until 1949. Even during World War II, when the NFL was shorthanded, no blacks needed to apply. They knew bigotry barred the door for them. Demand for able-bodied men for the war effort depleted NFL rosters. Many nonprime-time players were brought in. Teams reduced their rosters by five players to survive. In 1943, the Steelers of Pittsburgh and the Eagles of Philadelphia became the Phil-Pitt Steeler-Eagles, called the "Steagles" by fans. The Chicago Cardinals and Steelers merged in 1944 and 1945, as Card-Pitt, a team so mediocre its own fans called it the "Carpets." The Brooklyn and Boston franchises fused in 1945, becoming the "Yanks."

In 1939, at the University of California, Los Angeles, Jack Roosevelt Robinson led the nation in rushing, with a dozen yards a carry. The NFL was segregated. Major League Baseball was segregated. Thus, the man they called "Robby" played in the Negro Leagues. With the help of Branch Rickey in 1947, Robinson shattered baseball's color line as a member of the Brooklyn Dodgers. There is no telling how good a player he would have been in the NFL, but all estimates are that he would have been very good.

The all-white NFL Cleveland Rams moved to Los Angeles in 1946. Their plan was to play games in Memorial Coliseum, a venue supported with public funds and one that could not be leased to a segregated team. Under pressure, the Rams signed former UCLA standouts Kenny Washington, a running back, and Woody Strode, a receiver. Both had been teammates of Jackie Robinson at UCLA. It was reported that all hell broke loose among NFL owners at the signing. The signing was revolutionary. Washington and Strode were the first African American players after 13 years of a whites-only atmosphere in the NFL.

The Chicago Bears were a whites-only team their first 32 seasons. Although the New York Giants came into being in 1925, the first blacks they signed came in 1948. The Pittsburgh Steelers featured only white players from 1934 until 1952.

On October 22, 1939, the first televised professional football game was transmitted in the New York City area, when NBC broadcast a game between the Brooklyn Dodgers and Philadelphia Eagles at Ebbets Field. According to the Pro Football Hall of Fame, there were 500 television sets in the Big Apple during that time, and 13,050 fans attended the game. Nevertheless, that primitive beginning foreshadowed a future of promise.

Early technology was primitive. "Television was a child of radio," said Curt Gowdy. "We used one or two cameras, and we thought that was something" (Frommer, 1974, 43).

From the beginning, television positively affected the game's popularity, but the new medium had a negative effect on game attendance. In 1950, the Rams televised all games—home and away. Attendance plummeted. The next year, lesson learned, they only televised road games. Attendance boomed to more than 234,000. In 1953, the courts upheld the NFL's right to black out home games.

Commissioner Bert Bell only allowed road games to be broadcast, explaining, "When you televise a road game, you are getting free advertising. When you televise a home game, you are competing with your own ticket sales. The home gate must be protected or the game will die. You can't sell what you give away free" (Frommer, 1974, 54–55).

> HOWARD COSELL: The blackout was the single most important thing. You don't give your product away. Football used television properly.

A major turning point in the history of professional football took place at Yankee Stadium on December 28, 1958. In a game broadcast nationally by NBC, the New York Giants matched up against the Baltimore Colts. Against a backdrop of temperatures in the high 40s, Baltimore kicker Steve Myhra powered a 20-yard field goal to make the score 17–17 and send the game into sudden-death overtime—the first in NFL championship game history. A touchdown by Baltimore's Alan Ameche gave the Colts a 23–17 triumph.

The thrills and suspense of that competition and mesmerizing effect on the millions who watched it play out earned the contest the label of the "Greatest Game Ever Played." One viewer was Lamar Hunt, whose father, Haroldson Lafayette Hunt, was founder of Hunt Oil and one of the wealthiest men in the world.

The young Hunt, heir to his father's billions, had cast about for months, jockeying back and forth, and trying to make up his mind about whether to attempt to purchase a Major League Baseball franchise or pro football team. By game's end, he was sure.

"My interest emotionally was always more in football. But clearly the '58 Colts–Giants game, sort of, in my mind, made me say, 'Well, that's it. This sport really has everything. And it televises well.' And who knew what that meant?" (MacCambridge, 2004, 115).

One of the stars of the "Greatest Game Ever Played" was New York Giants running back Frank Gifford. He remembers what it was like.

> **FRANK GIFFORD: After the game, the sport had it made. There were stories in the media. Advertisers became really interested in football, the networks cared. That game enabled the sport to self-generate itself nationally.**

All of a sudden a line of businessmen got into the act, seeking to own a team of their own in the National Football League.

In 1956, the owner of the Chicago Bears, George Halas, said the NFL would expand from 12 to 16 teams within a decade. In 1957, NFL commissioner Bert Bell was optimistic about the league increasing the number of franchises in 1960. Bell appointed Halas and Pittsburgh owner Art Rooney to a committee to explore expansion in 1958.

Around that time, Lamar Hunt and Bud Adams, owner of the Ada Oil Company of Houston and son of the chairman of Phillips Petroleum, both ambitious young men and very sports minded, also attempted to acquire the Chicago Cardinals and transfer the team to Dallas. The duo was rebuffed in their efforts. The reaction of NFL owners was, "What? A pro football team in Dallas, what next?"

Self-effacing—some would say almost self-deprecating—Lamar Hunt did not back down. Against the advice of his highly successful father, the former second-string pass receiver at Southern Methodist University, called "Games" because of his love of sports, decided to create a football league of his own.

"There had been a National League and an American League competing side by side for 60 years," Hunt told reporters. "I was encouraged because pro football had become so tremendously popular and because I knew there were cities interested in backing a competitive league. I felt that an American Football League, side by side with the National Football League, could be a success" (Frommer, 1974, 58).

Other rivals to the NFL had sprung up throughout the decades, including the American Football League (1926), another American Football League (1936–1937), and yet another American Football League (1940–1941), as well as the All-America Football Conference (1946–1949); however, none of them had the financial muscle and organizational skills that Hunt, the new kid on the block, had in his American Football League.

Joe Foss was put in place as AFL commissioner. A World War II Medal of Honor winner who shot down 26 Japanese planes as a U.S. Marine pilot in the Pacific and a man who was born in 1917, on a farm without electricity in South Dakota, a state he later became governor of, the amiable Foss seemed a perfect choice.

Charter AFL franchises included the Boston Patriots, Buffalo Bills, Dallas Texans, Denver Broncos, Houston Oilers, New York Titans, Oakland Raiders, and Los Angeles Chargers. Original owners included Lamar Hunt of Dallas; Bud Adams of Houston; Ralph Wilson, a Midwest insurance and trucking power broker, of Buffalo; Barron Hilton, son of the founder of the hotel chain that still bears his name, of the Los Angeles Chargers; Max Winter, sports promoter and part owner of the Minneapolis Lakers basketball team; Billy Sullivan, sports publicity director and businessman, of the Patriots; Harry Wismer, famed sports broadcaster who had been part owner of the Detroit Lions and the Washington Redskins, of the Titans; and Bob Howsam, former World War II test pilot and a man with a feel for running sports franchises, of the Denver Broncos.

NFL owners tried to persuade AFL owners to switch leagues. Apparently only Max Winter was listening. He moved his Minneapolis franchise to the NFL. Businessman F. Wayne Valley set up shop for a new team in Oakland as a replacement for the Minnesota franchise.

AFL team owners were actually at meetings in Minnesota on the day that Winter joined forces with the enemy. That night, over dinner, the outspoken owner of the New York Titans stared down Winter. It was reported that he slowly and carefully said to Winter, "Nice going, Judas."

Annoyed, Winter stood up. Wismer was fond of telling everyone what happened: "I got him with one line when I told the other owners, "Boys, this is the last supper."

AFL owners referred to themselves as the "Foolish Club," a backhanded (some would say), realistic acknowledgment of the challenge they knew was before them going against the established and powerful NFL. No other league in history had faced off against the NFL and survived.

This varied and ambitious group took on the fight with the old league with gusto. Part of the AFL's strategy was to try and outbid the NFL for top players. It was viewed as a crucial component of survival by AFL owners. So was finding players who had been overlooked, not given a chance, who came from nontraditional outlets,

The AFL landed a powerful blow against the NFL early on by signing Billy Cannon, the 1959 Heisman winner out of Louisiana State University. The number-one draft pick of both leagues, the bruiser of a ball carrier signed with the Houston Oilers. That signing underscored the future—the push and pull for players, the virtually uncontrolled bidding, and the payment of huge sums of money to untested collegiate stars, making them wealthy and angering established veterans. In the 1960 draft, the AFL signed 75 percent of the NFL's first-round picks.

The Texans of Dallas situated their offices in the Mercantile Securities Building. AFL offices were also in Dallas. Sharing the Cotton Bowl with the Dallas Cowboys, the Texans won the attendance battle, drawing about three thousand more fans that season than the NFL club. Ticket prices were more affordable for the AFL team, which also put forth a more attractive team. That initial season, Hunt's team charged $4 for reserved seats.

General admission was $2. High school students paid 90 cents. The Texans won 11 of 14 games—and the AFL championship.

> LAMAR HUNT JR: My father was taking on a powerful, entrenched league. He had a fight on his hands. There were the big signings like Billy Cannon. The AFL was able to identify, at a sort of deeper level, players that were either sitting on benches, or getting cut, or released, who had some ability, like a Len Dawson. And I think tapping into the African American player, looking to those colleges for people like Otis Taylor.

From 1960 to 1962, AFL teams averaged 17 percent more blacks on their teams than NFL teams. Several AFL clubs had 10 or 15 black players on their rosters.

Seeing the force and determination of Lamar Hunt in action, the NFL offered him the expansion franchise in Dallas. All he had to do was turn his back on the other seven franchises and their owners in the AFL.

> LAMAR HUNT JR: My father was a quietly powerful person, just very determined. I would say he was loyal, sometimes loyal to a fault. When he turned down that NFL offer he said, "No, we're just going to go ahead and do the league. We are going to do it." I think that was good loyalty. It was good character.

> ED LOTHAMER: I'll give you one example of what kind of guy Lamar Hunt was, what his character was like. We used to play at Municipal Stadium in Kansas City. And Mike Livingston and I drove up one day. It was like December and five below zero. And we parked and were walking toward the stadium entrance. And here's Lamar standing there, and you could tell he was just freezing.
>
> I said, "Lamar, what's the matter? Why aren't you inside?"
>
> He said, "Well, this guy here at the gate, he doesn't know who I am, and I didn't want to make any waves so I was just waiting for somebody."
>
> That was Lamar. He loved athletics. His nickname at SMU, where he played behind the great Raymond Berry, was "Games." He sure loved the game of football and knew an awful lot about it.
>
> Modest, not pushy, but honed in completely with everything the team was doing. He flew with us every time on the plane. He was just there.

There, in January 1960, were all the NFL team owners in Miami at the famous Kenilworth Hotel. Their main agenda item was choosing a new commissioner to succeed the respected Bert Bell, who had died from a heart attack while attending an Eagles–Steelers game at Franklin Field in October 1959.

Choosing a new commissioner was the main focus; however, there were also other grave concerns: the AFL challenge, the slim and unpredictable attendance for some NFL teams, the television exposure that was not prime time. Hughes Sports Network, not a household name, was transmitting Cleveland Browns games.

Some owners favored staying with the steady, practical approach that had been followed by Bell. Others sought to install a commissioner with modern ideas, marketing skills, and the savvy to fuse the old league with the new world of television and computers, a person with skills to steer the NFL's expansion.

There were two equal in-house favorites: Austin Gunsel, treasurer and acting commissioner, and Marshall Leahy, chief legal counsel. Day after day there were meetings and discussions held, disagreements voiced, and ballots cast. Neither candidate was able to gain a clear advantage, and newspaper reports made fun of the futile efforts, lack of progress, and sense that there was a pervasive aimlessness.

Various names were suggested and rejected. Vince Lombardi, general manager and coach of the Green Bay Packers, was mentioned as a candidate, but his candidacy never gained traction. It was against this backdrop—caught between the past and the future—that owners haggled, debated, bluffed, and tried to reach a consensus between the two candidates for NFL commissioner. Leahy, annoyed with and frustrated by the goings on and lack of movement, made his own move. Leaving his name in nomination but not his contact information, he boarded a plane and headed back to his native San Francisco.

Unable to reach unanimity on any candidate, a movement began to find one that everyone could compromise on. Pete Rozelle, just 33 and general manager of the Los Angeles Rams, was the choice of both Wellington Mara of the New York Giants and Paul Brown of the Cleveland Browns. Both men thought of Rozelle as a choice that would be agreeable to the majority of the owners. It was suggested that he leave the premises—that it would be best if he were absent while his candidacy was the main topic at the meeting.

So the dark horse of all dark horses—he was even referred to in a *Miami Herald* story as "Pete Roselle," a face in the crowd, an in and out of the scene personage in the hotel lobby, a young man with a nice tan—hung out in the men's room for a couple of hours, adjusting his tie, looking away, and washing his hands when anyone entered. Rozelle later guessed that he had washed his hands 35 times while waiting.

Finally, on January 26, 1960, after 11 days and nights of little sun and fun, and much dread and deadlock, after 22 ballots, by a 7–4–1 vote, the NFL's youngest general manager—Alvin "Pete" Rozelle—was chosen.

Paul Brown and Wellington Mara came to Rozelle and told him that he now had a $50,000 a year job—commissioner of the National Football League.

In a backhanded and witty reference to his time spent nervously washing his hands in the men's room, Rozelle quipped to the owners, "I can honestly say I come to you with clean hands."

It was thought that the 33-year-old general manager of the Los Angeles Rams was a bright and unassuming man, one who would not be hard to handle.

"They finally picked Pete as a compromise," said longtime Dallas Cowboys executive Tex Schramm, "because both sides thought they could control him. But they were wrong. Pete was a lot stronger than any of them realized."

"I was totally shocked," Rozelle recalled, "because I was so young and because they'd considered so many other people who had so much more experience in football than I."

Born March 1, 1926, in South Gate, California, Rozelle's youth was spent in the Los Angeles suburb of Lynwood. He played tennis and basketball at Compton High. Sun-kissed California was his playground, his backyard, his work station. The era's patriotic events and spectacles, floats, marching bands, balloon drops, fireworks, and Technicolor movies fascinated him and would shape his outlook on sports and entertainment for the rest of his life.

After serving in the U.S. Navy in the Pacific from 1944 to 1946, Rozelle enrolled in Compton Junior College. The Los Angeles Rams practiced at Compton. Helping out in the publicity department of the Rams, Rozelle began a long-term relationship with Rams public relations director Tex Schramm. By 1957, Rozelle had been appointed general manager. Affable, ambitious, and efficient, the young Rozelle became a popular figure in NFL circles.

So when he was picked to serve as commissioner of the NFL that day in Miami, the native Californian had paid his dues, made his contacts, and had all kinds of experience in football, media, and public relations. He was more than ready for the next big thing. It would be the challenge of his life.

In 1960, each NFL franchise was valued at about $1 million. Some franchises were struggling to get by. According to Howard Cosell in *I Never Played the Game*, the half-filled stadiums and few teams with television contracts symbolized deep-rooted problems. The 12 teams had very different agendas and vastly different resources. All had different histories and contrasting needs.

Yet, if there were differences among NFL clubs, the contrast between the two leagues was even greater. The AFL was new school. The NFL was old school. The old league was the establishment. The new league reflected the 1960s, when it came into existence. It was an era of things outrageous, outspoken, hip, innovative, and fearless. Some said the "other league's" game strategy—pass first and score a lot of points—resembled a "flag football league."

> **HOWARD COSELL:** The AFL was made by television. The television contract, although the NBC sponsorship lost $40 million in its first five years, was the key to parity between the leagues.

PAUL ZIMMERMAN: The NBC contract with the American Football League put them in the ball game. The size of the television contract showed that the AFL would be able to survive.

Television network income was shared by all AFL teams. Television coverage had cameras in motion, not the stationery shots from the 50-yard line favored by the NFL. A scoreboard clock kept the official game time. A two-point touchdown conversion, the names of players on the backs of jerseys, a Thanksgiving Day game in a different city each year—all were American Football League innovations.

"The feeling," Pat Summerall noted, was that it was that it was the "major leagues against Triple A's. Most people connected to the NFL didn't think too much of the AFL. As the game progressed we realized these guys were just as big, just as quick as the NFL players."

Not only did Pete Rozelle have the challenge of an "outlaw league"—as some called it—going toe-to-toe with his, but he became aware right from the start that the NFL was much more of a mom-and-pop operation than he realized. Its inadequate offices were situated in Bala Cynwyd, outside of Philadelphia. Understaffed and out of touch, the offices had provided easy access for the late Bert Bell from his home. For others, it was a trek.

In 1961, Rozelle moved the NFL base from Bala Cynwyd to Manhattan's Rockefeller Center. That accomplished, what he wanted was closer communication between the NFL and the television and advertising industries.

In place when he took office was a national television contract for the NFL championship game. Rozelle wanted more than that. Each NFL team had separate television packages with widely differing valuations. In 1960, for example, the big-market New York Giants pocketed $350,000 a year for television rights to their games. The small-market Green Bay Packers were paid a tenth of that. This was actually an improvement over the earlier days of the game, for instance, 1948, when the Baltimore Colts received $50 to televise a game in Washington and $100 to televise it in Baltimore.

In June 1960, the AFL struck a five-year television deal with ABC for $10 million, getting the attention of the NFL and Pete Rozelle. It was a great deal of money for that time.

"Without ever having played a game, each of the eight teams in the AFL entered the 1960 season guaranteed to earn more in television revenues than five of the venerable, established franchises in the National Football League" (MacCambridge, 2004, 133–34).

FRANK GIFFORD: Professional football with color, with night games in attractive stadiums, with management dressing things up— all these things were able to make the sport on TV more appealing. There is something subconscious about a jam-packed stadium that's important to the game. People looking in at a full house get a feeling of satisfaction that there are that many people watching.

In 1961, Rozelle convinced owners to let him negotiate a single television deal, with teams sharing proceeds. The two-year league-wide agreement with CBS was valued at $9.3 million—also a great deal of money for that time. The small-market NFL teams were very pleased.

"What Pete Rozelle did with television receipts," Green Bay's Vince Lombardi said, "probably saved football in Green Bay."

Jim Kensil, on the scene as an aide to Rozelle, remembered, "He said that for the strength of the league, they had to share the money equally or the league would go to hell" (Sandomir, 1996).

> **FRANK GIFFORD: The pooling of television money, regardless of attendance, was a tremendous factor in spurring television's growth.**

Despite the hype and hoopla and, at times, herculean efforts and vast sums of money expended, the AFL had little to brag about in those early years.

AFL players were a real mix in ages. Some were rejects from the NFL and the Canadian Football League. Some were young guys fresh out of school. Some came from colleges where attendance at games was triple that of the AFL. One player noted, "It was almost like going back and playing before high school crowds." The league lost almost $4 million in its first season. Lamar Hunt's Dallas Texans lost $1 million.

As the story goes, a reporter asked Hunt's father about the losses. "What do you know about that?" the billionaire oilman smiled. "At this rate my son Lamar will go broke in a hundred years."

Lamar Hunt did not go broke, but in 1960, the NFL broke his heart by placing the expansion Cowboys in Dallas. And even though the Texans of the AFL won more games than the Cowboys and won the league championship in 1962, the zeal of Dallas fans was for the Cowboys. It was clear. There was no way two pro football teams could coexist in Dallas. In 1963, Hunt's Dallas Texans started anew as the Kansas City Chiefs.

> **JERRY IZENBERG: When the AFL started up, I was still working at the *Herald Tribune*. In fact, I think I covered one of the first Titan games in the Polo Grounds. What they used to say about those games is that the owner, Harry Wismer, would count the number of legs sitting in the park and then multiply by four instead of dividing it by four to get his crowds. So I was there through it all.**

Sportswriter George Vescey had a great line about the Titans and the Polo Grounds: "People came disguised as empty seats" (Olderman, 2012, 161).

"It was like war," Lamar Hunt recalled of those times. "And I think it made the AFL a viable league. The cloak-and-dagger stuff captured the public's imagination."

Not quite cloak-and-dagger stuff, but the scene at the famed 21 Club in Manhattan in 1962 was intriguing. A birthday party for AFL commissioner Joe Foss had been organized by MCA talent agent David A. "Sonny" Werblin of Flatbush, Brooklyn. His client list included such "A" names as Jackie Gleason, Alfred Hitchcock, Jack Benny, Benny Goodman, and Johnny Carson.

Among those in attendance for the birthday celebration was Wismer, former famous sportscaster, a narcissistic and unliked presence. His New York Titans were a flop. Playing in the decaying and dreary Polo Grounds, the former home of the New York Giants, attendance for Wismer's team was 114,682 in the AFL's first season. By 1962, only 36,161 fans showed. The team was panned and ridiculed by the New York City area media.

It was said that Sonny Werblin and Harry Wismer never liked one another. They went back and forth with food and drink, teases and taunts in the posh Manhattan restaurant. Then Wismer crossed the line when he called Werblin a "kike."

There never was any risk of the two physically going toe to toe, but Werblin had the last word. "Someday," he told Wismer, "I'm going to *own* your team!"

"Someday" turned out to be a couple of months later.

Just before Wismer declared Chapter 11, Joe Foss sold the Titans to a five-man group for $1 million. Heading the group was Werblin. He quickly went to work.

In came Weeb Ewbank, a man who had experienced success with the NFL Baltimore Colts, as the new coach. In came new colors—green and white. Out went the team's home stadium, the decrepit Polo Grounds. In came Shea Stadium, home of the brand new Mets. And out went Titans. In came the team's new name—Jets.

Still hustling, still dealing and wheeling, Werblin negotiated a new television contract with NBC, putting the eight (soon to be 10) AFL franchises on more solid financial footing.

> **BOB MOORE: At that particular point, the AFL was engaged in a fairly acrimonious situation with the NFL. For Sonny Werblin to come in and negotiate the contract with NBC was one of the key pieces of the AFL's existence.**

Getting Werblin was the (AFL's) turning point," Lamar Hunt said.

In 1964, the NFL signed a two-year deal with CBS for $28.2 million, about $1 million per team. It was clever negotiating by Commissioner Pete Rozelle that got CBS to triple its rights fees to $1 million per year per club—a financial arrangement that broke new ground for television sports.

In what appeared to be a death blow for the AFL, ABC cancelled the final season of its four-year television contract with the new league. With connected Sonny Werblin working front and center, as well as backstage, NBC picked up the AFL, shelling out $1 million a year to each team for five years. The deal more than matched the NFL's package and was considered by some the worst television deal ever made.

"I still don't believe it," an unnamed AFL coach remarked. "NBC could have had us for 15 cents, give or take a nickel."

"NBC did the smart thing," Lamar Hunt said. "Most of our clubs needed big money from TV to compete with the NFL. It was a smart business move for NBC to have a strong AFL, and Werblin was the guy who made them realize that."

Money, money, money.

Poor Denver was another story. Early on, the AFL's Broncos played their games adorned in secondhand uniforms purchased from a Copper Bowl college team. The most annoying aspect of the uniform was the glaring yellow socks with vertical brown stripes. Players offered to purchase more suitable socks. Their request was turned down. Finally, on opening day of the 1962 season, a bonfire did the socks in. A pair of socks was saved. One sock was kept for old time's sake, while the other wound up in the Pro Football Hall of Fame.

> JERRY IZENBERG: The babysitting war was another story, a story in many ways more exciting than the games! I mean, it just went on and on. All kinds of strange things happened.

> BILL MCNUTT III: It was a real war within a war, drafting, hiding, and signing players in those days.

NFL scouts identified the nation's top players. Staff employees called "baby-sitters" kept an eye on them. Out of the way hotels and resorts were mainly used to keep players away from AFL teams until NFL teams could lock them up. During those "war years," approximately $7 million would be disbursed in rookie deals.

> CHRIS BURFORD: The NFL teams, they didn't believe people would go to the AFL. I got an ultimatum from the Cleveland Browns, who said, "Sign with us by Friday or we'll withdraw the offer." Yeah, their $8,500 offer.

> BOB LONG: I was out of Wichita State and was drafted in 1964, by the San Diego Chargers of the AFL and the Green Bay Packers of the NFL. I went out just to watch the Chargers practice. And I'll never forget this as long as I live.
>
> I said, "Who's that number 19? Young guy jumping all around, running great patterns, and great hands."
>
> And the guy beside me said, "This is our new young receiver Lance Alworth. He's a Hall of Famer to be."
>
> I called Green Bay, and I said, "Send me a program." I personally was going to go to the team that had the oldest receivers, and Max

McGee, I think then was 30, and Boyd Dowler was 29. This was three years or so previous to Super Bowl I. That is how I wound up in Green Bay.

FRED ARBANAS: I landed at the airport in Dallas. I was greeted by Texans owner Lamar Hunt and his father, H. L. Hunt. Jim Tyrer, my new teammate, who accompanied me on the flight, and I picked up our bags to walk to the car. It was a 1953 Hudson. It was parked in the back where you didn't have to pay. I thought that was kind of strange.

BILL MCNUTT III: Prior to being old enough to work at training camp, my Dad and I would pile into a big Chrysler car with Lamar Hunt and Lamar Junior, and we would drive from Dallas to Liberty, Missouri, and spend a few days at training camp. The car was a loaner to Lamar from the Chrysler Corporation, who gave each AFL owner a big four-door vehicle to drive.

Lamar had a big Chiefs sticker showing a running Chief with a four- or five-state area behind him, put on both doors! Mr. Hunt liked to speed and was aggressive behind the wheel. The big sticker that said KC Chiefs got him out of some speeding tickets.

The first Chief training camp in Kansas City, in the hot summer of 1963, was very memorable. So were the 1964 and 1965 training camps due to the amazing talent that came to the team because of General Manager Don Klosterman's ability to identify talent and Mr. Hunt's big wallet!

SMOKEY STOVER: I went to the University of Louisiana Monroe. It was a state college then called Northeast Louisiana State College. It was just a small college, like a 2A college. I knew of the Hunts because of the oil business. But other than that, I didn't know that Lamar was as involved in football as he was. I had never met Hank Stram before, never heard of him or anything.

I came in on a tryout basis in Dallas, Texas, at Jesuit High School. This was July the fifth, 1960. They brought a bunch of us in and tried us out. You wouldn't have believed it. It was mass confusion right at first! Cowboys, farmers, truck drivers, all sorts of people showed up for those tryouts, more than a hundred people.

That first day about 60 dropped out in the first hour and a half. We had two-a-day drills through 10 days, working with no pads. As the practices moved along, more and more dropped out. It got hotter and hotter.

Finally, the upshot of it all was that only two of us made the Dallas Texans out of that bunch, myself and a guy named Al Reynolds. I played seven years with the Chiefs, '60 to '66. I was one of the original originals that played for the Texans/Chiefs.

ED LOTHAMER: I got married the day I got drafted in 1964, and I didn't think I was going to get drafted by anybody. So I just went off on my honeymoon, and I get back to find that Baltimore and the Kansas City Chiefs had drafted me. I was the 64th pick by the Colts, the 26th by the Chiefs.

I went to Baltimore to meet with owner Carroll Rosenbloom, and I'm sitting at this big long table and we're talking. It went very well. I felt comfortable.

And I was also down on the field that day, and I got to meet Johnny Unitas and Raymond Berry and Ordell Braase and Gino Marchetti, all these guys I'd grown up with in Detroit, you know, that I was just fascinated by them and the NFL, the established league also.

I said—and they gave me a good offer and a decent time track— "Look, I'm going to come here, but I have to meet this guy, Lamar Hunt. I don't know who he is, but I know he has a lot of money and he is coming to see me!"

They said okay. So I went back to my campus at Michigan State and was in my room waiting for Lamar Hunt to show for the appointment. Actually, he was late. He knocked on the door, I opened it, and here's this guy who looked like Wally Cox with the torn car coat and all this stuff.

He says, "I'm Lamar Hunt."

And I'm thinking, it's some kind of a graduate student joke.

And I said, "Yeah, yeah, I know, and I'm Santa Claus."

And I shut the door!

Then he knocked on it again and said, "No, no, I'm really Lamar Hunt."

So he came in and we talked for about 20, 30 minutes. And he told me, "We watched you, we're going to give you this, and we're going to give you that."

It was a lot of money. I kept listening.

Lamar was a great guy, but he wasn't an overwhelming personality. I think he understood that he wasn't a real personality. I mean, he said, "Don't do anything yet until Mack Rankin comes to see you."

And I said, "Okay, how many days will that be?"

He said, "He'll be here tomorrow."

Lamar Hunt, as rendered by artist and writer Murray Olderman.
Courtesy of the artist

I had expected Lamar to be this big, robust Texan and all that stuff, but he just wasn't. But this Mack Rankin was. He came in, and this guy, he was obviously a closer.

I got an $8,000 bonus and a $14,000 contract, and he told me, "Boy, this is a lot of money for a defensive lineman."

And I said, "Okay, I believe you!"

I think we closed the deal on a pair of cowboy boots with walking heels on them instead of riding heels.

Rankin's official job description with Hunt Oil in the early 1960s was "landman." He was sometimes characterized in newspaper accounts as a "scout" for Hunt's Dallas Texans. His desk was located close to that of Hunt. He was actually a "recruiter" and, more often than not, a "closer."

He had signed Texas Tech legend E. J. Holub without any problems. Rankin targeted Ed Budde by sending the football player's wife two dozen roses as soon as the Chiefs drafted the Michigan State standout. Rankin was still talking about it when Budde signed up only four days later.

> ED BUDDE: I was out of Michigan State and was drafted in the 1963 Draft by the Philadelphia Eagles, fourth overall. And that was quite an accomplishment. I was picked by the Chiefs in the first round of the 1963 Draft, eighth overall. The reason for going to the AFL was I liked Lamar Hunt, I liked Dallas. They had a great team, were building a great team too, because they were the AFL champions in 1962. I played for $15,000 the first year, and I got $8,000 for signing.
>
> I also chose the Texans because of Fred Arbanas, the tight end. I thought that he was one of the finest tight ends in professional football, ever. I really respected him, and he was a Dallas Texan, and he was telling me about all these great guys and the wide-open offense, which kind of cemented the deal that I would play in the AFL.

None of the signings, none of the headlines—and there were many—compared to the frenzy that the bidding war became in 1965. That was also the year a national survey indicated that football had passed baseball for the first time as America's favorite sport.

> MARTY GLICKMAN: TV was used well by football. It made more fans. Baseball just didn't come across on television. It was too slow, too limited. That is what pushed football into the forefront as the top sport over baseball.

> MICHAEL MACCAMBRIDGE: Pete Rozelle very consciously and privately all thru the 60s would open a bottle of champagne the day after the World Series ended. Because from that moment on in the calendar he knew his National Football League had center stage and would have it thru the end of the football season.
>
> At some point that ritual no longer was necessary because pro football had much of the stage even during the end of the baseball season. Pete Rozelle knew the power of television and what it could do for football and what it could not do for baseball.
>
> By the end of the 60s, baseball no longer was the national pastime, aside from in the minds of a lot of people who were baseball

lovers and could not, would not realize things had changed. The ratings told the story, documented it. That's I why I named my book on football *America's Game.*

In the 1965 draft, highly regarded University of Alabama quarterback Joe Namath, dubbed by his legendary coach Bear Bryant the "greatest athlete I ever coached," was selected first by the AFL Jets and 12th by the NFL St. Louis Cardinals.

The player who would be known as "Broadway Joe" signed with the Jets for $400,000, the richest contract in professional football to that point in time. It was the most important AFL star signing since Billy Cannon had been signed for $100,000 by the Oilers in 1960. A pot sweetener for Namath included scouting jobs at $10,000 a year for his three brothers and brother-in-law, a green Lincoln Continental for him, and other assorted extras. The money shelled out for him was minimal compared to what it triggered. Not many realized Namath would become the next big thing for the Jets and his league, a mighty star set to shine in the Big Apple, the media capital of the world.

With the signings, with the vast sums of money being expended by both the AFL and NFL, things were swiftly moving out of control. There were many who thought a merger of the two leagues was the only thing that could save the day. Quite a few NFL owners (and Pete Rozelle in the beginning) opposed a merger, believing the AFL would ultimately cave in. Rozelle knew that despite the affiliation with rival leagues, there was mutual respect and a good friendship between Tex Schramm of the Cowboys and Lamar Hunt of the Chiefs. The NFL head man quietly arranged for both men to begin talking about a framework for a merger. In early March 1966. Schramm and Hunt spent more than two hours talking in the back of the Dallas executive's car.

In April 1966, the battle of the leagues heated up. Genial Joe Foss was replaced as AFL commissioner by the anything but genial Al Davis, out of Brooklyn's Erasmus High School.

"I guess they thought I'd be a catalyst. It was a situation that called for constant pressure from the other side," the fiery Davis is quoted as saying in a *Sports Illustrated* piece from January 22, 2001.

It was business as usual at the NFL owners meeting in Washington, D.C., in mid-May 1966. The meetings generally generated news; however, no one expected the blockbuster news generated by New York Giants owner Wellington Mara. Rocking the world of professional football on May 17, Mara announced that he had signed Buffalo Bills soccer-style placekicker Pete Gogolak. It was the first time a NFL team had raided a player from an AFL roster, ending a time-honored, unspoken agreement between the leagues. Mara explained that he was annoyed and angered at the signing of Namath by the Jets. The Gogolak signing was retaliation.

"That got everybody's attention," said Al Davis, "and I'm sure hastened the merger" (Olderman, 2012, 5).

Hunkering down in his posh pad at the Hotel Plaza in Manhattan, elated at the turn of events, excited by the acrimonious scenario, and perceptive enough to realize what the

Gogolak signing meant, former Oakland Raider general manager Al Davis announced, "We just got our merger."

Counterattacking was his specialty. He prodded AFL clubs to sign NFL free agents, quarterbacks especially, the more the better, the bigger the better.

AFL Oilers owner Bud Adams roared, "If that's what they want, that is what they will get."

Fury was on parade throughout the AFL and NFL. Davis, in office as commissioner for just a month, made it clear that his league was primed for a "no-holds-barred bidding war." "Futures contracts" would be made available to NFL players.

The Raiders signed quarterback Roman Gabriel of the Rams to a four-year contract worth $300,000 on May 27, 1966, just a couple of weeks after the explosive Gogolak signing.

Football was on its way to self-destruction, Tex Schramm noted. Both sides were exhausting treasure, moving rapidly into a red zone near bankruptcy. Only four teams could possibly sustain themselves and remain competitive.

"Teams were drafting players not on the basis of whether or not they could play, but whether they could be signed," Schramm explained. "Whenever that happens, then your sport is in trouble, and that's the way we were headed then."

The NFL sought a truce. On May 31, Lamar Hunt and Tex Schramm were feverishly working to put the final tweaks and touches on a framework for the merger of the two warring leagues.

MICHAEL MACCAMBRIDGE: Rozelle admittedly did not favor a merger in the beginning; however, once owners decided to merge, he did as good a job as anyone could do in carrying that out. There would be fits and starts, but as commissioner he carried things out in an evenhanded fashion.

The war between the two leagues was awful, and there were teams in both leagues who almost went out of business, but collectively the in-fighting and struggles helped the profile of football, made the game more popular. Everybody liked the cloak and dagger, the good fights, the bigger-than-life personalities. Pro football was on the sports pages almost year round, whereas previously it had been like hockey and basketball, seasonal.

HANK STRAM: After six years of rivalry, it became apparent to even the most conservative NFL owners that the new league would not conveniently disappear. Unlike several previous attempts to found a second professional football league, the AFL was going to succeed. Perhaps the main difference between our success and the failure of the previous All-American Conference of the late 40s was the impact of television. First ABC and then NBC had pumped significant sums of money into the league in return for the rights to televise its games. Despite slim crowds during the AFL's formative years, several teams who otherwise might have floundered managed to survive because of television money. And telecasts of our games eventually served to develop fans and attract them to the parks.

JERRY IZENBERG: I had inside knowledge that a merger was going to be announced. I called Pete and I said, "Listen, I know you're going to have the merger, and I know you're waiting until the last second to tell us where and everything else, but I'm going to write about it right now. So that's why I'm giving you a chance to say something."

And he said, "I'll tell you what Jerry, I would rather you didn't write it."

And I said, "Well you've got some chance."

Pete was a great newspaper man in his way. And he said, "I'll tell you what I'll do. If you write this now, what're you gonna write? That they're gonna meet, that they're gonna merge? That's two paragraphs. Then you're going to write the same shit you've been writing for the last 'X' number of years because they'll wanna fill up a tremendous amount of space. If you hold off and don't write it, I'll sit down with you and Tex Schramm (the negotiator) the morning after, and I'll tell you every single thing that happened, inside stuff, about the meeting and everything else."

I think I would've been an idiot to write it! So I didn't.

JOE BROWNE: I have often told my two sons that I played a very significant role in the AFL–NFL merger announcement in 1966. Jim Kensil, who was Pete Rozelle's right-hand man, called (Peter) Hadhazy and me into his office the afternoon of June 8. He told us there was a very important press release that he wanted us to deliver by hand from our Rockefeller Plaza league office to AP and UPI. Hadhazy selected the AP assignment because it was closer. I had to walk all the way down to East 42nd Street to the UPI offices. Hadhazy would remind me for years that he got the more important assignment to deliver to AP, which served more papers than UPI in those days.

Kensil told us to call him when we reached our respective offices so he could synchronize, and the big news would be given to both wire services at the exact same time. We did that, dropped the press releases on the sports desks, and the rest is history.

There had been no news leaks about the merger announcement, so it received wide newspaper coverage the next day. I was a college sophomore at the time and only a part-time NFL worker. I did not take the news that seriously. I remember upsetting Kensil because I stopped for a Nedicks hot dog on the way back to the office from 42nd Street. He wanted to know how the news was received at UPI. I was more concerned that my lunch that day had been delayed due to the historical assignment.

The press release contained the following main points:

Pete Rozelle will be commissioner.
A world championship game will be held for the season.
Existing franchises will be retained.
No franchises will be transferred from present locations.
Two new franchises will be formed no later than 1968.
Two more teams will be founded as soon thereafter as practical.
Interleague preseason games will be held in 1967.
A single-league schedule will be issued in 1970.
A common draft will be held the following January.
Two-network television coverage will continue.

The press conference was staged on June 8, 1966, in the Essex Room of Manhattan's posh Warwick Hotel. Jammed with all manner of media, the room was divided into two sections. NFL loyalists sat on one side, while AFL zealots were on the other.

Explaining that an armistice had been agreed to by the two warring leagues, the commissioner announced that agreement had been reached to merge into an organization of 24 teams. Throughout the seven years of friction and fighting there had never even been a scrimmage between teams from the AFL and NFL. Now there would also be a championship game.

> JERRY IZENBERG: I was at that press conference. Oh yeah, it was packed with reporters and lasted well over an hour. Rozelle took questions on a sofa. Flanking him were Tex Schramm and Lamar Hunt. There were a lot of questions because there were a lot of sub-plots. First of all, NBC wanted to know if they were going to get stuck with all the bad teams to televise.
>
> One of the "bad teams" was Denver, which had to fight like hell to save its franchise. At first they were playing in an old baseball park, the Denver Bears minor league baseball park. Then they had Mile High Stadium. They just kept adding on and adding on, and it was the worst-built stadium in the world. NBC didn't believe Denver would draw national audiences, and there were a couple other teams

they felt the same way about. NBC hoped it could get a couple of the other National League teams to come over. Too bad for them that didn't happen until three years after the merger. And they really had to fight for that.

But the interesting thing about all that happened was that a single city was not lost in the merger. I think everybody came in on both sides, which is not the way it was with the old All-American Conference. So that was good.

There was unbalance after the merger. The NFL had more teams. There was some concern about that because of voting, but it all worked out.

Howard Cosell, a self-promoter allied with Al Davis and the AFL, "conspicuously sat in the front row of the press conference. . . . Coming off like the lawyer for the younger league, Cosell asked if the AFL had forced the merger secretly by making huge offers to NFL stars.

"'You know that it's true,'" he impudently told Rozelle.

"'No I do not know that it's true,'" Rozelle replied, trying not to look miffed.

"'I know that it's true,'" Cosell volleyed (Ribowsky, 2014, 168).

Announcing that he spoke for the American people, badgering Lamar Hunt, insisting that he go through all the steps that created the merger, Cosell was like a battering ram.

The mild and dignified Hunt raised his voice and got back at Cosell. He also apologized to him for the voice raising. Cosell was flummoxed.

In what can be looked back at now as gross understatement, Wayne Valley, owner of the Oakland Raiders, concluded, "The merger was desirable and necessary" (Fortunato, 2006, 74).

NFL owner Art Modell said, "The merger will allow the league to expand scientifically, giving it stability and insuring that no franchise will be moved."

Owner Art Rooney of the Steelers said, "It was inevitable. We felt that for the good of the public this was the only way the game can be presented to the entire country."

AFL owner Bud Adams of Houston said, "It will end the financial strain on pro teams."

JOE BROWNE: The merger helped change my life because Pete Rozelle and our small office quickly transitioned from being responsible for just 14 NFL teams in '65 to being in charge of 24 AFL–NFL teams in the '66 season. Rozelle told me at the end of that summer that if I kept my nose clean, there would be a full-time NFL job for me after I graduated. That was a turning point in my life.

A Murray Olderman caricature of Pete Rozelle, ever-present cigarette in hand.

Courtesy of the artist

A highly interesting take on what the merger meant came from Mel Durslag in the *Los Angeles Herald Examiner*:

The American Football League owners have, by luck or by cunning, emerged with the long end of the stick in the negotiations. . . . You begin with the simple reminder that the charter members in the American Football League picked up franchises six years ago for the grand sum of $25,000. . . . For the investments, they wind up in the big tent with properties worth at least $100 million." (Olderman, 2012, 17)

One of Commissioner Pete Rozelle's suggestions for the name of the new game was "The Big One." That name never caught on. "Pro Bowl" was another Rozelle idea. Had the name been adopted there would have been confusion, for that was the name used for the NFL's all-star game. Another name floated was "World Series of Football," which died quickly after being deemed too imitative of baseball's Fall Classic.

There was no Super Bowl Committee, which some said was part of the problem. There was also a game that had no location and no name. That, too, was part of the problem.

It was Rozelle's idea to call the contest the AFL–NFL World Championship Game. While the name was made official, it never took off. It was too cumbersome, a mouthful, no good for newspaper headlines.

BOYD DOWLER: We thought it was kind of funny they called it the Super Bowl; that was a feature of the media more than anybody else. But the AFL–NFL Championship Bowl Game, yeah, that's a lot more words than necessary. Super Bowl is a lot more practical.

SHARRON HUNT: The name AFL–NFL Championship Game was too unwieldy, hard to get straight.

Two days after the hullabaloo about the merger, *New York Times* sports columnist Arthur Daley wrote about what the future had in store: the "new super duper football game for what amounts to the championship of the world."

The *Los Angeles Times* reported on September 4, 1966, that the game was being "referred to by some as the Super Bowl."

The *New York Times* sports section's lead story that same day headlined, "NFL Set to Open Season That Will End in Super Bowl."

A week later, the *Washington Post* reported, "The brash upstarts who will tackle Goliath in professional football's ultimate production, a highly appealing 'Super Bowl' that promises extra pizzazz at seasons' end."

LAMAR HUNT JR: My parents got divorced, and my dad would come over and pick us up. And I remember showing him the Super

Ball, the "Whammy" super ball, and saying, "Hey look, this will bounce over the house, this ball."

You know my dad was not going to be preoccupied with toys that were given to children. You know, he might have bounced the ball. We just remember demonstrating it.

But then what happened going forward is my dad was in an owner's meeting. They were trying to figure out what to call the last game, the championship game. I don't know if he had the ball with him, as some reports suggest.

My dad said, "Well, we need to come up with a name, something like the 'Super Bowl.'"

And then he said, "Actually, that's not a very good name. We can come up with something better."

But "Super Bowl" stuck in the media and word of mouth.

It kind of came out of my dad's mouth. What do you want to call it? Power of suggestion or just an idea or whatever, it stuck. And the inspiration was that Super Ball. I feel blessed to be the son of the guy who really came up with the name.

BILL MCNUTT III: I became very close friends with the Hunt children. We would go over to Dallas, and I would play with that ball with them. We were just amazed at this ball. It was the most popular toy of its day.

The Wham-O Super Ball was introduced in 1965. Invented by Norm Stingley, a chemical engineer at the Bettis Rubber Company in Whittier, California, the ball was made of Zectron. The "Super Ball" could bounce six times higher than any regular rubber ball. Millions were sold, and it remained a craze through the 1960s.

PAUL ZIMMERMAN: The National Football League hierarchy frowned on the term "Super Bowl," but the fans and the media liked it and used it, and Super Bowl would become the name to represent professional football's championship game.

SHARRON HUNT: It was something else that a toy a child was playing with could have inspired the name.

JERRY IZENBERG: The afternoon of the merger, the switchboard rang at the NFL offices, and the guy said, "I want 20 tickets for the title game."

They said, "We don't even know where it's going to be."

And he said, "I don't care, I want to buy it right now!"

> The championship game was not an afterthought to the merger. They were trying to get games played. Even in the merger they negotiated things like, "When will we play exhibition games against each other?"

By October, with the 1966 pro football season at full throttle, a site for staging the AFL–NFL World Championship Game, scheduled for January 8, 1967, still had not been selected. There was agreement by members of the NFL site selection committee that the game should be played in a warm-weather location.

Growing up in Southern California, Rozelle knew that January weather there could generally be counted on. He also knew that comfort for the crowd and a game that could be well televised were crucial. The native Californian also knew that a field where players could get solid footing would better showcase the talents of everyone who played in the game. His reasoning was that a Southern California venue, with a field that was not frozen and not impacted by weather, would be fair to everyone.

Arthur Daley of the *New York Times* agreed, writing, "Under no conditions should this classic-to-be ever be entrusted to the whims of the weatherman. By mid-January, it's possible that snow in Green Bay or Buffalo might be piled higher than the goalposts."

Initial prospective sites for the game included the Rose Bowl, the Coliseum, the Astrodome, Rice Stadium in Houston, and the Sugar Bowl in New Orleans. Other venues in Texas and Miami also came under consideration.

The committee representing the Rose Bowl objected to its use for a professional football game because they felt it would lessen the prestige of their long-running enterprise; however, as the first world championship football game drew closer, Pasadena's City Council tried to reenter negotiations with the NFL, but it was too late. Anaheim Stadium also came onto the scene too late.

On December 1, 1966, after much wrangling, many false starts, and all kinds of jockeying about, it was announced that Los Angeles Memorial Coliseum would host the event. Two weeks later, news broke that NBC and CBS had each signed a four-year, $9.5 million package to telecast the Super Bowl.

On November 7, the Chiefs defeated the Chargers, 24–14, giving them the fast lane to the AFL West crown. What made the game unique was that Pete Rozelle attended his first-ever American Football League game.

The clinching of a deal to merge was not official until the NFL received a special antitrust exemption from Congress. Rozelle, driven and charming at the same time, pushed a bill through Congress making single-network contracts for pro sports leagues legal. There would now be a league-wide agreement replacing the individual television packages of 12 NFL teams.

Some Washington, D.C., legislators had claimed a merger would make for a NFL monopoly. Promises had been made and broken. Helped by a crucial vote by Louisiana senator Russell Long, the NFL was finally given antitrust exemption. What clinched the deal was a promise by the NFL that its next expansion franchise would be located in Louisiana—and that's how the Saints came marching in.

The scrambling and shuffling resulted in the creation of a never-before-staged television doubleheader on New Year's Day. The AFL Championship Game from Buffalo was scheduled for 1:00 p.m., Eastern Time. The NFL Championship Game was slotted to start at 4:00 p.m., Eastern Time, from Dallas.

It was not until the end of December that the league formally announced that the AFL–NFL World Championship Game would be played at Los Angeles Memorial Coliseum. The date of the game was changed from January 8 to January 15.

> **HANK STRAM: The AFL had been lobbying for a championship game from the beginning since we had nothing to lose. The NFL had resisted that idea because they had everything to lose. But by 1966, the difference in quality of the two leagues had narrowed to the point where a playoff game became inevitable.**

The name "Super Bowl" was not officially used until the third championship game. The first game in 1967 was officially known as the "NFL–AFL Championship Game"; however, fans, the media, and players referred to the first and second games in 1967 and 1968 as the "Super Bowl." And that it became.

Green Bay Packers Hall of Fame head coach Vince Lombardi talks to
assistant coach Phil Bengtson on the sidelines during Super Bowl I.
AP Photo/Vernon Biever

The Coaches
Vince Lombardi and Hank Stram

I firmly believe that any man's finest hour—his greatest fulfillment to all he holds dear—is that moment when he has worked his heart out in a good cause and lies exhausted on the field of battle—victorious.

—Vince Lombardi

Pump it in there, baby. Just keep matriculating the ball down the field, boys.

—Hank Stram

Still evolving at the time of the first Super Bowl were Hank Stram's philosophies and strategies, and he was still looking for the personnel to fully implement for him, whereas Lombardi was at the zenith of his coaching powers.

—Michael MacCambridge

Vince Lombardi, as rendered
by Murray Olderman.

VINCENT THOMAS LOMBARDI was born June 11, 1913, in Brooklyn, New York. He died in Washington, D.C., on September 3, 1970. Henry Louis "Hank" Stram was born in Chicago, Illinois, on January 3, 1923. He died July 4, 2005, in Covington, Louisiana.

The two men were matched up against one another for the first time in a football game on January 15, 1967. Stram, the Kansas City coach, was 44 years old. Lombardi, the Green Bay coach, was 53, although he seemed much older. Both men began their professional football coaching careers at almost the same time.

VINCE LOMBARDI

Vince Lombardi was the first born of five children of a father who was a meat wholesaler and butcher. His mother came from a family of 13 children. Lombardi studied to become a priest for two years, but sports proved more beckoning. Awarded a football scholarship to Fordham University from 1934 to 1936, the young Lombardi gained fame on the team as one of the "Seven Blocks of Granite." It was a bit hyperbolic, but the nickname caught on.

As head coach at St. Cecilia High School in Englewood, New Jersey, for eight seasons, his teams won a half dozen state titles, racking up a 36-game winning streak. In 1947, Lombardi returned to Fordham as a freshman football coach and law student.

Army head coach Earl (Red) Blaik lured Lombardi away from football and law studies at Fordham, hiring him as offensive assistant coach (as the position was called then). At West Point, Lombardi was heavily influenced by military tenets. He was also especially taken with Colonel Blaik, who, along with his father, was one of the two most important influences on his life.

In his five years at the Point with Blaik, the young Lombardi was particularly impressed by the long hours the head coach spent studying game film; however, the ambitious Fordham grad was frustrated that no head coaching job was made available to him.

Lombardi stayed at the Point until 1954. He then moved on to become a member of the coaching staff of the New York Giants. His official title was offensive backfield assistant coach. He was much more than that. He was head coach Jim Lee Howell's top lieutenant, in charge of the offense. The Giants won two divisional championships—in 1956 and 1958—and the NFL championship in 1956.

With the New York Giants, Lombardi and Tom Landry, on the scene as a defensive assistant coach, were an odd couple. One was a born-again Christian, the other a rough around the edges, devout Roman Catholic with the accents of New York in his voice. Landry was calm and reserved. Lombardi was, in Landry's words, "Mr. High Low" (MacCambridge, 2004, 97).

Flush with the thrill of their 1956 championship season, Giants owner Wellington Mara, Landry, and Lombardi were sitting atop the world of professional football.

Sitting at the bottom of the pro football world were the legendary Green Bay Packers. Owned by its shareholders and in one of the smallest markets in sports, the team had won half a dozen NFL championships under Curly Lambeau. Unfortunately, the glory seasons of Lambeau were the stuff of memory. The franchise had fallen on hard times, failing to post a winning record since 1947. Rock bottom for the Pack came in 1958, with 10 losses, 1 win, and 1 tie. Ray "Scooter" McLean, the head coach, resigned under pressure after presiding over the Packer's worst record in 40 seasons in the National Football League.

> **SUSAN LOMBARDI: I was in fourth grade when we all got into the family car, a Pontiac, I think, and drove to Green Bay. It was a long ride. It was late January, and there were piles of snow everywhere. I cried.**

Dominic Olejniczak, president of the Packers, explained, "Vince Lombardi has the background to be a good administrator. We know that from a couple of long interviews with him. He was our man without a question of a doubt."

Out of Sheepshead Bay in Brooklyn, an altar boy at his local parish who had seriously considered the priesthood and a man with no pro football head coaching on his resume, Lombardi was highly recommended by Olejniczak to the Executive Committee of the Green Bay Packers.

Some members reacted by asking, "Who the hell is Vince Lombardi?" It was a logical question. Lombardi had never held a head coaching position beyond the high school level. According to some, there was prejudice against him stemming from his Italian heritage, his New York City ways.

On February 2, 1959, the tough-talking, determined 45-year-old had a meeting with the Packer Executive Committee. Never one to hold back his thoughts, he quickly got to the point, saying, "I want it understood that I am in complete command here."

Two days later, Olejniczak put the built-like-a-pit-bull Lombardi in place as not only the fifth head coach in Green Bay Packer history, but also as the team's general manager. The 13-member Executive Committee had handled many of the duties that Lombardi would now take over as general manager.

Maintaining that he had too much respect for the New York Giants organization that he was leaving, Lombardi explained, "I have about 10 men in mind as assistants. I will not take along any of the Giants' assistants."

> BUD LEA: Vince Lombardi would turn the Green Packers into a NFL dynasty. He had complete control of the team, its Executive Committee and Board of Directors, the media, everything.

> TOM OLEJNICZAK: My father was chairman of Board of Directors. Although he was the one mainly responsible for the hiring of Vince Lombardi, he and my dad were not chums. They were both strong willed people. But they worked well together.

> BART STARR: Until Coach Lombardi came, I was just one of the quarterbacks there. We were being rotated and moved around.

In June 1959, the 5-foot, 8-inch, 180-pound head coach assembled his quarterback candidates: Babe Parilli, Bart Starr, Boyd Dowler, Bob Webb, Joe Francis, and LaMar McHan.

> BOYD DOWLER: I came there as a rookie the same year as Coach Lombardi came in to the Packers. I was a quarterback in college. That was my very first trip to Green Bay. I was the 25th guy picked in the draft. In those days, that was pretty high. There were only 12 teams.
>
> Oh yeah, Lombardi impressed me as a person. When you first met him, he was almost scary. He could look a little threatening. The minute he started talking, you kind of think, "I better pay attention and listen to what's going on here."
>
> And then you get to listening to him and you realize that he had a tone about him, that Eastern New York accent.

But he was very genuine, you knew what he was saying. And if you did what you were told, and you did it the way he wanted you to do it, he respected that. We got along pretty good.

I was approaching my time there as competing for a roster spot as a quarterback. We basically just went through the playbook and talked about some stuff he had up on the board. He got up there and talked about the offense. After a day or so of that—we were there for about three or four days, he said to me as we were going out on the field, "Oh, and by the way Dowler, you're a flanker."

I kind of shrugged my shoulders because I had played in the College All-Star Game as a receiver, and I'd played in the East–West Shrine Game as a receiver. I didn't play quarterback in any of those games. So I kind of thought that I could and would end up being a receiver in the NFL anyway.

BART STARR: Lombardi was a great, great leader. I was so impressed with him from our initial meeting in Green Bay. We were brought in to meet him and to get acquainted with the system and so forth and so on. There were about a dozen of us, and we're seated around a few tables and he's standing up in front of us. And he opens the session by thanking the Green Bay Packers for that opportunity.

Now immediately, that told me something about this man's character and class. Then he quickly turned to us after making that statement. He directed his next comments at us: "Gentlemen, we're going to relentlessly chase perfection knowing full well we won't catch it because nothing is perfect. But we are going to relentlessly chase it because in the process we will catch excellence. I am not remotely interested in being just good."

It almost jarred us out of our chairs. Now, this is his first session with us, and this is how he opens it. God, I didn't even need a chair the rest of the day. So we were really primed. Yes, we were really lucky to have him.

There were reports that Lombardi did not initially feel lucky to have Bart Starr in place as his quarterback, that he was not very impressed with the 25-year-old, whom he thought was too gentlemanly and on cruise control. Mainly a sideline spectator his rookie year, as the Pack went 4–8 in 1956, by 1958, Starr was sharing the quarterback position with Babe Parilli.

Aware that opportunity, environment, and coaching had shaped Starr, Lombardi made up his mind that he would give the still-young quarterback a chance. It would be one of the most important decisions the supreme judge of talent and character would make as a coach. It would be a life-changing experience for Starr. It would prove to be a significant change of direction for the Green Bay Packer franchise.

A 17th-round pick in the 1956 draft, Starr learned as he went along. Lombardi's toothy grin grew wider and wider as he helped the future Hall of Fame quarterback progress in the development of arm strength, touch, and timing—the total package.

> **JIM TAYLOR:** Lombardi's leadership, his ability to recognize and use talent, his way of putting his players together, making them be effective and productive to play the game at a very high level—all were part of his success story. He established all of this after my first year with Green Bay, where we won just that one ball game in a 12-game season.

> **CLIFF CHRISTL:** My background was in Green Bay. In 1957, I got a season ticket kid's section in Lambeau for $2.25 as a ten-year-old. By the time Lombardi arrived, I was 12 and followed them even more, and by the time he departed I was a sportswriter covering the team.

Change was everywhere as the "Lombardi Way" became a way of life for the Packers of Green Bay and their adoring fans. The way the team looked, the way it played, the way it thought—all were given makeovers. Displeased with the look of the uniforms, Lombardi ordered changes that lasted, with current Packer uniforms closely resembling the remake of the old ones.

"Football is a symbol of what is best in American life," Lombardi said, "a symbol of courage, stamina, coordinated efficiency, or teamwork. It's a Spartan game, a game of sacrifice and self-denial, a violent game that demands a discipline seldom found."

Coming off of a five-year tenure at Army, where cohesion and community were paramount, Lombardi was displeased that the team he inherited was made up of cliques, lacked spirit, and was accustomed to losing.

Assembling players for the first time in training camp to begin the 1959 season, he told them, "There are trains and planes going out of here every day, and any man who doesn't want to work will be on them."

Determined to build a winning team, during his first preseason on the job, Lombardi signed Fred Thurston, who had been cut by three other teams. The signing paid off, as Thurston ended up becoming an All-Pro left guard for Green Bay. Lombardi also traded for players who became fixtures on defense, including Henry Jordan, Willie Davis, and Bill Quinlan.

Out of Lisbon, Louisiana, and Grambling, Willie Davis came in a trade from Cleveland in 1960. At first, he was very unhappy that Lombardi decided to convert him into a defensive end.

"I consider speed, agility, and size to be the three most important attributes in a successful lineman," Iron Vince told him. "Give me a man who has two of these and he'll be okay. But give him all three and he'll be great. We think you have all three" (Pro Football Hall of Fame site).

It was common talk among the Packers that, "Challenging Lombardi was like challenging God." The driven Lombardi drove himself and everyone around him. In his first training camp with the team, his powerful voice assaulted the players' ears. "GET BACK OVER THERE! Mister, we don't walk around here—we run!"

Imposing an almost monkish lifestyle on players in training camps, "regimented monotony" one player called it, Lombardi believed in drill and discipline paying dividends and more drill and discipline paying more dividends.

Punctuality was something the sturdy coach insisted on. It became known as "Lombardi time." He fined players who missed curfew or came to practice or film sessions late. The new coach and GM was fond of the expression, "I have never been on a losing team, gentlemen, and I do not intend to start now."

True to his word, Lombardi would never know a losing season as head coach. In eight NFL seasons leading up to Super Bowl I, he would post an 80–25 record, with three ties.

> **JERRY KRAMER: Lombardi ran the show, and he was way bigger than anything and anybody we had ever seen.**

Lombardi's hard work paid off. His first triumph as head man of the Packers was the first game he coached, a grind-it-out 9–6 decision over the Chicago Bears in City Stadium, which opened in 1957, and was later renamed Lambeau Field. At game's end, the stumpy rookie coach was lifted onto the shoulders of players and carried off the field. Using many of the same players from the 1–10–1 team from the year before, Lombardi steered his Packers to a 7–5 record in 1959, winning unanimous Coach of the Year honors.

The Pack surprised the league in 1960, winning the Western Conference title. In the NFL Championship Game, the Pack lost, 17–13, to the Philadelphia Eagles at Franklin Field. Although they were defeated, the former lineman had sent a clear message: We are losers no more.

> **BOYD DOWLER: Football wasn't an exact science of Xs and Os for him. It was a way of life. I think that's why the first championship game we lost to the Eagles in 1960 was the only one. He told us, "As long as we're together, we'll never lose another one. Quit fussing about this. Put it behind you. We'll come back and win one."**

> **JERRY KRAMER: We really began to believe him after the game in Philly way back in 1960. We came off the field and he said this year we played in the championship. Next year, we win the championship.**

Everybody on that team at that moment believed in him. The feeling in my house was that we had better win it all, the grief that guy was putting us through, how hard we were working. I began to believe in him after the Eagle game, knowing we were a better team and should have won that game.

JIM TAYLOR: Lombardi's leadership was on both sides of the ball. He was not going to let individuals and people be "all about me." We're just going to suppress that. We are not going to let you get a foothold in this football team.

We were going to move the chains and use the short passes; this was our philosophy. I'm going to get the ball 25 times a game, and I'm going to give you a good run for your money. I'm going to have plus yardage. And Bart's going to hit the dump passes. We are going to work as a team and chip away.

In '61 and '62, we played the Giants and were successful, and won those two games in Yankee Stadium. We went 11–3 and 13–1 in those two seasons. So we felt like we were the best team in professional football. The 1961 NFL championship was the Green Bay Packers' first title since 1944.

Lombardi just pushed you and enlarged you, and was the leader, and moved you to become a better player. He worked very hard on eliminating mistakes and errors, and making you be serious about playing your position and being the best player you could be. He made us a family.

CHUCK LANE: They were like a family. Exactly. According to Frank Gifford, who was coached by Lombardi, Vince had done a great deal of that with the New York Giants, establishing a sense of family with the players and coaches out there before coming to Green Bay.

In pep talks during practices or before games, the man few called Vince, generally with notes at the ready, made good use of his index finger, vigorously jabbing the air, making dramatic gestures to emphasize a point.

In practices, he used his foghorn voice to his advantage, urging players to hit and hit harder and harder. Like a bantam rooster, during games he moved up and down the sideline, screaming out suggestions and critiquing players as they came off the field.

"Nobody tackling out there."

"Get your head into the game."

There were many times he quoted from the scriptures, invoking the exalted language of religion.

JERRY KRAMER: Vince had a knack for making all the saints sound like they would have been great football coaches. He was a very strong believer in conditioning and execution.

Elevated on the blocking sled, Lombardi was fond of exhorting his players to do "Nutcracker" drills. Blood flowed freely. The Packers worked out with cracked ribs, broken bones, and torn cartilage. Dehydrated players were sometimes sent off to the hospital.

BOB LONG: Coach Lombardi's favorite training camp drill was the "Nutcracker." Players lined up for the one-on-one blocking, offensive player against a defensive one. Receivers had to go against the linebackers, Nitschke, Lee Roy Caffey, and Dave Robinson. And no one wanted to try and block Ray Nitschke.

Another part of the "Lombardi Way" was a training camp regimen that mandated that each player, no matter his status with the Packers, was required to complete a two-mile run in less than 15 minutes. Those who couldn't pass were required to do the run again after practice—the "Lombardi Way."

Running a few plays in different formations, running them over and over again, using simple and compressed language, something he had learned at West Point, Lombardi drilled his players in the theory and practice of basic power football.

Isometric exercise was always in favor for the Packer leader. He took his turn straining at the pulley during training camp and other times against strongmen like 215-pounder Jim Taylor, out of Louisiana State University.

"Visual education" was a big part of the 70-hour workload of Lombardi. Using videotape technology to record practice, he supplemented it with wide-angle projections to view the entire playing field.

Lombardi, ever the teacher, and some would have said ever the tyrant, graded each player on each and every play. A three was the highest grade. At film sessions on Tuesdays, mistakes were replayed as many as 50 times, punctuated by the booming voice of Lombardi.

During game situations, players would return to huddles saying, "Crap, my block was just a 1." "Damn it, I could have run faster than a 2."

BILL CURRY: We would be chastised for our errors. I was a baby, and he was forcing us to grow up, and I wasn't ready. A lot of the other guys looked back on each year positively, even though we may not have enjoyed the process. The result was so outstanding.

BOYD DOWLER: He could be very direct in watching the films from Sunday. And if you didn't have a good game, he wasn't bashful about letting you know. He didn't handle you with kid gloves. Everybody heard what was on his mind, and he didn't have any problem chewing you out. Now, certain guys he could be a little harder on than others.

BILL CURRY: Lombardi coached through fear. Most of the Packers were afraid of him, of his scoldings and sarcasm. It's a form of motivation that works for some people. But it didn't work for me. When I made a mistake, I would dread Tuesday mornings when coaches reviewed film.

CHUCK LANE: I played college football myself, so I was really a fan of the Xs and Os, and it's amazing that in those film sessions with Lombardi and his team, there was some ranting and raving—but when they were preparing a game plan, it sounded like they were plotting and planning the invasion of Normandy. I mean, everybody had input, everybody was saying, "Coach I think we can do this. . . ." "Carroll, do you think you can break that off and get open underneath?"

When the Pack triumphed in a game, when they ran up the score, when players were exultant with victories, the Italian taskmaster still critiqued, still pushed for more from his players.

A strutter on the sidelines of any football field he ever coached on, Lombardi made prime use of his ample vocabulary and booming voice. Depending on the game situation and the performance of his players, criticism, coaching tips, encouragement, and directions—all were part of his verbal bag of tricks. The words "grab, grab, grab" still ring in the ears of many of those who played for him.

BILL CURRY: I remember Lombardi saying, "Winning isn't everything—it's only thing." You might hear that every day for three weeks. He never deviated.

But that most famous phrase associated with Lombardi was not original for him. "Winning isn't everything, it's the only thing!" came from the 1953 movie *Trouble Along the Way,* from the lips of famed actor John Wayne. Even though the Green Bay leader might have adopted that phrase, he had many original sayings of his own.

"Fatigue makes cowards of us all."

"The harder you work, the harder it is to surrender."

Pro football is a "game that requires the constant conjuring of animosity."

Vince Lombardi was a man of many sides. There was the dark-sided Lombardi, the compulsive work force, the one who blotted out anything that was a distraction, the pusher for success no matter the price. He could be abusive to his family members, colleagues, players, and the media.

There was Vince Lombardi the charmer, the man who liked to laugh, the emotional Italian who could also turn on a warm, gracious personality, tell stories, and enjoy the company of others.

TOM SAHARSKY: He was a caring person, involved with his players. If a player had a problem with alcohol, Coach Lombardi would take them to church and take them under his wing.

JERRY KRAMER: He could be very caustic. I almost hit him in the mouth one time. Actually, there were actually three, four times of almost. He actually apologized to me. Through it all, we became pretty close.

PAT PEPPLER: I was an assistant coach at Wake Forest. I knew about Vince Lombardi, of course. I reported to a number of NFL teams, giving them scouting reports, and was paid a hundred dollars for each report. Dick Voris was a friend of mine and was Green Bay's outgoing scouting director. He recommended me to Vince and said Lombardi would be calling. Lombardi called. We met in one of the prominent downtown hotels in Manhattan that the NFL used.

It was January 1963 in New York and cold. I checked into the hotel. I didn't have much of a wardrobe and was not very flashy in my best day. We met in the big lobby. Lombardi was down to business immediately. I learned fast that Lombardi was always to the point. He knew my background and what he wanted.

We talked about the job. He said the salary would be $10,000—I was making $8,000 at Wake Forest. He added there would be $1,000 more for the College All-Star Game that the Packers would play in. I was impressed going from a winless college team to the 1962 NFL champs.

I told him I was married and had a lot of children. He said, it doesn't matter. But what religion are you? I said I was not Catholic like him, just careless.

We shook hands. He said, you stay overnight in the hotel—everything's taken care of. I have promised two other guys that I will interview them. Unless they impress me more than you have, you will have the job.

Very early the next morning he called and told me, "You have the job. Get down to Green Bay and check into the YMCA. Everything's covered."

The YMCA was not exactly a place of royal splendor, but it was warm. Outside it was colder than a well digger's behind—11 below zero. I ran the five blocks to the Packer headquarters.

On January 28, 1963, I was hired as the director of scouting. It was just a few weeks after the Packers beat the Giants in the NFL Championship Game. Lombardi said we will work hard to keep the talent coming to Green Bay. I had to settle in on the job and also bring my wife and kids there. I was on to my new adventure.

I was director of scouting by myself. We had two defensive coaches and three offensive coaches who scouted on the weekends. Vince was very much a part of the scouting operation, as he was with everything to do with the Packers—hands on.

Charts, film, opinions, evaluations, Vince was involved with all of that, and he had strong feelings about who should be drafted. He wanted players with good character. Some of the guys we picked were not exactly Sunday school teachers, but he was able to handle all types.

My first day on the job he told me I'd be doing contracts. He never mentioned that in the interview. All I really had to do was present the offer Vince wanted to the player. I dealt with Vince on a daily basis in the team's office. He was all business. Vince was short and concise, and if he called you into his office, you'd better be prepared. There was a very low level of small talk.

He really was an emotional person. He'd get mad as hell, and then he could be happy as hell. But he had the same butterflies the players had before a game, maybe worse.

Vince said to me, you never get nervous or upset. I said, "Coach, I have five kids and a high-maintenance wife at home. This stuff is a piece of cake."

His wife Marie was the one to smooth a lot of things over. Marie would talk to the young players, and she was very good with the wives and families. She was a good lady, and I felt very comfortable talking with her.

"Coach had a knack for pulling the best out of you," Marv Fleming said. "He pulled me aside in 1963, when I started, and said, 'Marvin, I'm going to be on your butt, but I'm going to make you a good football player. I'm going to make you a star in this league.' I said to myself, 'Make me a star and you can be on my butt all you want.'"

MICHAEL MACCAMBRIDGE: Lombardi held a central role for the National Football League owners at that time. He was a crucial ally of Rozelle. Rozelle made that decision in 1963 to suspend

Hornung and Karras for betting on games, and it was crucial that Lombardi be on board, and he was. He recognized the authority of the commissioner.

A disciplinarian, a man with a strong code of conduct for himself and those he coached, Lombardi did not suffer fools gladly and did not hesitate to levy fines on his players for infractions of any kind.

TOM SAHARSKY: Some of the money Coach Lombardi collected from fines he levied on players was given over to the Norbertine Order just outside of Green Bay. He was strongly an advocate of that organization.

JERRY IZENBERG: There is a story, and I know it to be true. Vince was sitting on the floor in his house in the living room playing marbles with his grandson. Marie, Vince's wife, a smart lady, was on the couch. And the kid started to cry.

"What's the matter?" she asked.

The kid sobbed, "Grandpa is winning all my marbles."

Marie leaned over to Vince and out of the side of her mouth said, "Let him win, Vince, let him win."

And Vince answered, "That's not the way the world is."

PAT COCHRAN: Vince was one day, "Hi Patty." Next day he would walk right by. You never knew where you were with him. My husband's relationship with Vince was stormy but phenomenal. Coaching under Vince was roller coasterish. After a while my coaching husband could not take it anymore. Too many disagreements. He walked out of it.

Fond of his lucky camel hair coat, the neatly groomed Lombardi favored crisp, white button-down shirts.

SUSAN LOMBARDI: Dapper Dan he was. All his clothes were custom made for him. He had an extremely large chest.

Not a sophisticate but extremely intelligent, the former Brooklynite was a lover of the television show *McHale's Navy*, which he watched as often as he could through his thick-lensed glasses.

He arrived for every meeting on time—sharp. Lombardi was an addicted chain smoker, three cartons of Salems weekly for a long time. When he finally kicked the habit after going through great discomfort, he gained 20 pounds. He never went back to smoking.

Golf was also an obsessive interest for him, but he never gave up the game.

> SUSAN LOMBARDI: My father's life was golf. He loved golf. My mother hated to go with him to vacation spots like Bermuda and Puerto Rico because she knew he just wanted to golf.
>
> We lived in a very simple house. My parents had built it—four bedrooms, two and a half baths. My mother had decorated it to the nines—she was very good at it. We lived a not so simple life. As I started to grow up, I had to be home on time for dinner every night. If I wasn't, I would be punished. I had to be there because he had such a great love for the family. It was God, Green Bay Packers, and then the family.
>
> Because when he was coaching he came home from work and never left work. He'd scream out, "Hornung!" He'd yell, "Kramer!" And I wondered, what is he calling those names for? And then it clicked, he wanted me. He couldn't remember my name.
>
> My father was a modest, humble man. He was also a very tough man. And I can vouch for his toughness.
>
> I traveled with the team. I was just a young kid. My mother went to every game and couldn't leave me at home. My friends would ask, "What's it like standing next to Hornung? What's it like standing next to Bart Starr?"
>
> None of the players ever came to the house. Only Paul Hornung, whose mother and my mother were friends.
>
> My mother and I never missed a practice, every game. I was loved by the players' wives. I played with their kids, hide-and-go-seek, any kind of game. The wives trusted me to take care of their kids, and they loved watching their husbands.
>
> When games ended, my father was already telling the team, "They are all going to be gunning for us, and we have to start preparing." "We better watch out," he would say, "They're coming after us."

> JERRY KRAMER: Coach Lombardi would kiss one of the coaches good-bye instead of his wife. He was so wrapped up in himself. He'd leave the house with his pants unzipped and all kinds of things.

The great Jerry Kramer characterizes the great Vince Lombardi in his diary of the 1967–1968 season, writing that he was a "crude, tough, gentle, miserable, wonderful man whom I often hate and often love and always respect" (Kramer, 1968, xiii).

Always full of maxims and philosophy, Lombardi was fond of telling his team,

Winning is not a sometime thing here. It's an all-the-time thing; you don't win once in a while. You don't do things right once in a while; you do them right all the time. There's no room for second place here. There's a second-place bowl game, and it's a hinky-dinky football game, held in a hinky-dinky town, played by hinky-dinky football players.

BOYD DOWLER: Coach Lombardi motivated constantly through constant life lessons. Everything was in the context of football, but he used a lot of other references other than football. Like family. He was a very strong Catholic. He came up with scripture, used it, and referenced it as motivation.

JERRY IZENBERG: The owner of the New York Giants, Wellington Mara, classmate of Lombardi at Fordham, told me, "In another life he could have been a general, the president of the United States. He could have been the pope."

BOYD DOWLER: He was a great leader. You would get in the foxhole with him if that was the venue. He could have been a politician, a general, and lots of things. He knew a lot about history. That was a surprising thing to many of us and gave him a completely extra dimension.

DAVE ROBINSON: I'm a little bit of a historian, was a history minor in college. And I'm a firm believer that if you don't study history and you don't understand it, you're going to become victims to it. And football's the same way. Vince Lombardi was a historian of football. He was a great source of knowledge. I used to talk to him all the time about it.

He also had an amazing knowledge of the game, and he answered my questions always explicitly and told me things I didn't know about the game and philosophies.

CHUCK LANE: He shifted players from one position to another, changing careers.

FRANK GIFFORD: When Vince arrived as an assistant coach for the New York Giants, he changed my whole life. I had been a single wing tailback at USC. Made All-American. Made All-Coast as a defensive player. But I was not happy with my role with the Giants. I was actually getting ready to quit football. He took me off defense and put me on offense. He turned my career around, and I helped his.

CHUCK LANE: Lombardi versus whomever. He just willed victory, and those Packer players loved him, respected him, and played like hell for him.

I met Lombardi for the first time in the kitchen at the office. I stuck my hand out and introduced myself to him and said, "Coach, as long as I'm working for ya, I think I probably should meet ya."

And I asked him, "Do you want to be called Mr. Lombardi, or coach, or . . ."

And he laughed and said, "Whatever's comfortable for you."

I called him "Coach" primarily. I never called him "Vince" a day in his life. Very few people would ever refer to him as "Vince." I think it was just a sign of respect that everybody had for him.

Lombardi was my father figure. Very, very inspirational. I had a great deal of respect for the man. I really liked him. Of course he would holler, and he would rant, and he would rave, and he would carry on, but as mad as you'd get at him, you never lost respect, which I always thought was an interesting balance.

Yep, he could outwork the horse.

And he expected it of his troops. There was a great deal of respect that existed there. And it truly was in the strongest respect imaginable. It was a family of warriors, and I think one of the major reasons for success arose from that atmosphere within the locker room.

In the Packer locker room at Lambeau Field there was a big sign that read:

What You See Here
What You Say Here
What You Hear Here
Let It Stay Here
When You Leave Here

BILL CURRY: Standing in the Packer locker room as a young guy gave you a strong feeling that everyone in the room could push you over the wall.

During a game, Coach Lombardi would do little on the sidelines but praise and scold. Some of the Packers called him the "most useless guy on the sidelines." But the consensus was always that he prepared his team for any game situation, that no one did it better.

KEN BOWMAN: I was an eighth-round draft pick back in '64. Since I was a member of the College All-Star Team, I arrived late to training camp. I was there a few days and hanging out with Bob Skoronski, an offensive lineman. It was before supper. We were coming back from the Dairy Bar. We both had big double-dipper ice cream cones. We were walking, shooting the breeze. Suddenly, here comes Lombardi on his way to the chow hall.

I'm walking along enjoying my ice cream cone. I look at Skoronski. He had no cone. I said, "Bob, where the hell's your ice cream cone?"

Bob said, "Oh, I threw it in the bush back there."

He didn't want Lombardi to see him eating an ice cream cone.

BOB SCHNELKER: I always admired him from the time he coached me when I was in New York with the Giants. I knew what he expected, and I knew that you couldn't be stupid. You had to know exactly what you were doing; if you did, he'd let you alone, let you do your job, never bothered you. But if you mentally screwed up the basics, he was down on that.

I always thought he was the greatest motivator there ever was. Xs and Os, he was like anybody else. But when it came to getting the players ready to play, there was nobody better. He knew exactly when he was going to do it, but nobody else did. He might have done it on a Monday, he might have done it on a Friday, and he might have done it prior to the game on Sunday.

He would get players ready to play. All of them weren't the greatest players in the world, but they played better than they were, some of them, because of him, because of the way he could motivate them. He had a great speaking voice and a great vocabulary, you know, he studied to be an attorney at Fordham.

He could be a little tough to deal with, too. He was demanding, but once you understood that you came to work every day and it didn't make a difference. Winning became a goal, a way of life, something we strove for, and he did, too. We knew what to do.

JERRY KRAMER: No question there was some theatrics in his methods. If he wasn't pissed off he would pretend to be pissed off and put on a little performance. He felt he had to do it to keep you on edge and not be satisfied.

BOB SCHNELKER: Vince ran the whole show, and he ran it well. He was very well organized. He didn't use profanity in his pep talks. The only time he did was in the heat of battle. He used a few words on the sidelines, especially at officials, but I think he was doing it on purpose to get them to his side. In practice he did, and things like that, but not in meetings other than maybe to correct somebody that wasn't paying attention.

BART STARR: It was a fabulous experience all of us had playing for him, being coached by him. I could hardly wait for the next morning to get into the meeting to start that day off. He made everything so exciting, so challenging. He was a brilliant teacher, and because of it he was a fabulous coach.

BILL CURRY: Bart Starr was one who had the guts to take on Coach Lombardi. On one occasion after we had had a bad game, I remember coach was standing up and he said, "None of you guys have the guts to take responsibility. Everybody's pointing your finger at other people. Every quote I see is that, 'Oh, we couldn't stop anybody,' or, 'It's somebody else's fault.'"

This rustle came from the back of the room, a stir, and everybody turned and Bart was on his feet. "Let's get it right, mister. I was quoted widely that I made serious mistakes, I took responsibility. Don't be saying things like that when you don't know what you're talking about."

Everybody thought, "Dear God!"

Vince said, "Okay, one guy took responsibility."

But he didn't take Bart on. Of course, Bart didn't do that very often, but he would do that during a game if coach was over there yelling. Bart would quiet him down. He became our role model.

Vince coached through fear. He told us he was going to do that. He said, "I'm going to use fear, I'm going to use whatever it takes, and I'm going to see that you hate the opponent. And if you don't hate them sufficiently by Thursday, I'll be sure that you hate me by Sunday so that you are in an angry mood when we play." I really didn't like any of that. The guys moaned and complained about it all the time.

FORREST GREGG: He had the offensive line out in the worst weather trying to move a blocking sled that was frozen to the tundra. Players grasped, groaned, some fell to their knees. Lombardi screamed, "You guys are just feeling sorry for yourselves."

KEN BOWMAN: Lombardi would stand up there and he'd give us a little lecture. "Gentlemen, I was thinking the other night, and do you realize that the quality of a man's life is directly proportional to his commitment to excellence? The more committed you are to being excellent, the higher quality of life you will have."

The Packers hated to face second-division teams because Lombardi, figuring they would take the team lightly, had us practice in pads instead of sweats all week and would rant and rave, hoping to increase motivation.

We were down one game at halftime. I think he knew he'd overworked us that week. We had just played miserably. I don't think anybody had any legs. Everybody came in at halftime figuring he was going to just start chewing butt.

He sat. He looked out at us. "Gentlemen, last night I was reading my Bible—and Paul, you ought to pick up that book because there's a lot of good stuff in there—and I was reading St. Paul's letter to the Corinthians, and St. Paul says this, 'There are many runners that run the race, but there is only one that runs to win.'

"And, gentlemen, St. Paul says, 'Therefore, run to win,' and that has been the tradition of the Green Bay Packers from its very inception under Curly Lambeau." He went on and building and building with that big, booming voice to a crescendo.

By the time he was done, you had players trying to take the door off without opening it when we were on our way out for the second half of the game.

Everything to him was a sign of weakness. Coach Lombardi was not really mean, though. He was fair. The first 20 minutes of his practices were probably the toughest 20 minutes you would go through. He wanted you dead tired, barely thinking, and then he wanted to see if you could rise above that and get your brain working. Make an adjustment, make a play. React.

He would also get you mad at him. We used to do these up downs. Running plays. He would say people are paying spas $200, $300 a day for this. I am doing this for you guys for nothing. By the 70th or 80th up down, he would get you where he wanted you. He would start preaching. He would tell us that the superb conditioning he was putting us through one day would win a game for us.

And at the end of the practice we used to run the sweep. We ran it better than anyone. Everybody had their sweep, but we ran ours better than anybody else. In practice we ran it over and over and over again.

He would be preaching, "This is our play. This is the play that defines the Green Bay Packers." He instilled a lot of pride in us. It was all psychological.

When Lombardi first came on the scene as coach and general manager he announced, "You can't play for me if you have any kind of prejudice." He banned his players from frequenting segregated restaurants and hotels. During a time when speaking out against racism was not the norm, Lombardi spoke out and also insisted on fair and equal treatment of players who were gay. His brother, Harold Lombardi, who was gay, died in 2011.

> SUSAN LOMBARDI: My father was discriminated against as a dark-skinned Italian American when he was younger, when he felt he was passed up for coaching jobs that he deserved. He raised his family to accept everybody, no matter what color they were or their sexual orientation.

Defensive tackle Henry Jordan quipped, "He's fair. He treats us all the same—like dogs."

> CLIFF CHRISTL: Green Bay was a lily white city when Lombardi came in 1959. There were basically two shoeshine men at the two big hotels and a sprinkling of other blacks. And that was it.

The population of Green Bay in 1959 was 62,000, and only 128 blacks lived in the county that encompassed the small midwestern city.

> CLIFF CHRISTL: The Packers then basically were an all-white defense, all-white team. There were three blacks on Lombardi's first team—Em Tunnell, who was a 12-year veteran brought over from the Giants; Nate Borden, a holdover defensive end; and A. D. Williams, a backup who rarely played.

Borden came to Green Bay in the 1955 NFL Draft. At that time, the few black players on the team had to stay at the YMCA because they couldn't find other housing. Tunnell and Borden stayed at the Astor Hotel after Lombardi came to town, and it was anything but plush. Tunnell called the hotel a "place where you wouldn't keep your dog." In short time, Lombardi found better lodging for Tunnell and worked on open housing so his black players could stay in some of the new apartment buildings that started springing up in the early 1960s.

By embracing the black athlete and the football skills they possessed, Lombardi was helping make little Green Bay, Wisconsin, "Titletown, USA" and a major player in professional football.

Dave Robinson, Herb Adderley, Willie Davis, and others later wrote that Lombardi did more for diversity than any other person in the history of the NFL, that he was color blind, that there was an entirely different kind of atmosphere for black players in Green Bay than a lot of other cities. He also changed the culture of the city.

WILLIE DAVIS: Coach Lombardi told me, "I consider speed, agility, and size to be the three most important attributes in a successful lineman. Give me a man who has any two of those dimensions, and he'll do okay. But give him all three, and he'll be great. We think you have all three."

There weren't many blacks on the football field at that time, probably even less in the community! You know to go through that and kind of survive it without incident, major incidents anyway, that was pretty special. Coach talked to me about racial discrimination. And he talked to me straight up, too. He didn't try to necessarily convince you to do anything but accept the fact that we had the problem, and that if you focus on the problem, it probably could destroy you.

It's true if I had listened to all the problems, there's no way I probably could have played the way I did. And good ole' Green Bay, then considered the Siberia of football, all that stuff never entered my mind.

Oh yeah, yeah there was prejudice. I'm not one to want to beat Green Bay up for some of its shortcomings, but I can tell you in many ways what I said not too long ago to somebody, Coach Lombardi, as far as that was concerned, did more to promote diversity than any other coach in the league at the time. And that really in many ways was what probably, ultimately, caused us to come together and be a team that wouldn't be denied.

Green Bay fans were fantastic all around. I'll tell you, the one thing about Green Bay fans. Wherever we went, we packed the house. Half the people wanted to see us win, half the people wanted to see us lose. Like the famous story Muhammad Ali said. A little old lady came up to him and said, "Saw your fight, I came to see you get your butt whooped. I hate you!"

DAVE ROBINSON: I was drafted in December in '62, and Vince was getting ready for the 1962 championship game against his old team, the Giants, in New York. And if you knew Vince Lombardi, nothing comes before a championship game.

And so Vince Lombardi, even though I was drafted by him, I never met him 'til after I signed. There was a lot of pressure for us to sign prior to December 31st so that our bonus would be in one salary in one year and our salary would be in the next year income tax wise.

I did sign on December 30th, and then I finally went to Green Bay to meet Vince Lombardi for the first time. You know, guard from Fordham College, one of the "Seven Blocks of Granite," you know what the expectation for a young kid, 20 years old, was to see this hulk of a guy. From Brooklyn too, that's another thing! Tough Italian guy, real good friends with Joe Paterno, who was the assistant coach who had told me so much about Vince before I got there.

In fact, Joe Paterno used to like to say that he was the one that told Vince to draft me. But he said, "I didn't tell him to do it in the first round." Because in 1963, it was not common to draft black ball players in the first or second round. Black ball players usually were saved for the third round. And when Vince drafted Herb Adderley in 1961, in the first round, that was the first Green Bay Packer African American ever drafted in the first round.

And as the story goes, according to Lombardi, somebody on the Board of Directors said, "Vince, I'm not telling you what to do, but we think you're wasting draft choices drafting black guys in the first round."

To which Vince reportedly said, "Listen, I don't draft by color, I draft by football. There's only two colors in Green Bay, and that's green and gold. You guys handle the finances, and I'll handle the football end of it."

JERRY IZENBERG: This is a true story. Willie Davis and Em Tunnell come to Lombardi and told him they would have to miss practice on Thursday. He said, "Why can't you go after practice?"

"We have to go to Milwaukee to get a haircut."

"What do you mean you have to go to Milwaukee to get a haircut?" Lombardi asked.

"We can't get a barber here to cut our hair."

Lombardi said, "Oh really. You're not going anywhere and you are coming with me after practice."

After practice, Willie and Em go with him to the barber shop. Lombardi sits in the chair. The barber says, "What'll it be? A little trim coach?"

He said, "No. Cut their hair!"

And he did.

BOB LONG: Without a doubt, Lombardi ushered in blacks to Green Bay and, in a way, was the breaker of the color line there. Lionel Aldridge, defensive end, went to Utah State. He was the first black player in the state of Utah. Now think about that. That's how groundbreaking he was. He might've been looking for a date at Utah State, but how are you going to have a date when there's no other blacks there. So, he dated a very good friend of mine, Vicky.

Lionel gave her an engagement ring, but she couldn't wear it. She hid it, feeling she couldn't tell anyone she was engaged to him.

I learned from Vicky that Lombardi told Aldridge, "I don't care who you marry, as long as you play good football (and) you keep your nose clean."

Vicky said Lionel called me and said, "Wow, I walked out of there shaking my head. My gosh, I still have a job. So we can get married."

And that's how it started. And that was the support he gave to every player he got, every black player he got. Herb Adderley in the '63 draft. Willie Davis. The year before I got there he drafted Dave Robinson, a Hall of Famer. He drafted Lionel Aldridge, starting defensive end, Marv Fleming. Talk about great players.

I'm not saying we wouldn't have had a great team without those black players, but we were certainly even better with them.

PAT PEPPLER: In a league that at that time did not want too many black players, Lombardi was sort of a pioneer. We were encouraged to scout at the small black colleges. There was no color line on the Packers.

BILL CURRY: Coach detested racism or any other prejudice. He wouldn't tolerate it. He had experienced it because of his Italian American background. Other teams had quotas; they would only have one or two African American players. And Coach Lombardi didn't believe in that stuff. We had 10 guys at times that were African American.

He didn't care what your pigmentation was if you could play, and that was a great lesson for a southern kid coming up. I had never been in a huddle with an African American until I got to Green Bay, except for a couple of those All-Star Games. Never teammates until I got there, and then I met some of the greatest people I've ever known.

Green Bay is a white city. It is more integrated now, but there's not a large African American community, and at that time there were virtually no African American people other than the Packer players.

JERRY KRAMER: Coach had his methods, his secrets, his ways. We played the last two games of the season on the West Coast. One season I had busted a couple of ribs against the 49ers, and we were getting ready to play the Rams the following week. I came out of the game, missed one play.

I see the team doc on Tuesday: "Doc I got a couple of busted ribs."

"Oh, you got a pulled muscle Jerry."

"Doc, I know a pulled muscle. This is busted ribs."

"Jerry, don't worry about it, won't hurt ya."

Another time Fuzzy and I had just had a wonderful write-up in the *Chicago Trib*—best guards in the NFL.

Now understanding this was too much exposure for guards who now thought they would be worth a lot more money next year.

Lombardi was always thinking as coach and GM. We had contract problems before.

We were running a sweep in the game and there was a rookie guard out there. As an offensive guard you've got to belly a little bit to get past the back who is making a block on the defensive end. And if you don't belly, the back will trip over you and the play will be a mess and everything will be a tangle. This rookie did not go deep enough. The back stumbled over him. The ball carrier stumbled over him, and I did too, and the whole play was a mess.

Lombardi had been waiting for something like this. He comes running across the field and he says, "Best guards in the NFL, my ass! We have got the worst guards in football, the worst."

I got up off the pile, and I had done everything I could do to make a contribution and I am hurting. I start walking back to the huddle and I tell myself, "I'm gonna hit this son of a bitch, bust him right in the mouth."

My subconscious is saying, "You'll be suspended, you'll be traded, you'll probably be out of football."

And I said, "Bullshit! I am going to hit him right in the goddamn mouth."

I am standing in the huddle with my arms folded, and he won't look at me. I am not bending down in the huddle as I normally do. I glare at him. I have pretty much lost it. He won't look at me, he starts pacing back and forth.

Bart calls a play. I go to the line of scrimmage, bend over at the waist. They run a play, and I do not move. I go back to the huddle and look at the coach again, arms folded, glaring at him. I am still out of control.

I walk out and yell to Fuzz to get in there. I walk down the sidelines. Vince waits precisely the right amount of time to communicate with me. Vince is exquisitely aware of everything we are doing. He is waiting 'til I cool down just enough.

Here he comes down the sidelines. He slaps me on the back of the neck, messes up my hair. And he says, "Oh, come on, I didn't mean you. What's the matter with you?"

To me, that was a classic example of how he controlled his emotions and how he tried to control our emotions. He didn't want us angry long term. He wanted to piss us off and get us emotional—if he went too far he was not letting his emotions dictate the situation. He would come back and apologize if he went past the line. He would say he was wrong and pat you on the back. Whatever he had to do he did to keep the team focused.

He was always in control of his emotions to the point where if the player took exception, he would make adjustments. He was always able to control his emotions, and he tried to control us and our emotions. He could and would subjugate his ego and emotions to the team. And that was what he asked of us.

He ultimately got us on a quest for perfection. What happens is that you are never satisfied because you can't get there. But if you try to get there, then that salves the ego, takes care of the arrogance, takes care of keeping you humble, working, focused.

SUSAN LOMBARDI: A special time was Thanksgiving dinner after the game against the Lions in Detroit, held with players and coaches and their families and friends. The environment was very happy. It was festive. Especially if we won the game, which at that time we usually did.

PAT COCHRAN: Wives and children would dress up. It was a bonding time.

TOM OLEJNICZAK: For Vince Lombardi, the Packers were his family. No one was excluded from the Thanksgiving dinners. Hundreds showed: players, kids, wives, coaches. The Packers–Lions game in Detroit would be at 11:00 Central Time. The team would get back to Green Bay about six o'clock, and we would all go to dinner. It was always Packers–Lions in Detroit, every season back then.

TOM SAHARSKY: Any parties he hosted, Thanksgiving, the Five O'Clock Club, he was a salesman for the Green Bay Packers and the NFL.

BOYD DOWLER: We always had a real close relationship with everybody, with the whole town as far as Green Bay and Packer fans are concerned. To this day I think that probably the Packer fans are the best in the whole league. We always got along with the local media—if we didn't, Lombardi would get after them!

JERRY IZENBERG: Lombardi was a very good interview for New York and New Jersey guys. The other guys had all kinds of trouble. Milwaukee and Green Bay media were terrified of him.

BUD LEA: I never felt comfortable talking to Lombardi. It was always a tense atmosphere. He was on guard, never giving out any information you could develop into a meaningful story. He had absolutely no patience with anyone asking what he said were stupid questions.

Possessing an extroverted personality, an ability to tell stories, Lombardi knew socializing with others was the best way for him to relax and get away from the pressures he always seemed to have on him.

MICKEY HERSKOWITZ: Lombardi was great at a late-night session in a bar around the piano with a group of guys. One of his most memorable times of getting away from pressure had been back in 1950, when he was with the Giants. It was a time when pro football took a back seat in popularity to baseball and boxing. Training camp for the Giants was staged in Vermont. At five o'clock, there was a social hour. It was a time for Lombardi to have a drink, swap stories with the press, kick back. He never forgot that time.

DAVE ROBINSON: Oh yeah, everybody heard about that Five O'Clock Club, that people were just relaxing and socializing. We didn't really know what was going on.

JERRY IZENBERG: Lombardi brought the routine of camaraderie of that time in Vermont to the Five O'Clock Club in Green Bay. He saw it as a way to stay in the good graces of the media and also as a way to resume to even keel after the intensity of his practices and games. He also claimed he thought it helped him keep his sanity.

BOB SCHNELKER: The assistant coaches were invited to the Five O'Clock Club. It was held generally in the basement in St. Norbert's in the recreation room. They had hors d'oeuvre and whatever you wanted to drink. It was right after practice and before dinner most times and a time to relax after a long day.

TOM OLEJNICZAK: Vince Lombardi was fond of sitting down from five to six p.m. and drinking scotch with his intimates, cronies, enjoying the moment and adulation. That was his lighter, his back-slapping side.

BUD LEA: The Five O'Clock Club was held by Lombardi in his hotel suite on road games. The media traveling with the Packers were invited to attend. Drinks started at five and stopped exactly at six. There was no lingering. Vince's wife Marie was always there with him at the Five O'Clock Club. He wanted her there. He was more personable around Marie, more pleasant.

SUSAN LOMBARDI: At the Five O'Clock Club those who were there were allowed one or two drinks. There were priests, media, friends, coaches. A lot of stories, a lot of jokes. My father had a great sense of humor and could tell a story like no one else.

I was at the Five O'Clock Club. I couldn't drink because I was too young, but as I got older my father would let me have a beer. The club was generally held in a small conference room in a hotel. After a while, when the drinking was about done and the talking slowed, my father would just break it up and everyone went their separate ways.

JERRY IZENBERG: The Five O'Clock Club was a gathering where you drank and talked. There was no pontificating. Writers were allowed to come. You went because somebody might say something. Everything you heard and saw at the Five O'Clock Club was off the record.

CHUCK LANE: I was invited to the Five O'Clock meetings. Lombardi would loosen his tie. And that was when he was really at his most charming self and when he would let his guard down a little bit with people.

Remember Chuck Connors, the old rifleman. I had never seen nor heard of Connors before other than his television performances, but somehow he had wrangled an invitation. I don't know how Lombardi knew him, but Connors showed up and, I hate to say it, kind of made a horse's butt out of himself. He was performing in front of Lombardi and his assistant coaches and whoever else was there, the media. I think he was a Lombardi fan. You know, Coach Lombardi had a following that was just incredible.

BILL CURRY: Some who went to the Five O'Clock Club, I thought they were his classmates from Fordham, but they may have been priests. They and Vince used to play some game, these name games; I never got how they worked. That's the only time I saw Vince laugh before a game. These guys could make Vince laugh.

They had sideline passes. They rode the team bus from the hotel to the stadium with us. There were two buses, and all the veterans would get on the second bus and the rookies on the first bus. But the first bus was like a morgue with tombs. Nobody said a word. Vince Lombardi was old school. No laughing, no levity going into the game. Second bus was the veterans! Sometimes it was rockin' and rollin' back there ahead of the game!

But when these guys got on the plane, these friends of his—for the East Coast games, they always went to Baltimore. Vince would smile with them and laugh with them; not big belly-washing, but a mild chuckle, which was unusual for Vince.

CHUCK LANE: He would travel with one or two of his good priest friends, one of whom was Father Burke who was president of St. Norbert College. And he would have some of his friends from New York City who were in the priesthood who would travel with him on occasion. They were great characters, great personalities. It was almost like the old English gallantry or the English royalty who would travel with their soothsayers and all their advisers. They were usually given sideline passes. And they'd be at the Five O'Clock Club the night before, and they'd have a mass the night before, et cetera. I think it helped sustain him through all the pressures that he went under.

SUSAN LOMBARDI: When the game ended, he was already telling the team, as he told them every year, they are all going to be gunning for us and we have to start preparing.

BOB LONG: For sure, Coach Lombardi was the greatest coach in the history of pro football and also, without a doubt, the best motivator of all time. He could motivate in any situation.

BART STARR: Lombardi wanted to win every game very badly. It was never, "What if we lose? It was we must win. We can't lose." Because Coach Lombardi trained us so well it was just a joy to compete on a Sunday afternoon, it really was. You could hardly wait to get out and play the next opponent.

SUSAN LOMBARDI: At home games we always had A1 seats on the 50-yard line. When we went to away games, the seats were good but nothing like Lambeau. I had gone to all the games before. I traveled with the team. I was just a young kid. My mother went to every game and couldn't leave me at home. I was too young.

BART STARR: Zeke Bratkowski, my backup, was very, very talented. He was a fabulous teammate, and I'll always be grateful to him for that because when he and I would study film together—it was not tape in those days, it was film—when we would study the film, it was just a great experience to listen and see and feel how his feelings were being reflected to you. Absolutely, absolutely he could pick up things on the field also through a quarterback's eyes. You had another set of eyes working for you.

It was Coach Lombardi who also set up that kind of a scenario. And I was very grateful.

KEN BOWMAN: That first Super Bowl team was a typical Lombardi team. We loved one another. There were guys that did not hang around with each other, but still there was a feeling of being a team, being in a foxhole together. That feeling that we got as a team came through this guy at the tops two-a–days, which were killers. They asked Fuzzy Thurston once if he worked out during the off-season, and Fuzzy said, "No, I know Lombardi is going to kill me anyway, so why should I work out?"

BOYD DOWLER: We weren't what you call "cliquey." It wasn't that kind of a chemistry or attitude in our locker room or otherwise. We all had a good time together, we all liked each other and got along with each other on and off the field. It was an unusual chemistry blend of players that came together. And a lot of that was due to Lombardi.

Once you became one of "his guys," we had a bunch that were, and some of them were there for all five world championships, if you were one of his guys, he went down the line with you. He was smart, he demanded. He'd at least try for perfection. He was a good man. Good man.

WILLIE DAVIS: The players that probably didn't get close to the man for whatever reason, in my opinion, they lost an opportunity to meet someone that was so dynamic, so right in his approaches to getting things done. I feel like today in running my radio stations, there's probably a little bit of Lombardi still in everything I do.

I would have to say honestly that when I got picked to be the defensive captain, it was, "Oh my God" to me. I couldn't believe that I had climbed the mountain the way I had.

And I even said to myself, "I can't believe that I'm in Green Bay. I am one of the first co-captains in the league that was a black American."

He would simply say, "If you play the right kind of football, you've got a place here." But if you didn't, there was no place for you. And that was true whether you were white or black.

DALE STRAM: Dad first met Vince Lombardi when he was at Army and dad was at Purdue. Lombardi was sent by West Point to a seminar on passing the ball being conducted by my dad.

They sat down, according to my dad, one-on-one. And all Lombardi wanted to talk about was the sweep. Lombardi spoke for about an hour about his philosophy of running the ball, but he had no interest at all in the passing part of the game.

"I had watched Lombardi at a practice in 1955, when he was still a Giants assistant," recalled Hank Stram. "I couldn't believe that one man could yell and scream and shout so much profanity."

Offense favored by Lombardi was basic and methodical. His most famous play, now mostly referred to as the "Lombardi Sweep" or "Packers Sweep," had Paul Hornung or Jim Taylor following pulling guards Jerry Kramer and Fuzzy Thurston. In full force, it was exquisite, timed to perfection, the gut peak of Packer performance. Lombardi's best-selling book, *Run to Daylight*, explains it. Other teams who practiced to cope with it knew it was coming but were still mostly helpless against it.

CHUCK LANE: The power sweep—guards pulling out, leading the way and providing interference for the backs, was his signature offensive weapon employed over and over again with great success.

BILL GUTMAN: Jets running back Matt Snell told me, "The Packers were so basic. They would tell the world they were going to run the sweep and dare anyone to stop it. That is how perfectly they did that." He said, "I can picture Hornung running behind those guards just going patiently and waiting for the hole to open up, as he knew it would. They had the blocking down to a science, and it was a thing of beauty, especially if you were a fan of the Pack."

John Madden told me early on when he was coaching in junior college he attended a clinic in Reno that featured Lombardi as guest speaker. Madden remembers it this way: "I thought I knew everything about coaching, but that day Lombardi spoke for eight hours about one play—the Green Bay Sweep. I learned then and I never forgot it about how much knowledge goes about the simplest of things. Lombardi was truly an incredible coach."

DAVE ROBINSON: He was the boss. I was one of 40 players, and Vince Lombardi was the head coach and GM. No doubt about it. I knew my place.

CHUCK LANE: Of course he would holler, and he would rant, and he would rave, and he would carry on. But as mad as you'd get at him, you never lost respect, which I always thought was an interesting balance. Yep, he was a workaholic. And he expected his troops to be the same way.

A great deal of respect existed there. And it truly was in the strongest respect imaginable. It was a family of warriors, and I think one of the major reasons for success arose from that atmosphere within the locker room.

For everything you can say about Lombardi, the contrary is probably true also. He could be just absolutely charming at those Five O'Clock Clubs or after a game in his basement in Green Bay. He was fun, he would tell stories. Nobody would laugh any harder at his stories than he would. He was just a typical Italian, warm, outgoing. He was everything you could possibly imagine and then some. There was profanity thrown in, too. Yes there was.

Here I am in Green Bay, Wisconsin, 50 or 60 years later, and I've got a picture of myself with Coach Lombardi. There's only one I ever had, and it's sitting here framed on my wall.

HANK STRAM

He was a piece of work.—Ed Lothamer

Standing just a bit taller than five feet, seven inches and weighing a bit less than 200 pounds, Henry Louis Stram was called the "Mentor" by himself and others.

Murray Olderman's take on Hank Stram.
Courtesy of the artist

ED LOTHAMER: Hank was short and stout but pretty well-built. He was strong.

Born in Chicago on January 3, 1923, Stram grew up in the "Windy City" and Gary, Indiana, and was always deeply interested in sports, especially football.

DALE STRAM: My grandfather was Polish-born. His name was Henry Wilczek. He was a tailor and sold door-to-door for a company. He also was a wrestler. The guy who trained him was German.

My grandfather was built like my dad, very strong. His trainer called him "Stramm," which meant strapping, strong. So my grandfather dropped one "m" and took the name "Henry Stram, the wrestling tailor."

Growing up my dad was known as Henry Stram, but he was born Henry Louis Wilczek. In 1943, my dad went into the service. They saw "Henry Louis Wilczek" on his birth certificate and asked if he wanted to change it legally to "Stram," the name he used. That was how he evolved into Hank Stram.

A halfback at Purdue, where he had also played baseball, Stram had gigs as an assistant coach at Southern Methodist University, Notre Dame, and Miami. When Lamar Hunt founded the American Football League and took over as owner of the Dallas Texans in 1959, he went about the task of finding a head coach. An offer was made to Oklahoma's head coach, Bud Wilkinson, but the legendary footballer declined the opportunity. New York Giants defensive coordinator Tom Landry also turned down the proposition. Hunt turned around and hired Hank Stram, whom he had known as an assistant coach at SMU when Hunt had been a backup on the team.

> **BILL MCNUTT III: Hank predicted that he would become the winningest coach of the winningest team in the history of the American Football League.**

Stram's teams would win three AFL championships and play in two of the first four Super Bowls, winning one.

"We were awfully lucky," Hunt would say, reflecting on hiring Stram. "He had never been a head coach before, and you never know how that's going to work out. In our case it worked out tremendously. I think it worked out great for his career, too, because he ended up in the Pro Football Hall of Fame.

"Hank was really symbolic of the coaching style and the coaching personality of the American Football League," Hunt continued. "Maybe he never would have gotten a chance anywhere else. Hank personified the American Football League. He was a salesman. He was an innovator. He wasn't afraid to try new things."

"If you look at NFL Films as the film arm of the league, Hank was our Errol Flynn," said Steve Sabol, president of NFL Films. "He was the first swashbuckler, the first coach who really understood, more than any other coach, that football was also entertainment."

> **ED LOTHAMER: He was a piece of work. There were times when he had practices and a band playing. He knew a lot of people and many celebrities. If an entertainer or celebrity was in Kansas City, often they would call Hank, and Hank would invite them to come over and watch practice. People like Muhammad Ali, Jim Nabors, Al Hirt, Eydie Gorme, and Steve Lawrence all watched us practice. You never knew who was going to pop up.**

> **ED BUDDE: I really respected him. Hank Stram was ahead of his time: We had a rollout, we had an "I" formation, to confuse the defense we had people in motion. He was a great coach, and we all loved him. He was like a father figure for us.**

The inventive coach was the architect of a system he called his "movable pocket." He was confident it would confuse other team's pass rushes. Stram had his quarterbacks moving out to throw from behind either right or left tackle. It was, in Stram's words, "Something to keep the other team guessing, reducing their pass rush effectiveness by 50 percent. They cannot groove their rush."

The first pro football coach to use a moving pocket for the quarterback, Stram was also the first to put in play a two-tight-end offense and a stack defense, linebackers lining up behind the defensive linemen rather than between them. Creating mini-camps and bringing players in monthly during the off-season was another Hank Stram innovation.

ED LOTHAMER: Hank was probably one of the true promoters in football. Hank was always upbeat. What we heard—and I don't know if this was true—is that players would watch films with Lombardi, he would chastise people and kind of get tough with them: You know, "You weren't good on this play" or whatever.

Hank never did that. Hank had this little flashlight thing with an arrow on it. And he would just put the arrow on you on the screen. He'd never say a word, he'd just be running back and forth, and he'd put the arrow on you on the screen. Everybody knew that they'd screwed up. Everybody knew that there was a change to be made, an adjustment to get better.

BILL MCNUTT III: Hank was full of idiosyncrasies, marvelous ideas, and special ways of having things done. He was brilliant.

I was a ball boy all those years in training camp. Every Chief player that ever played for Hank Stram had to have his shoestrings changed after the last preseason game. Hank, earlier in his coaching career, when he was an assistant coach, felt that he lost a game because a key player broke a shoestring.

Now, remember it was usually just a cotton shoestring, and equipment wasn't as tough and well-designed back then as it is now. So this would be a common thing for people to break shoestrings. By golly, we put new laces on. That's a monumental task because then these players would show up for every game with two or three pairs of shoes based on the conditions because there was no artificial turf.

Well, Bobby Yarborough was supposed to be the shoestring guy, but everybody was. But my point is, we were the ones that had to do that. Even today, I amaze my children at how quick I can tie a shoestring.

Another thing was that Hank always wanted a stick of white spearmint gum and a stick of yellow Juicy Fruit gum in every locker. He thought that if players chewed that gum, it would calm them down a little bit.

DALE STRAM: My dad had a lot of confidence about what he could do and what his team could do. If there was a guy you wanted for a money putt, he was a man who had enough confidence he could make the putt. He was so competitive. He believed in what he did. He was also such a great salesman to the players that he was able to sell what he believed.

He was incredibly organized, prepared. He always said that the best way to give his players the chance to win was by getting them organized and following a plan to the letter.

BILL MCNUTT III: Coach Stram's attention to detail was evident in everything, like having Dial yellow soap in the showers. He thought it reduced infections. Like practicing over and over again the right way for a punter to give up a safety in his own end zone, to how the team would run out on the field to warm up, to replacing every shoelace in every shoe prior to every game, to all kinds of rituals and beliefs. Like the owner of the Chiefs, Lamar Hunt, he knew the power of repetition.

Sherrill Headrick, who was the Chiefs' middle linebacker, was famous for working himself into such a lather that he would vomit prior to every kickoff. When Hank would hear Sherrill Headrick regurgitating in the bathroom, that was part of the signal for Hank then to go over and talk to the team, give them their pregame speech.

Respect for Hank Stram was part of the deal. He treated his players like men, was aware of their needs, and made them aware of his.

TOMMY BROOKER: Hank would let his kids and the kids from all the guys on the team onto the field to run around at Saturday practice. It wasn't more than 45 minutes long most times, just a walk through. And we were always flexible and loose on the field.

SMOKEY STOVER: We had some times when we were on break and Curtis McClinton would get up on a chair or table and sing. He had a deep and rich voice. He had been trained in classical music. It was just glorious, a great break from hard football work. Hank was always there enjoying it.

TOMMY BROOKER: Hank couldn't chew you out, couldn't fuss at you. He never tried. He was a rah-rah coach who believed in making some noise and making some things happen. He was very well organized and detailed and reminded me of Paul Bryant, who was my coach at Alabama.

DALE STRAM: I used to go and watch film during training camp with the offensive line. Dave Hill had a habit that if the whistle blew or was about to blow and he was not engaged with a defender, he would simply take a position on the ground. I asked him why.

He said, "Hank would be mad at me if the play ended and I was not on the ground or blocking somebody in a different color jersey." It was the truth and shows how players felt about Coach Stram, but it did look funny on the practice film.

BILL MCNUTT III: Lamar Hunt Jr. and I back then, 1966 to 1975, worked as ball boys during Chiefs training camp at William Jewell College in Liberty, Missouri. In those days, we worked for room and board. A few years later somebody brought to the attention of the organization that this was not legal and the ball boys started actually getting paid! We washed the laundry, shined the shoes, and put in the laces, ran water at practice.

After a year or two, I got promoted into the tower with Hank. I was just a kid, but in practices I charted plays in the tower with him. There were only two people Hank would invite up to his coaching tower, Lamar Hunt, the team owner, and Tex Maule, the *Sports Illustrated* NFL writer of that era. Man, did I learn a lot about football and judging talent listening to his comments, to their comments.

He would look at a rookie and say things like, "We are going to put a little disappearing cream on him this week," or "A great running back has a hind quarter just like a thoroughbred race horse."

One of the players Hank Stram had a special regard for was the toughest person on that team, Fred Arbanas. He was just one absolutely tough individual. He was the only one-eyed tight end in the history of the NFL. He was involved in an off-season incident, some kind of street brawl or altercation, and he lost his sight in one eye.

I remember that Lenny Dawson and Fred lived close to each other, and they just went to a public park and he learned how to catch the football all over again. I think Fred was the toughest, and I know Mr. Hunt felt that too. I heard him say, "I think my toughest football player is Fred Arbanas."

Hank Stram talking to the team prior to the kickoff of Super Bowl I.
Courtesy of Dale Stram

FRED ARBANAS: I played for Hank for 10 years, and I loved the guy. He was more like a father figure to you than anything else. He never yelled or screamed. I don't think I ever heard him cuss. And most of the staff was the same way. And everybody went about their business. If you busted your butt for him, he would do the same for you. I couldn't have played for a better person.

DAVE HILL: Hank was always an upbeat guy. I mean, he was that kind of guy, that "rah, rah" guy. Sometimes it could overwhelm you a little bit, but he was always a real optimistic person. And I don't think he ever thought he could lose even though he did some. He had that persona you know, "We're going to win. We're going to win."

And he tried to get us to believe that, too. You can't go into the game and not think you're going to win. I don't think we ever went into a game that we didn't think we could win. I know I didn't. Of course, we didn't win them all.

PHYLLIS STRAM: Hank was confident. He was very confident, upbeat. Yes, indeed. I don't think I've ever seen him go out the door to a game that he didn't think he could win. He was a very positive thinker.

Shoes always spit shined, ties perfectly matched to what he wore and knotted to perfection, suits in the latest style and dry cleaned perfectly, Stram cared about each and every detail of his apparel. Some said it was a way of life he had picked up from his father, the haberdasher.

LEN DAWSON: His father was the one who got him started, you know, about "your appearance," and how important it is. I think his dad came over from Poland and grew up in Gary, Indiana. You had to be tough to grow up in Gary, Indiana, I can tell you that.

ED LOTHAMER: Hank had our clothes tailored by a guy named Verl Becker. The name of his business was Verl's Custom Tailoring. He did most of our travel uniforms. And we looked like a boys' school when we were on the road.

Everybody had on the same exact outfits. The pants being like small checkered, black and white, and the coat was black. We had two coats; we had red sports coats. Then when Verl started doing it we went into the black ensemble.

CURT MERZ: Hank was an immaculate dresser. Hank never met a suit he didn't like! I went over to his house once, and his wife Phyllis took me into the bedroom and showed me this giant whole wall that was solid closet space with all his suits. He was a character, but he won!

ED LOTHAMER: Hank always roamed the sidelines wearing a black suit jacket and tie, a matching bright red vest, and handkerchief to match the color of the Chiefs' uniforms. He was real dapper. He liked to look nice all the time. We players noticed it.

The great thing about Hank is, he'd always figure out an angle where he'd go down and see somebody and say, "Hey, you know, I'd be glad to do some advertisement for you if you give me four or five sports coats."

SMOKEY STOVER: We called him Dapper Dan. He was a sharp dresser. You can't take that away from him.

DALE STRAM: Dad was known as such a dapper guy, and people would want him to wear their clothes. He would get solicitations: "If you do some ads for us you'll get some coats." He was dear friends with the Haggars, Joe Haggar and Ed. And they would send him clothes all the time.

BILL ADAMS: Stram, he was the opposite of low key, pretty cock-sure. He was effervescent, confident. He was the epitome of sartorial splendor. He made friends with the local haberdashers.

JERRY IZENBERG: Hank was the best-dressed coach in football at games and not at games. He was a dandy.

PHYLLIS STRAM: My husband was so particular about how he looked and how his players looked. He had tailor-made jackets and pants for the players when they traveled.

CURT MERZ: He had us all dressed up in little red blazers, which was fun because we'd go into these hotels and people thought we were like the bellhops. They'd hand us the bags!

ED BUDDE: We were playing Denver, and we were all hanging out in the front. Well, Bobby Bell was alone, and as the story goes, a cab pulled up in front of the hotel, and a woman got out of the cab. Bobby was maybe 10 or 15 feet away, and she says, "Hey, could you . . ." And he did it! It was so funny, he put all the luggage in the cart and escorted her up to the room. It probably looked like he was working for the hotel!

PHYLLIS STRAM: My husband had enough clothes so that if he were marooned on an island, he could probably last two months without wearing the same thing twice. He wanted to be well-dressed. He was always meticulous about his appearance. He would pack a lot of stuff, but he ended up wearing pretty much the same outfit with a clean shirt the whole time.

BOB MOORE: It was always that way. The jackets were worn as early as Dallas, and the only change came in the patch on the pocket, which went from the Texans logo to the Chiefs when the team moved to Kansas City in 1963. They were red and changed to black jackets around 1967.

SMOKEY STOVER: It was pretty impressive on the road. We all wore the same outfits, the same colors. Uniforms were sharp.

PHYLLIS STRAM: Hair could not be any longer than the hem of the helmet. No long hair, no long sideburns, no facial hair, period. He was

The Dallas Texans before they became the Kansas City Chiefs. Lamar Hunt and Hank Stram are in the red blazers at lower left.

Courtesy of Dale Stram

afraid that if they did get injured or cut on their face it would be difficult for them to suture, and he just liked the clean-cut look.

ED LOTHAMER: Your hair could not touch your collar—that was one of his rules—and you couldn't have any sideburns below your earlobes. And you could have no facial hair whatsoever.

SMOKEY STOVER: I still have my letter from 1961 telling me when to come back to camp, what date and everything. That letter told us not to have long hair, no sideburns, no beard. And if you came back that way, he would tell you to cut it off or get out.

PHYLLIS STRAM: During the national anthem—this is something I don't see any more and it just breaks my heart—he had the players from number 99 to number 1 line up in numerical order, all in a row, with their helmet cradled in their left hand and their right hand over their heart. They'd even practice that, from getting all together and getting into numerical order. The huddle was constructed in the choir formation instead of the usual circular arrangement.

ED LOTHAMER: Hank was also big on fining. If you were late for a meal or if you were late for a meeting, there were pretty expensive fines. If anybody ever got caught with somebody in their room who wasn't supposed to be there while we were out on the road, it was a real big fine.

CURT MERZ: Stram had tendencies to be strict in the sense where we used to call him "Little Caesar." He had all these rules and regulations. He fined me $50 once down in Houston for smoking a cigar in the hotel lobby. I thought I was hidden behind a pillar where he wouldn't see me. He was screaming from across the room, "It's gonna cost you 50 bucks, Merz!"

Tough rules and fines underscored the controlled and conservative approach of Hank Stram. But for all his strictness and rules, the Chiefs were the most racially diverse team in professional football. Roommates were not chosen by color but by playing positions.

DALE STRAM: The AFL gave a whole lot of people opportunity, a lot of castoff players, a lot of guys who didn't get a chance to play much in the NFL, a lot of blacks.

Dad did not see color. But he had to live it. Lloyd Wells, first black scout, was actually hired to scout the small black schools. He was a true talent scout. He was amazing. Dad had a nickname for everyone, and he called Wells "Outta Sight," which I learned came from Wells's habit of telling my dad, "Coach, you must see this guy. He's out of sight."

Wells scouted all the small southern all-black schools. He ended up getting us cornerback Emmitt Thomas from Bishop, defensive tackle Buck Buchanan from Grambling. It was when he became pro football's first black full-time scout in 1965 that he managed to get the great wide receiver Otis Taylor from Prairie View for Kansas City. All these great, great players from these small black colleges. In 1969, eight of Kansas City's eleven starters on defense were black—four of them from historically black schools.

CURTIS MCCLINTON: Lloyd Wells was a unique personality, a unique affiliator who came out of the Southwest Conference, out of Texas and the Negro colleges, and he happened to know all the trees in the forest. He knew the right plums, the right peaches, the right grapes. And he was able to pluck them and pull them into the attention of Lamar Hunt, who had a sense of trust and affiliation and cognitive respect for Lloyd Wells, who was respected for his ability to denote talent. He also was an individual who had great affiliation skills with his culture, with the black players. He also had the ability to interact at the highest level, whether it was the president of the university, a coach, an assistant coach, or a player. He could move and gather knowledge and information like no one I ever knew. He could also not be deceived.

ED LOTHAMER: Hank was an offensive genius. Hank really could put together offenses really well. He knew his personnel, he knew what they could do, what they couldn't do.

For me, Hank was probably one of the best offensive-minded coaches in history. We really basically had the San Francisco offense way before anybody else did. Because he had coached Lenny (Dawson) at Purdue, he knew Lenny was extremely good at short passing. He was all right passing long, but his real game was short passes. So he went out and got these big wide receivers, and we ran a California offense—short patterns, accurate passes, hope the guy comes up and misses the tackle and the big receivers could shake them off, and then they'd go down for a touchdown.

LEN DAWSON: Hank was a very personable guy. You know, he had a terrific sense of humor. But when you get down to business in the football business, he was very serious about that. But he could laugh at himself, that type of a guy. I can't imagine Lombardi being that type of a guy, but Hank Stram was that way.

And very innovative. He was doing that at Purdue, trying to find ways to improve the offense and probe all different ways to improve the defense as well.

Everybody was straight back in the pocket; there wasn't any spread formations back in those days either. He decided, "Well, wait a minute. We can move the pocket. We'll need somebody who can throw on the run, and get out there and get set and do that."

And I was able to do that. It was just his way of presenting more problems for the defense that he was facing. And he was big on play-action passes as well, because we had a good running game. And off of the running game, the play-action passes really helped. He was always trying to be innovative.

Restaurant owners hated to see him come into their place if they had cloth napkins on the table, because he'd be diagramming plays while he was at dinner. They'd give him a pad of paper and say, "Here, write on this coach, not on the good napkins."

But he was always thinking about how to improve things. That's what made him a heck of a coach.

I didn't know Lamar before I went with the Dallas Texans. I know that he and his brothers would sit around training camp and see who should be on the team and who should be cut. They cut me several times before Hank Stram decided I was going to be the starting quarterback. That's what I was told by Hank. I didn't believe everything that Hank told me all the time, because he might have sometimes a tendency to exaggerate things.

DALE STRAM: My dad was watching game film one day when he noticed how quickly defenses were charging after running backs even before the handoff. He thought what would happen if Len Dawson faked the handoff, then hesitated a half-second or so and passed the ball to a receiver behind a defender racing toward the line to stop the runner.

Dawson followed dad's plan. It was a great success. It was something brand new in football at all levels. It was the play-action pass. Who made up the name is a mystery. But there is no mystery about its impact on the game of football.

In that era, the Chargers had a large defensive line, with guys like Earl Faison, six foot and five inches tall and 290 pounds, and Ernie Ladd, six foot and nine inches tall, 300 pounds. Lenny could not throw the ball against guys like that. He had balls knocked down. Dad had to neutralize these two guys, had to invent something. He invented the moving pocket. He also went for players equally as big and competent as these guys.

The chess match was always in play. In the rivalry with the Raiders, we had the great wide receiver Otis Taylor. The Raiders got a player who could cover him—Willie Brown. We had Buck Buchannan. The Raiders had to get back so they got Art Shell, Gene Upshaw.

It was all about plugging the gaps and being able to win your division. Squads were small in those days, so you had to be quite specific on who you drafted to plug in holes right away.

Always on the lookout to improve his team, always staying in touch with his network of contacts, always open to taking a chance, always seeking to gain any edge he could on the field, Stram maintained a unique relationship with Len Dawson, who he had coached at Purdue. But Dawson had languished after being drafted by the Pittsburgh Steelers of the NFL.

> LEN DAWSON: I had serious doubts about my ability. In five years in the NFL, I had never played two games in a row. I never started and finished a game. I had to ask myself why. One conclusion was that I was not good enough.

His former coach disagreed. Stram reinvented and reconstructed Dawson's mechanics, and by 1962, Dawson had become a confident and capable quarterback.

> LEN DAWSON: Hank Stram saved my career; I wouldn't have had a career if it hadn't been for him. Hank Stram was the assistant football coach at Purdue University. They didn't have titles in those days, but he would've been considered the offensive coordinator. Stu Holcomb was the head coach. I knew Hank from after the time I graduated from high school and was in college for four years, so my relationship with him went back a long way.
>
> I was the number-one draft choice of the NFL Pittsburgh Steelers and was with them for three years. I really didn't get to play much. I think I started one game in those years there. I played behind Earl Morrall the first year and then Bobby Layne came over from Detroit.
>
> I ran into Hank, who was in Pittsburgh at a coaching convention/clinic. We had lunch. He was the head coach then for the Dallas Texans. He was asking me how I was doing, and he could see I was not very happy because I hadn't had an opportunity to play.
>
> He said, "If you ever get free, let me know. I'd love to have you on the team." So I got to thinking. I was now with the Browns, traded from Pittsburgh to Cleveland. I went to Paul Brown and asked for my release, asked to be on waivers. And he did. He did it in June.
>
> Back in those days, the assistant coaches took a month off before going to training camp, and that month was in June generally. They didn't have scouting staffs and other stuff that they have today. So many of the teams didn't realize that I was on waivers. So I cleared waivers. I called Hank. He came to Pittsburgh and signed me.

Stram was surprised by Dawson's sloppy fundamentals in the early weeks of training camp.

> DALE STRAM: Lenny Dawson came in and looked terrible, and dad remembered in his mind's eye how great he had been at Purdue

and now how these skills had seemed to have eroded, become diminished. At the beginning of the year at the training camps, dad put Cotton Davidson in as the starting quarterback. He was that the year before.

Stram overhauled Dawson's fundamentals—his footwork, his throwing motion.

> DALE STRAM: There began a quarterback controversy as Lenny started to improve. Dad announced that Lenny would be the starting quarterback that season. Controversy developed when Lamar Hunt traded away Cotton Davidson without consulting my dad, who was so angry he did not speak to Lamar for weeks and was tempted to resign since dad made all the football decisions.
>
> We did not have a skilled punter due to the Cotton Davidson trade. Dad had to modify the whole offensive plan and do things with higher risk. We did not have a skilled kicker in that '62 season. The good news was that the trade yielded the number-one draft choice in the '63 draft, and that turned out to be Buck Buchanan.

"At that time," Buchanan told the Associated Press, "I was the first player from a small black school drafted in the first round. It said a lot for a player from the Gramblings, the Prairie Views. That was important to me."

> HANK STRAM: A big guy will be strong, and he might be quick, but he is rarely fast. Or sometimes he's strong and fast, but not quick. But Buck had it all. Plus he had a great attitude.

> LEN DAWSON: There was more throwing in the AFL. When I was in Cleveland for two years, they had Jim Brown and Bobby Mitchell. Now, what do you think they're going to do? They're going to run the ball. They had some classics against the Giants back in those days.
>
> After being with the Browns in '60 and '61, I was rusty. When I got to the Dallas Texans training camp, I hadn't thrown and hadn't competed in five years since I got out of Purdue.
>
> And fortunately Hank knew me and had worked with me in college and had stayed with me, and was an excellent quarterback coach. Well, first and foremost Lamar Hunt did save my career. He founded the AFL. But it was Hank Stram who gave me a career.
>
> I ended up being the starting quarterback for the Dallas Texans, 1962. We went into the championship game against Houston. We won it.

BILL MCNUTT III: For those seven summers, I was the only person up there with Hank Stram in that tower. It was like getting a pro football tutorial. You learned a lot from a man like that, about football and also about people.

I learned particularly how to evaluate player personnel and talent. One of the many things he told me was that kickers and quarterbacks were the most undercoached players on a national professional football team. He felt that one of the reasons that Lenny Dawson made such progress when he became a Dallas Texan was because he started receiving coaching again. He felt like Leonard didn't get much coaching during the four or five years that he was with the Steelers, but that was not an indictment of the Steeler organization, it was an indictment of a time when people really didn't coach kickers, and they really didn't coach quarterbacks.

Hank was his own offensive coordinator, and he personally worked out all of the quarterbacks that ever played for him.

SMOKEY STOVER: Coach Stram was a super duper guy. Very innovative. Very good at getting you fired up psychologically. He was a great mind reader. He could feel the pulse of a game pretty quick. He was an honest guy.

He never berated you in front of people. Now, he would call you in the office, and he would berate you and just make you feel like you weren't worth a whole lot, but when you walked out of that office and that door shut, he'd put his arm around you and say, "Hey, so how are you doing? What about the kids?"

And he'd bring you right back up, you know. It was told that he was very much so opposite of Lombardi.

BILL MCNUTT III: Hank loved to tease people, but he did it in a good-natured way. Now, the subject of the tease did not always see it that way. Jack Steadman was named the GM of the team in 1966, after Hank was already a coaching legend. When it came time to take the team picture for the Christmas card, Hank told Mr. Steadman he was not allowed in the picture. Mr. Steadman took it hard and went to Lamar, who just giggled and said, "Jack, get in the picture, he does not mean it."

DALE STRAM: My dad was a very devout Catholic and would go to church before games every Sunday. In the mid-60s, the Chiefs had flown into Boston for a game. Right near the hotel they stayed at was a Catholic church. Dad went to Mass after Communion, and after the service the priest came running over to him.

"Hey, aren't you Hank Stram?"

"Yes, I am, Father."

"Are you here for tomorrow's game with the Patriots?"

"Yes," dad said. "Would you like to go?"

"I'd love to go. Can I bring a friend along?"

My dad said, "Sure," and arranged for sidelines passes, and they went to the game. This was the beginning of a lifelong friendship!

The monsignor attended and paid his own way to all the big games. He would never take a reimbursement for his expenses. A little man, he was about five feet, six inches, with a fair build, about 145 pounds. He had black hair. Under his vestments he would wear a Kansas City Chiefs T-shirt. There were times he would lift his garment and show off the shirt to anyone interested.

We would have Masses before games, and the bigger the game, the more players would attend. E. J. Holub was usually the altar boy. Monsignor Mackey would give his homilies with special reference to the Chiefs: "Now Lord please let Lenny's arm be strong and accurate. Bless Buck. May Otis's hands be sure and true."

My dad wanted every advantage that he could get. Monsignor Mackey was one of dad's best friends and a special good luck charm. The monsignor took pleasure being on the sidelines during big games and wearing a Kansas City jacket. During the game, he would position himself on the sidelines next to dad, his rosary in his pocket, and dad would talk to him and sometimes say, "Monsignor, you better start strumming those beads. We need a little help!"

Vince Lombardi and my dad were strong students at university. Both were strong Catholics of great faith. Hank got Lamar to let him travel with his own team priest, Monsignor Mackey from Boston. Unlike Notre Dame University, Hank was not allowed to have an "offensive priest" and a "defensive priest." He only had Monsignor Mackey. The Catholic Church is a very top-down organization, and that was the way Hank and Vince ran their professional football teams.

The "Mentor" nickname for my dad came about from Monsignor Mackey, who coined the term. Dad liked it and held onto it and used it. And others used it to describe him.

JERRY IZENBERG: Hank had a supreme ego. He would always give long answers when interviewed, which is what you wanted as a writer. Hank was a very affable guy. He could talk the talk.

BILL MCNUTT III: Dad and Lamar used to refer to Hank as the "Little Corch." They said "Corch" instead of coach because that was the way Hank used to pronounce it! Hank had a way to slightly mispronounce words in a way to emphasize what he wanted to say and add character to the way he communicated.

DOUG KELLY: I started with the Chiefs as assistant director of public relations. There were all these "Stramisms." One of them was "birdseed." He always wanted to know what the "birdseed" was. "Birdseed" was a euphemism for information. Hank, in the Internet age, would've been incredible! He just had a very insatiable appetite for knowing what was going on around the football team. Information from another team was highly valuable.

There were those who called the irrepressible Stram innovative, inventive, and intuitive. Green Bay's Fred "Fuzzy" Thurston told a *Baltimore Sun* reporter, "I have no idea what kind of a coach Stram is. But if he is better than Lombardi, he is God."

Anything but laid back, loquacious, a guy who loved to talk, a wisecracker on the sidelines, self-assured, Stram had his own special vocabulary. In addition to calling himself the "Mentor" and "Co-Ach," Stram coined the term *play-action pass* and called his coaches the "Rats" and his players the "Boys." The Chiefs didn't drive the ball. According to Stram, they "matriculated" the ball. The refs were referred to as "sausage stuffers."

"You marked it good! You marked it good!" he would scream to the officials.

"How could six of you miss a play like that?" was another of his favorite lines.

DALE STRAM: Jim Schaaf was the public relations man for the Chiefs. My dad, who had nicknames for everybody, called him "shaky," because he was always nervous.

ED LOTHAMER: Everybody that played for Hank, I think, believed that he cared about them. Years after I played I'd get a call from Hank every month: "How are you doing? What do you hear about this guy, what do you hear about that guy? How's Johnny Robinson doing? How's Curt Merz doing?"

It's hard to say, but I do think the guy really considered the players that he was with a family. You have to remember, back in those days we all stayed together a long, long time. It wasn't free agency guys coming and going every year.

LEN DAWSON: His whole life was football. That's what he was born for, I think. He had a passion for it, not just a liking. He was really sincere when he talked about the team being a family. Everybody really loved him.

DALE STRAM: We were always like a big family, and as time went on, I used to hear my dad speak as training camps would begin. Dad would say to the guys, "Look, we will only be together for a very short time as a team, but we will always be together as a family."

AFL CHAMPS 1966 1ST SUPER BOWL TEAM

The 1966 Kansas City Chiefs, showing the kind of decorum that Hank Stram insisted upon.

Courtesy of Hank Stram

Chapter
THREE

Santa Barbara and Long Beach

Lombardi warned us all week long. He was walking on eggshells. He had a short temper. He would not let us sink.

—Boyd Dowler

I felt we could score on them. If we scored enough—maybe three touchdowns and a field goal—we would win. Football often is that simple.

—Hank Stram

DURING THE first year of the American Football League and National Football League championship game doubleheader on New Year's Day 1967, the Buffalo Bills hosted the Chiefs at 1:00 p.m., Eastern Time. The Dallas Cowboys played against the Packers at 4:00 p.m., Eastern Time.

The Packer–Cowboy battle, played in the Cotton Bowl, was a matchup of old colleagues, Tom Landry and Vince Lombardi. Played on a dry field before a sellout crowd of 75,504, the game was telecast on CBS, and the announcing team of Jack Buck, Ray Scott, and Frank Gifford was at the top of its game.

The Packers defensive coordinator, Phil Bengtson, spoke about the game, calling it "one of the most exciting 60 minutes in the history of football," adding, "but to this day people remember only the first four minutes and the last four."

In the waning minutes, with everything on the line, Green Bay won, 34–27, copping its second straight NFL championship and its fourth in six years.

It was the first NFL title game played after the merger of the NFL and AFL, the 34th annual championship contest since the NFL originated title games after the 1933 season.

> JERRY KRAMER: At that time, the World Championship Game was our Super Bowl. The whole world of pro football was tuned in to what happened, always. It was the biggest thing that had ever happened to any of us. We proclaimed ourselves world champions. It was huge.

When Green Bay held off the Cowboys, NFL fans felt that the true champion had been crowned. Back then, the NFL Championship Game ranked second only to the World Series among sporting events in the public's mind.

> PAUL HORNUNG: Winning the NFL World Championship was our Super Bowl. We proclaimed ourselves football champions of the world.

To get into the AFL Championship Game, Hank Stram's team sailed by San Diego, 24–10. A few weeks later, on a muddy and sloppy field, KC battered the two-time defending Buffalo Bills, 31–7, to win the AFL championship.

On January 7, snowplows in Green Bay worked hard to clear the field of play for the final practice of the Packers. Except for linemen, the practice was noncontact. Blocking sleds were no longer visible, buried under four-foot snowdrifts.

SANTA BARBARA

The next day, the team, along with support staff, boarded a charter jet. Leaving the frozen tundra of Wisconsin, the Packers flew west. Lombardi had kept his charges working away in the bitter cold of the Green Bay winter as long as he could. When the Packers finally arrived in California, Kansas City had been there for four days.

BUD LEA: As beat writer for the Packers for the *Milwaukee Sentinel*, I never asked Lombardi for a favor except once. I asked him if I could travel with the team to Santa Barbara under the conditions that the *Sentinel* would be prorated for my travel expenses. Two days before departure, Lombardi told me, "Okay, you can come with us on one condition. I don't want any of my players disturbed on the flight. I don't want you interviewing any of my players."

The day before we left Green Bay, there was 14 inches of snow on the ground. In California, there would be warmth and sunshine.

Vince Lombardi, his wife Marie, and the assistant coaches settled into the first-class section of the jet. I sat with the players in the coach section. Throughout the flight, Vince would make several trips to assure himself that none of his players were being interviewed. Of course, I interviewed players on the long flight to the West Coast, but every time he passed by, I would pretend I was reading a book or sleeping.

About an hour before landing in Santa Barbara, a scream came from the back of the plane. Some of the players had taken off their shoes and were playing cards when someone accidentally stepped on Elijah Pitts's foot.

That someone was Susan Lombardi, Vince's daughter.

"I didn't mean to," she pleaded to her father when he raced back to see what had happened. He scolded Susan and ordered her back to her seat. And when he passed me, he gave me a look that said, "None of this will be reported in the *Sentinel*." Nothing was.

The plane landed at the Santa Barbara airport on January 8, 1967, a week before the kickoff for the AFL–NFL World Championship Game. Players came down the ramp, dressed in suits with shirts and narrow ties. About a thousand cheering fans ran down the runway.

DAVE ROBINSON: There were people near the plane that lived out there who were Packer fans. In Green Bay, there used to be a sign that said, "Green Bay: Titletown of the USA, population 50,000" (or whatever it was). Somebody had the sign, the street sign from Green Bay, Wisconsin. It was being held up. The story was that some kid had stolen it and then taken it to Santa Barbara!

Annoyed and agitated by the hullabaloo, Lombardi relaxed a bit when the police escort finally showed up. Players boarded the buses, and the Green Bay contingent was driven to the Santa Barbara Inn.

BUD LEA: When Lombardi got a first sight of the majestic mountains that surrounded the plush Santa Barbara Inn and the oceanfront view, he was irked. That was all he needed—a luxurious resort, a vacation haven. He wanted something basic, barren.

He would correct things in a hurry. Forget the beautiful surroundings, he would make it like training camp all over again. One of the first things the man some called "St. Vincent" behind his back took note of was the swimming pool. He quickly declared it "off limits."

SUSAN LOMBARDI: We were no longer going to have league championships. My father was like, "Ooh, we gotta go play another game." We already won the championship was how he thought.

My father was calm but also nervous. He had all the confidence in the world that he was going to take care of the Kansas City Chiefs.

With the defeat of Dallas on New Year's Day still being savored, a determined Lombardi had wanted to remain at home in Green Bay, have his Packers practice there and arrive in Los Angeles the Friday before the game. Arguing that Green Bay's defeat of the Cowboys showed that his club was the best of the best in professional football, he maintained that it was entitled to a "home cooking" edge; however, NFL commissioner Pete Rozelle disagreed. Insisting that the Packers set up camp in the Los Angeles area, he reasoned that the team would be more accessible for media exposure. After some back and forth, the compromise was Santa Barbara, some 95 miles from LA. The compromise did not please Lombardi.

BOYD DOWLER: Until 1963, our last two regular-season games were always played on the West Coast. We would play the San Francisco 49ers and the Los Angeles Rams, or we'd play the Rams and 49ers. We always stayed at Rickey's Studio Inn in Palo Alto, and no matter whether we played the Rams first or the 49ers first, that week in between those two games we would stay in Palo Alto at Rickey's. I think that's probably what Lombardi wanted to do.

Ricky's opened during the post–World War II building boom. Owner John Rickey had created a new type of property, with lawns, shrubbery, gardens, fountains, pools, and swans. Its overriding concept was that of a garden hotel with residential-style housing. It was a concept that Lombardi liked very much.

The Packer top man told the NFL chief that his plan to practice in Palo Alto, about 350 miles away from the tumult of Los Angeles, would make it possible for Green Bay to have peace and quiet in a setting in the middle of nowhere.

BUD LEA: It was clear that Lombardi might have helped drum up more interest in the game if he had brought his team to Los Angeles the week before, as Commissioner Pete Rozelle had asked him to do. He refused, citing too many distractions in Tinseltown.

CHUCK LANE: I think Rozelle definitely could order Lombardi to train in Santa Barbara. In those days I'm sure there was a lot of give and take between Lombardi and Rozelle because of the respect they had for each other. But I think Lombardi understood the responsibilities that he had and the need for it. If it was an initial disagreement, I don't think it was that big a deal.

DAVE ROBINSON: No, I never learned why we trained in Santa Barbara instead of LA. I never asked Coach Lombardi, but we just assumed that he didn't want to be in LA in that rat race. But Vince had what he wanted. He had us sequestered, and he had control. Also, he didn't have to worry about nightlife, guys going down trying to party.

BOYD DOWLER: We pretty much stayed close to home. We had a meeting every night.

BOB LONG: There was hardly anything going on in Santa Barbara, but it was about the best place Lombardi felt he could take our team. I know he wanted to go to a place outside of San Francisco, but Santa Barbara was definitely the second-best place to go. Santa Barbara had just one place that remained open past 10 at night—the Western Union Office.

MICKEY HERSKOWITZ: I had tried to book the Packers and the Chiefs into hotels in downtown LA, but Lombardi wanted every edge he could get and wanted to stay as far away from media that he could. He did wind up going to Santa Barbara, but he also booked a hotel 20 miles away from the city center.

I got him a Southern Cal or UCLA practice field, one of the really good ones. He turned that down and picked a field that would provide his players as few amenities as possible, made them as captive as they could be.

Lombardi picked Harder Stadium. Built in 1966, on the campus of the University of California, Santa Barbara, it seated 17,000.

The cautious Lombardi, under pressure from all quarters, was wary of anyone spying on his team's practices during the time before the big game. So he specially ordered green canvas for a cover up of the end of the field's open storm fence.

> CHUCK LANE: Lombardi used to do that all the time in Green
> Bay. He was absolutely convinced that George Halas of the Bears
> had taken up residence somewhere in a high-rise. Of course, in
> Green Bay then a high-rise was about two stories high. But he
> was convinced that George Halas was watching every practice, so
> throughout his career in practices he switched the uniform numbers
> of the players.

Determined that his practices be as secret as possible, concerned that his mighty Packers would become too enamored with the beauty of Santa Barbara, the highly focused coach also ordered that plays be run at UCSB's new Campus Stadium, away from the appealing view of the nearby mountain range. His reasoning: less scenery, more concentration.

> JERRY KRAMER: We had accomplished a great deal. We were a
> mature group. Lombardi was in full control, no questioning of his
> methods or what he had to say. At that time we had gone into virtu-
> ally accepting everything he said as gospel.

> WILLIE DAVIS: Here you had a new guy challenging the old estab-
> lishment. We had a job to do, and my attitude was, "What better
> team than the Packers?"

> JIM TAYLOR: We all knew we had a burden on our shoulders. We
> were representing the National Football League, and we wanted to
> have a good showing.

The Packer roster contained 28 players who had played in at least two championship games. Nine of the starters had been participants in all five of Lombardi's championship games.

> JIM TAYLOR: We were practicing to get ready for another football
> game. It did not matter who the team was or where they came from,
> if they were from Canada, or China, or Russia, or wherever. It was
> just a matter of getting ready to compete. We felt like we were as
> good a football team that existed, and we felt we could compete with
> anybody anywhere. It's not rocket science or brain surgery; it's play-
> ing football and competing against another football team.

Sure, we were up for it, but we were not excited. You go out, and if you're man enough you win. You do what you have to do, and you don't make a mistake. You don't have to get excited. If you lose, the world goes on. It's not a matter of life or death.

Before the 1966 season started, talented starting halfback Jim Taylor had made it clear that he would not return to the Packers in 1967. He announced his plans to become a free agent and become a member of the new expansion team, the New Orleans Saints. Disgusted, infuriated, feeling a bit betrayed, Lombardi refused to speak to Taylor that entire season.

> JIM TAYLOR: There was all this animosity towards the AFL. I had no negative feelings to the other league. None. Their existence just opened up more jobs for the National Football League people. I took my shot at that. They had their league, and they were competing with the NFL, so it was a matter of the survival of the fittest. You just wanted good, high-class, high-level football.

> BUD LEA: It was not only the NFL against the AFL, but CBS against NBC. Ford against Chrysler. Even the writers who covered the respective leagues treated their press credentials like dog tags, assembling in trenches according to their league allegiances. It was NFL writers over here, AFL scribes to the back of the room. And this was all before the big game had even begun. This was the pregame atmosphere.

In Santa Barbara, on the surface, the usually intense Lombardi appeared amiable and agreeable. He was available to reporters, but he was quick to show annoyance with questions that seemed to him to always be the same: "Will Hornung be all right and play?" "What do you think of the Chiefs?" "Any special thoughts about their league compared to the NFL?"

The question that reportedly annoyed him most of all: "Is the NFL a better league than the AFL?"

In a growling voice he responded, "I'll answer that after the game."

A reporter asked, "Is this going to be the most important game you have ever coached?"

"Every game," Lombardi replied, "is the biggest to me. I like to win them all. If we lose the world won't end for Green Bay. But we like to talk about winning. And we don't care how we do it."

"What does the Super Bowl mean to you?"

"This is the first time it's been played," Lombardi said, "so I don't know. I think a game has to have a little tradition to have great meaning. Maybe next year this will be the biggest game in the world. Right now, it's just another football game. Incidentally, I hate that name. I wish you guys would change it to 'The Bowl.'"

Built like a pit bull and sometimes possessed of the same ferocious temperament, the head man of Green Bay made a point of emphasizing that Kansas City's success in its league against teams like the Oilers and the Patriots was a success that would not work against his Packers. There was a good deal of talent on KC, he claimed, but also individual technical imperfections.

That was what Vince Lombardi put out there for public consumption. In his heart of hearts, however, the intense pilot seemed to have feelings that were different from his public pronouncements.

> **FRANK GIFFORD: After Lombardi watched Kansas City on tape, he confided to me that he thought the Chiefs were really good and there was a chance his team could lose.**

Lombardi had been so preoccupied with the Dallas Cowboys that it took him a while to focus his thinking and planning on Kansas City—not until after the NFL Championship Game victory.

Packer chief scout Wally Cruise had been sent to Buffalo for the AFL title game to get as many insights as he could. When the Packers started to prepare for the Chiefs, Lombardi admitted to wishing he knew more about them.

"What I know of their personnel is from information I gathered from player drafts and from films of the Chiefs' last three games," Lombardi explained. "They've got some excellent athletes—players who were first- and second-round draft choices by the National Football League. You can go right down their roster: Mike Garrett, Curtis McClinton, Otis Taylor, Chris Burford—they all are top athletes."

Interestingly enough, while viewing films, Lombardi was struck by how much the Cowboys and the Chiefs shared offensive similarities. Lombardi also stressed that everything was relative. He made the point that it was difficult to evaluate the Chiefs because the Packers were unfamiliar with the teams they played against in the AFL.

> **DAVE ROBINSON: "Defense: These guys are probably bigger and stronger and more well-balanced than anybody you've faced all year," Coach told us at film sessions.**
>
> **"But our advantage," he said, "is going to be that they're so good physically that when they played against the other teams in their league, they were able to dominate the other teams using poor football techniques. I want you to study their techniques and take advantage of them."**
>
> **When I started studying them, I noticed that my man would lead with the wrong foot on the block and little things like that. I**

remember one play in particular they stopped the film where the center snapped the ball and kind of leapfrogged, leaped with both feet and hit the middle linebacker. I think it was against the Jets—right at the ankles below the knee. Cut him down like a weed, and they took off and ran the play around to their left.

Vince stopped the film and turned to number 66, Ray Nitschke, who would play his entire career as a middle linebacker for Green Bay.

"If that guy throws that block against you and it's successful, I'm coming out onto the field to get you." And Coach meant it!

What we knew was that they hadn't beaten any great teams, so they hadn't had to play great football.

PAUL HORNUNG: I remember very vividly watching film of the Chiefs. They made some mistakes that were kind of sophomoric. Example: Two of their safeties ran into each other.

JIM TAYLOR: Seeing that collision of safeties, Max McGee, who was always the wit, of course, he went, "Da, aa, dat a dah, dah, dah." It was a *Looney Tunes* and *Merry Melodies* kind of thing, and we were giggling and laughing. In truth, film gave us a superficial look at their team, but we didn't expect much. Maybe the propaganda between AFL–NFL that existed at that time, all the bad feelings were a little infectious. Quite frankly, we didn't expect that much of a ball game.

BOYD DOWLER: We had a lot of film to watch. You look at film, and a guy might be six foot seven, but he doesn't look that much bigger than the guy that's 6'3", 6'4". They were a big bunch, and they were good athletes.

Watching film we had a very firm belief that we could throw to the weak side, which was the position I played, and Max McGee, who backed me up, on the weak side.

BILL CURRY: As we went through our film study, in addition to the fact that we began to realize the Chiefs were really good players, we realized that their systems were such that we could not run our base offense. Just the simplest way to say it is that they ran an eight-man front in an era when most teams ran a seven-man front. For instance, the Packer Sweep, if it were blocked our traditional way, simply couldn't be run.

That was underscored by Coach Lombardi slamming off the projector and stalking around the room saying, "We're going to have to throw the damn football!"

He didn't want to do that. He wanted to hammer people.

JERRY IZENBERG: Lombardi did not really know anything about the Chiefs going into that game. He had films that he looked at and some scouting reports. There were some weaknesses that he thought he could exploit, but he still had that doubt because he had never been on the field against Hank Stram or this team. There was the factor of the unknown, and that factor meant that anything could happen.

MICKEY HERSKOWITZ: Being the truly great pro that he was, Vince Lombardi knew that anything could happen in a football game. He knew that teams flip-flopped in a split second and could catch fire and turn things upside down. That was his great concern. The lucky break, the breakdown, the unforeseen.

JERRY KRAMER: For years the public had been brought up to believe the AFL was an inferior product. Now suddenly it was up to us. We would be labeled the biggest fakes and phonies in the history of pro sports if we lost.

We didn't know anything about the Kansas City Chiefs except everyone expected us to beat them by five touchdowns. It was like preparing in a vacuum. All we kept hearing was how inferior the American Football League was and how those teams didn't belong on the same field with us. But we didn't know that. Unspoken was the fear that what if these guys are better than everybody thinks?

BOYD DOWLER: The Chiefs had size over us. We were a little bit cautious. I'm not saying we were scared, but when you're in a situation like that, it's you're damned if you do and damned if you don't—almost.

It's a case of we were carrying the National Football League banner as far as that particular game was concerned, and they were basically referred to as the "other league."

Green Bay Packers wide receiver Boyd Dowler.
Photofest

BILL CURRY: The game overall to us didn't feel big-time. We looked down our noses at the AFL and its teams. We didn't watch them, and we probably didn't respect them enough. And that went for the Chiefs.

BOB LONG: The NFL people didn't think the AFL had good talent or teams, but they did. It was more of a passing league then. To us it was almost like a flag football league they threw so much.

BOYD DOWLER: We felt that we were a better team, we were probably put together as a team better than other teams. We played more as a team. We never were guilty of labeling anybody as a "go-to guy." We never had a feeling that, "This guy has to play really, really well for us to win." We had stars, but we did not rely on our stars carrying us.

We had people miss games, parts of seasons. And we continued on. Jerry Kramer missed a block of a season here and there, and it didn't change anything. We didn't put anybody up on a pedestal or put anyone else down.

All parts of our team mattered. We were not at all what you would call "cliquey." It wasn't that kind of a chemistry or attitude in our locker room or otherwise. We all had a good time together. We all liked each other and got along with each other on and off the field. It was all able to be traced back to the Lombardi Way as a general manager and coach. It was an unusual chemistry, a blending of players who came together.

CHUCK LANE: Backup quarterback Zeke Bratkowski didn't get a lot of playing time with Bart Starr around, but he and Bart were the closest of friends. They were like brothers. They spent a lot of time socially, as well as professionally, together. Zeke never at any time tried to out-stage Starr or wanted his job. Zeke was one of those guys who was just totally content being a very, very effective backup. And his record was pretty darn good.

DAVE ROBINSON: In Santa Barbara, with all that was going on, I agonized over what would happen if we didn't win big. Vince would have killed us or, worse, worked us to death the next year.

Never one to tip his hand, Lombardi told reporters, "I really don't know who will start in the game. But I'm a great hunch player. The game will dictate who will play and who doesn't. I'm not going to say who will and who will not. I probably will not know until Sunday. We'll do about what we have always done. Why change? We've been successful with it this far."

At a required press conference that lasted almost an hour, the highly prepared and articulate Green Bay Packer coach responded to a question that focused on the way his players responded to reporter's questions: "Our guys have been around long enough to know better. I don't have to put words in their mouths. We haven't briefed them on what to say to the press. But if they say the wrong thing they will hear it from me."

The Packer boss man grew testy when a reporter suggested that the Packers should score an easy victory over the Chiefs.

"That was nice," Lombardi scolded the eager beaver journalist, continuing, "But those people on the other side of the field don't realize that the championship has already been won. This is their chance. For seven years we've been saying they aren't as good as we are. That's fine. But I think we better wait and play the game, if that's all right with the gentlemen of the press, of course."

Never one to suffer fools gladly, Lombardi was annoyed and disgusted by a question that he thought naïve about the "great speed" of Kansas City.

"They look fast on film," he responded, "but how do I know. I don't know how fast the film was shot."

> **PAT PEPPLER: I went out early to Santa Barbara to help set things up. We had a ton of film on Kansas City and no shortage of knowledge about their players and their strengths and weaknesses.**

Willie Wood was asked about the Packer film sessions and what went on there. He was also asked what it was like seeing the Kansas City Chiefs in action. His response: "We had them checked. It was a question of how emotionally involved we were gonna get" (Maranis, 1999, 391).

> **FRANK GIFFORD: I was a very good friend of Lombardi, having played five years under him in New York, and I looked at films with him during the week. He kept telling me how tough Kansas City was going to be. I kept telling him how ridiculous that was. But he was scared.**

"We had to win," said Green Bay's Phil Bengtson, the only assistant coach who would be on the scene from 1959 to 1967, Lombardi's entire nine-year tenure. "If we got complacent and let the Chiefs pull an upset, we'd go down in history on the same page with Goliath and the Spanish Armada."

Lombardi—prideful, determined, and driven—had his players doing up and downs and grass drills. Conditioning was a paramount priority. And even though his Packers were in great shape, even though the team was a finely tuned machine, even though they had been under great pressure in the past, Lombardi never took anything for granted and was never one to be overconfident.

"You can't be fatigued," Lombardi told his team. "Fatigue makes cowards of us all."

> BART STARR: Physically, the Kansas City Chiefs were a larger team than we were. They had been exposed to a fitness training schedule that was advanced from what we had.

> CHUCK LANE: We did have a much better team, but physically they were big. Buck Buchanan was just a huge individual, and those tackles were far bigger than Fuzzy Thurston and Jerry Kramer. But they didn't have Lombardi.

Driven, paranoid, testy, Iron Vince made sure all workouts were closed to the public. And although the Packer head man emphasized that his team had been working a grueling and demanding NFL schedule since July 10, he nevertheless put his charges right back on a training camp schedule—two practices a day, meetings at night.

> BOB LONG: Coach Lombardi didn't want any of our players sneaking out at night. Who knows what they would do, how far they would go. He would have a practice and a meeting in the afternoon. We would have dinner. After dinner we would have another meeting at say 7:30, 8:00. Curfew was at 10:30, 11:00. Well, you couldn't drive to Los Angeles to get in trouble and get back in time for curfew.

> BOB SCHNELKER: At Santa Barbara, the practices were fairly normal. Vince was the same as he always was, you know, very hardworking, had everything laid out that he wanted to do. He did his usual coaching. He was a great promoter, and he got the players to play.

Defensive tackle Henry Jordan seriously and jokingly tackled the question of pressure: "Take a look around you. How many bald heads do you see in here? How many grey heads? They've been there before."

> BART STARR: We were impressed with the Chiefs—with their schedule and their opponents. So we had extremely well-organized and committed sessions for observation and study. Coach Lombardi always knew what he had to do to get us as prepared as he could. Facing the Chiefs, we obviously had to have that because we had never played against them, so we needed as much of that information and exposure as we could get so we could be well-prepared.

FORREST GREGG: Lombardi certainly did not present the Chiefs as a team from a Mickey Mouse league when he was portraying them to us. He pointed out that backs Mike Garrett, Bert Coan, and Curtis McClinton ranked among the top 10 running backs in their league. Flanker Otis Taylor was a deep threat. Tight end Fred Arbanas was just one of a half dozen of their offensive players on the All-AFL squad. On defense they featured Jerry Mays, the huge Buck Buchanan, linebacker Bobby Bell, All-AFL safeties Johnny Robinson and Bobby Hunt, and defensive back Fred Williamson. He told us they had a lot. They did have a lot.

He did not want to take any chances. We all felt pressure. He put tremendous pressure on us. Extra practice, we watched a lot of film, a lot of film. He said he expected us to win, but it would be difficult.

In his book *Run to Daylight*, Vince Lombardi calls Forrest Gregg the "finest player [he] had ever coached."

FORREST GREGG: In Santa Barbara, Coach Lombardi pushed us like we were underdogs.

DAVE ROBINSON: It was overall relatively quiet for us. We had a lousy practice field at the UC Santa Barbara. It was not a great practice facility at all.

BART STARR: The field at the Santa Barbara stadium was not as bad as some of the guys said. It was actually one of the first to feature a new grass, called "Tifton Bermuda." The turf was closely cropped, soft, and very fast. After practicing for a week on the ice and mud in Green Bay, we welcomed a well-groomed field. It was a pleasure to feel the sun and run on that field. Everyone felt fleet-footed.

A main theme of that Santa Barbara time was Coach Lombardi never saying, "What if we lose?" But it was instead, "We must win. We can't lose."

There was the constant repeating by Lombardi: "We are here to win."

BUD LEA: Lombardi was so obsessed in his preparation for the game while in Santa Barbara that his wife Marie left for Las Vegas for two days, and it was said he hardly noticed she was gone.

"You mean," he said to her when she got back, "you flew over the mountains?"

"No, dummy. I flew under them," she replied, drawing laughs from everyone in the hotel suite but Vince Lombardi.

If anyone could put down Vince, it was Marie.

BART STARR: When we arrived in California, we had never been in an atmosphere like that before for a championship or playoff game. We had never seen so many media people. Never seen so many fans who would be gathered around the areas at the places where media gathering took place for us. It was quite an eye-opener. I'll always remember that because of the number of fans who were just everywhere! It may well have been a turning point in the exposure the NFL has gone on to experience.

DAVE ROBINSON: The media was there. And then every day poolside they interviewed you. You had to be careful what you said because everybody was trying to paw at you, find out something that had not been written about. It was really something. Really something to behold. Something to be there.

FORREST GREGG: We had been in a lot of big games. And we were accustomed to a lot of media. But nothing could ever compare in our minds at that time with the media that we experienced. Television, radio, newspapers—everybody from all over was there. We had interview after interview after interview, and of course we loved it. And it was not just sportswriters who were there.

But Lombardi said, "Don't let it go to your head," and we didn't.

For interviews, Lombardi would tell players to hang around their rooms. He would then hand out the rooming list to reporters and turn them loose.

Buffalo News sports scribe Larry Felser's punchy (if hyper) prose brings back the time: "If you wanted to talk to Bart Starr, he invited you to his room, brushed the jockstraps off the bed, and you sat down and talked to him."

JERRY MAGEE: A colleague and I went out to the Green Bay hotel. We went up to Bart Starr's room and knocked on his door. Starr opened it, saw who we were, and said, "Hey, come on in, fellas. What can I do for you?"

JERRY IZENBERG: We drove up to Santa Barbara from LA. The ocean there, palm trees, just beautiful. We pull up to the motel. It was two or three stories. Lombardi is standing out front, but not for

us. He didn't even know we were coming. He was wearing a Green
Bay Packer sweatshirt. They had a practice that afternoon.

He looks at us and looks surprised. "What are you doing here?"

I said, "Hello, Vince. How are you doing? What a beautiful place
to train a team." I knew that would set him off.

"Are you crazy? How can you get serious about a football game
with the sun, this weather, all distractions. Bullshit."

"Well, if that's what you have to say," I told him, "I am going to
see your players." The players were sitting around, taking the sun.

He looked at them. He couldn't stop us from going up, and
he was mad. He walked back toward the courtyard and shouted,
"There's a couple of writers coming up. And by the way I don't want
to see any of you guys in the pool today."

A reporter seeking a story usually went to the bar in the hotel lobby or interviewed a
player in his room. Lombardi mandated that his players be available to the media in their
rooms between one and three in the afternoon.

Most of the writers covering Green Bay stayed in Santa Barbara. A daily bus was
made available by the NFL from LA to Santa Barbara. Only one writer generally rode
the bus for the 90-mile journey. Thus, the bus was named "Jack Hand's bus," for that
Associated Press writer.

If you were not lodged in Santa Barbara and wanted to interview Vince Lombardi
and the Packers, you had to drive the two hours from Los Angeles, sometimes more.

Reporters were stunned by a Lombardi comment that he had never seen an American Football League game in person or on television.

> BUD LEA: Reminded by a couple of reporters that even Commis-
> sioner Pete Rozelle had seen the other league play, Lombardi replied,
> "Pete has a lot more free time than I do."

> CHUCK LANE: I was running down to Los Angeles. I was doing
> media interviews. I don't recall being out there at many practices.
> And quite frankly, the farther I could get from Lombardi I figured
> was good for my career. Saying Lombardi had a temper is like saying
> it's a little chilly up here in Green Bay in the winter!
>
> Lombardi was wound tighter than the nuts on a new bridge. He
> really was. I had never seen him that tight. He was always extremely
> serious when it came to the football operation, but in this particular
> week, he was extremely tight, more so than ever before. And I think
> it was caused by the pressures that were applied . . . you know, he
> was receiving phone calls and telegrams and whatnot beforehand.

People like Art Modell were encouraging him and wishing him well. He was being praised and pressured by the praise that he was the representation of the National Football League, and all that was held sacred by the NFL versus the AFL upstarts. It was probably more pressure than he'd ever seen. The players felt the pressure, also. It was evident that the game mattered!

FRANK GIFFORD: The calls kept coming from NFL owners. They were almost kind of casual at first, but at the end of every one, the caller would say, "Make it big, Vince. Stick it to those clowns."

DAVE ROBINSON: Vince said to us, "You can't win this game 14–12 or 14–10 or 17–13. You have to win convincingly." And so he worked us harder for that game than any other game. He said one time, "We got to win by 21 points to prove that the National Football League is superior to the AFL."

Then he said, "I don't think you guys can beat the Little Sisters of the Poor by 21 points."

Which prompted Lionel Aldridge to ask, "Who are the Little Sisters of the Poor?"

But anyway he was primed to coach that Super Bowl I game like it was, and it was the toughest game of our career.

JERRY KRAMER: Vince read us a bunch of telegrams from people like George Halas (Chicago owner) and Wellington Mara (Giants owner), NFL old guard. They were telling him, "You better beat those SOBs and you better beat them bad." We had a lot of pressure not only to win, but to win big. I think the NFL would have liked to have seen a 60 to nothing score. That would have made them happy.

Wrapped tight, tense, honed in, possessed by the moment, Lombardi was in a place that most of his players and the media had never seen him before, one that never seemed to have lasted so long. NFL owners, friends, and players he had worked with put pressure on him. Lombardi, in turn, put great pressure on his players and most of all on himself.

BUD LEA: Lombardi wasn't having the time of his life in Santa Barbara. He was on edge all week. He was carrying the weight of the entire NFL. The telegrams were arriving from the other NFL teams. They all said pretty much the same thing: "Go out there and show those clowns who's boss."

CHUCK LANE: It was ridiculous. It was an all-out war with the networks and their promotion departments. The media was all over the place, looking for an angle or a quote.

CBS and NBC were fixated on their upcoming task: televising the game. They turned Green Bay's team hotel into a makeshift studio and attempted to outhustle one another for player interviews. The networks were preoccupied with talk of "Super Sunday."

CHUCK LANE: The two competing television networks tried to get as much airtime, face time as they possibly could with Lombardi and the players. They had a contingent up there in Santa Barbara virtually every day. I had never been exposed to the "Hollywood" type of media. I just dealt with the sports media in my limited experience up until that point.

I'll never forget the day, I think it was the people from CBS who asked me if they could get Coach Lombardi to pose on a trampoline with some of the gals from that show (with Buddy Ebsen).

They said, "You wouldn't mind asking Coach Lombardi to do that, would you?"

And I said, "Yeah, as a matter of fact I would mind it a great deal, because he'd *kill* me if I asked him to do something like that!"

But, you know, they were all trying to do something that was just out of the ordinary, something extraordinary, something that was just off-the-wall to get them an edge on the other network.

FRANK GIFFORD: CBS and NBC spent most of the week before the game plotting strategy in secret. To some, it seemed there was as much of a rivalry between networks as there was between leagues.

Nine of 10 "experts" picked the Packers to win big, with an average score of 33–18.

BUD LEA: A 100–0 score was freely predicted. Tex Maule of *Sports Illustrated* wrote the Packers would win, 58–6.

This infuriated Jerry Magee of the *San Diego Union-Tribune*. Describing himself as an AFL apologist, Magee picked the Chiefs to win, 58–6.

CHUCK LANE: I think Lombardi cut some slack for the national media . . . Izenberg and Tex Maule from SI, and Dave Anderson from the *New York Times*. He would be a lot more lenient with these guys in their questioning. But God help the local media who would ask a question that Lombardi thought was not appropriate. He would just rip them a new backside in front of their contemporaries, which wasn't a particularly honorable way to deal with local media. But nonetheless, he did that.

Photo ops pervaded the atmosphere. Bart Starr was a favorite subject. A popular image depicted the quarterback grinning, holding a football with "CBS Sports" inscribed on it, flanked by smiling, tight sweater-clad young women in short skirts.

Relaxation, whenever possible, and fighting off all the pressure was paramount to Lombardi. Watching television and browsing the *Los Angeles Times* were favorite diversions for him in Santa Barbara. So were libations. Late one afternoon, Lombardi got up from watching television, called his right-hand man, Tom Miller, and ordered another scotch. In the time it took Lombardi to put in his drink order, someone had put in a change of television channels.

Returning, Lombardi bellowed in that foghorn voice, "Who turned off my program?"

He had been watching a Tom and Jerry cartoon. It was reported that no one ventured close to the television set again when the burly coach was in the vicinity.

For players on both the Packers in Santa Barbara and the Chiefs in Long Beach, anxious for relaxation after long days of practice, drills, and media exposure, television viewing was a release—sort of.

The television announcements of "Only four more days to Super Sunday," "Only three more days to Super Sunday" only accentuated the clock's ticking to the showdown game on January 15, 1967.

> **BUD LEA:** Practice was all business, grinding, serious stuff most of the time. There would be no distractions. Vince Lombardi made sure every minute was mapped out. The players really had no time for themselves. He took care of any extra time by telling them things like, "I want all players on the bus parked near the main lobby at 9:30 in the morning. Do you hear me? Nine-thirty in the morning."
>
> So all the players got there at 9:15, grabbed a seat on the bus, and were ready to go to practice. But Lombardi informed the driver not to leave until 10:00 a.m. It was his way of using up 45 minutes of their time.
>
> He worked his team so hard that the players feared, for the first time, that they were going to leave the game on the practice field. The schedule, the seclusion, and the discipline started to get to the players as Lombardi continued to push them.
>
> "He stopped several of us one morning after breakfast," guard Fuzzy Thurston would recall later, and said, "There is one more thing I want to stress upon you people. I don't care how many friends you have on that team. I don't care how many guys you played with in

college, or how many guys you played with in high school. I don't care. Understand? Sunday, there will be no brother-in-lawing."

Strictly business he wanted it to be.

And strictly business it was.

JERRY MAGEE: Vince Lombardi was never my favorite. He was an asshole, the way he treated people, his mannerisms. One day I went to Santa Barbara. Practice had ended. Lombardi was getting on Tom Brown, cornerback. He could speak very derisively, which he did on that occasion. He was not a pleasant person.

It was the first glimpse I'd had of Vince Lombardi in person. I had heard things about how badly he could treat people. I remember thinking that I couldn't believe how sarcastic he was, especially with his players.

DAVE ROBINSON: He told us this game was so big that if anything went wrong he would fine us $2,500 for a minor violation, such as being late for a meeting, and $5,000 for a major violation, such as being caught for sneaking past curfew. That stuff was unheard of, but that was the level of anxiousness.

PAT COCHRAN: He was pretty adamant that we were not going to let the National Football League down. There was no way we were going to lose this game. He told my husband that he wanted to make sure we were going to play the game at the height of our efficiency. Only playing that way, the Lombardi Way, was insurance that would make us win.

"Vince would have beaten those guys 90–0 if he could have," Max McGee said. "He didn't like the idea of that league infringing on the league's monopoly, and he didn't think there was a team in that league that could measure up to us."

Never taking anything for granted, checking off every detail, overly prepared, frenetically focused, all of that was a way of life for Vince Lombardi, the coach, the general manager, the man.

BOYD DOWLER: Fear of the unknown sometimes can get you. We had a pretty good idea every time we went out and played the Colts, with Unitas and those guys. Same way with the Bears, we played them most of the time three times a year, once in preseason and twice in regular season. We knew about them. The Chiefs were another matter.

We knew we could also cover. Our defense was pretty darn good! Our guys were not going to get tricked. Trick 'em stuff didn't get very far against us; we never did get fooled very often. Our players were experienced, trained carefully. They looked at and went where they were supposed to go on the field of play. They keyed who they were supposed to key. And they were all smart, they played together real well.

I had a shoulder problem that began the year before, 1965. It was basically just a separation. I had no surgery. It calcified and there was a big ole lump on my shoulder, and I played the rest of '65 and all of the '66 season. I didn't play very well most of the year. I had some other physical problems—I wasn't up to my standards or anyone else's, but Coach left me in the lineup.

Once in a while I contributed a little bit, in fact, in the game before, down in Dallas, I caught a touchdown pass and helped us win that game. That's about all I did. I think that was the only touchdown I caught that year. It was probably the worst season I had as a Packer. But I was part of the team, part of the Packer family, set to play in the NFL–AFL Championship Game.

CHUCK LANE: Lombardi was confiding in his assistant coaches and some of the Green Bay media—who of course were prohibited from writing this—and Lombardi was saying that Marv Fleming was gonna have just a banner day because of what the Kansas City defense was doing or not doing. According to Lombardi, they were allowing the tight end to free up and weren't whacking or shucking him at the line of scrimmage.

And Lombardi's statement was, "That SOB is going to be the player of the game, because he should catch a couple dozen passes." But I don't recall Marv having that big a day.

Some thought the toughest person on the Chiefs was Fred Arbanas, the only one-eyed tight end in the history of the National Football League. He was involved in an off-season incident.

FRED ARBANAS: It was 1964, and I was out at 33rd and Troost in Kansas City, looking in a store window about 9:30 at night. Some guy walked up and sucker punched me. A couple of days later I lost sight in that eye. I could see motion up close, but mostly light. Three attempted operations on my right eye did not work.

Lenny (Dawson) and I started meeting after work in Swope Park in Kansas City. We'd start 5 or 10 feet apart and work back. Then I would go home, and my son and I would throw a tennis ball around in the family room. With my son and Lenny nursing me along, I was able to start tracking the ball again and was running patterns again in the spring.

DAVE ROBINSON: This is a little cruel, but in the preparations Vince made in Santa Barbara, he focused a bit on Fred Arbanas, All-AFL tight end, who had lost sight in one eye. And Vince told Lee Roy Caffey and me to study the films. He didn't say, "Poke the guy in his left eye till the right eye cries." No, he just said, "He's got a problem, and we should analyze it and play accordingly." So we were set to overplay his good eye in the actual game against the Chiefs. I don't think he caught a pass the whole game. There were little things like that. Vince was so thorough, so exact in every little thing.

BART STARR: The Kansas City Chiefs were an outstanding team, and we saw it preparing for them. Hank Stram had done an excellent job of coaching. They had outstanding talent. Len Dawson was a quality quarterback.

We just had great respect for the Chiefs, and even though we didn't know that much about them because they were in a different league, because of Coach Lombardi's preparedness and his coaching staff and how well they coached and were capable of analyzing opponents, we were well-prepared for them because they were so good.

Deeply religious, loving his work, wanting to win more than anything else, feeling pressure from sources throughout the NFL, Lombardi used anything he could to rally his troops—humor, sarcasm, bullying, high praise, scorn, inspirational talk, prayer.

In their final workout prior to their game of games, the Packers knelt around their coach at midfield of the practice facility. In that familiar foghorn of a voice, the coach lashed out at them for looking sluggish and tense, a bit tired.

"What's the matter with you guys? Look at you, you look scared! What are you scared of?"

From the rear of the pack, backup receiver Max McGee, in a loud voice, said, "We're scared the other team isn't going to show up, coach!"

His teammates couldn't stop laughing.

Lombardi, feigning anger, yelled, "Get out of here!"

The players headed for the showers.

LONG BEACH

SHARRON HUNT: I cannot remember a time of my life that there wasn't football. I would fly on the team charter to games even when I was a little girl, the owner's daughter. I remember sitting in the row in front of big Buck Buchanan, looking at him. And he gave me a dollar. We had won that day, and he was in good spirits. That was a nice moment.

An even nicer moment was when we had beaten the Buffalo Bills and everyone went back to the hotel and we watched the Packers–Cowboys game and wondered who we would face in the championship game between the two leagues. There is a picture of me on my dad's shoulders. I am wearing white go-go boots. I was a very smart and happy little girl that we had won.

DALE STRAM: I was 11 years old. I traveled with the team, I'd go to all the games. After the AFL Championship Game against Buffalo, we didn't fly immediately back. We stayed at the hotel and spent the night to watch the Packers play the Cowboys. Normally after a road game was played we'd fly back to Kansas City. But we didn't do that, we watched the entire game.

SHARRON HUNT: Flying back the next day to Kansas City we landed at the airport. Fans had swarmed the runway and surrounded the plane, and I remember my father carrying me protectively off the airplane down the back stairway. There was this big, crazy crowd screaming, cheering the team on like the players were rock stars. I was seven years old. My dad was holding me. I wasn't frightened.

BUD LEA: The Chiefs qualified for the shot at mighty Green Bay by routing the Bills for the AFL championship on New Year's Day in Buffalo, 31–7.

"Pour it on, boys," Hank Stram had screamed. "There will be a lot more when we tear apart the NFL."

BILL MCNUTT III: Hank would have preferred to pay the Dallas Cowboys, not because they would have been an easier opponent, but the Stram family, like many of the players, felt run out of town when the NFL put the Cowboys expansion franchise in town.

PHYLLIS STRAM: It was heartwarming that our AFL team was the first one in the first Super Bowl. I'd been to home games, but rarely did we travel out of town with the team. It was a real treat getting out to California.

CHRIS BURFORD: There were a few media at the airport in Long Beach when we arrived, but I don't recall a media crush being anything overwhelming at all.

Nevertheless, the scene at the airport displeased Hank Stram. Taken aback by the 75-piece brass band, a group of entertainers, press, and public swarming about, the KC coach took charge. He ordered everyone into the buses.

The Kansas City Chiefs arrived in Long Beach, California, on January 4, eleven days before the big football contest. While Vince Lombardi had held his team back in Wisconsin, Hank Stram admitted, "We had come too early."

The Chiefs would take up residency in the Long Beach Edgewater Inn. Team workouts were set for Veterans Memorial Stadium, which had opened in 1948.

> PHYLLIS STRAM: Long Beach Edgewater Inn was rather old. The food was good, but the rooms were a bit shabby. Accommodations were really middle of the road or lower. No grassy knolls, and no golf course, and no trees—it was pretty industrial looking almost. Players were all there in their own rooms. The bar was the drinking, gathering, and interviewing place for the press.

> DALE STRAM: I thought it was kind of cool. There was a marina across the street with a restaurant, and the practice facility was within walking distance.

> BILL MCNUTT III: Many of the reporters and NFL and AFL owners did not stay in Santa Barbara or Long Beach. They stayed at the Beverly Hilton, the top place in town in those days. The coffee shop at the Beverly Hilton was full of Super Bowl talk. You could hear the range of accents down the counters and inside the booths, from the Bronx to chicken fried Southern voices, all talking NFL versus AFL, Packers versus Chiefs.

> SHARRON HUNT: The hotel my family stayed at in California was big. I spent a lot of time in the grand hotel pool. My brother and I loved the TV show *The Green Hornet*, so as a special surprise my dad got the lead actor in the show to come to the hotel and surprise us.

> BILL MCNUTT III: *The Green Hornet* was a very popular TV show in 1966 and 1967. Lamar's SMU football teammate, Buzz Kemble, played high school football in Fort Worth with the actor Van Williams, who played the Green Hornet, and Bruce Lee played Kato. We got to go to the movie lot and watch an episode being filmed.
>
> Going out to Disneyland you could see team owners and officials and their wives there. The big deal at Disney in those days was a coupon book. Most expensive was the series E coupon. Mickey Mouse would talk to you. And so that was certainly a must spot.

Usually tactful, Hank Stram expressed optimism about his team's prospects for winning the big game on January 15, but keeping in character, he also had nice things to say about the abilities of his opposition.

The KC coach said Lombardi did things the right way, carefully and fundamentally, and with great effort. The Green Bay players went all-out every second, Stram told reporters, but he added, "I am sure we can move the ball on their conservative defense."

Practices for the Chiefs, like those for the Packers, were closed to the public, open to the media.

> BILL MCNUTT III: Most of the players were always nice to ball boys. This is back when people viewed hydration differently. Water breaks in training camps were special, and if a guy played hard he might get a little more water. So they were always ultra nice to the ball boys because what they wanted us to do was sneak them ice in our towels! And let me tell you, Hank would get mad if he caught us sneaking them ice in the towels. But Buck Buchanan and Jerry Mays could not have been nicer to us, and it was primarily because we used to slip them ice in the towels.

A small incident took place one day that gave insight into Stram's makeup. The team bus took off for a practice session. Otis Taylor, the terrific flanker, was one of the best-known and most popular of the Chiefs, and he somehow missed getting on the bus. Taking possession of a motor scooter in the parking lot of the hotel, Taylor arrived a half-hour late on the practice field.

Four reporters were on the scene, three of them from Missouri, chatting away with Stram, who was apparently unaware that Taylor had missed the bus. Spotting his star coming onto the field late, Stram shrugged his head.

"Well, that's Otis," the coach said, smiling. There was no fine, no berating. It underscored Stram's levelheaded treatment of his players and the media.

> CURTIS MCCLINTON: In Long Beach, as everywhere, everything flowed back to our leader Hank Stram. The sense or order, discipline, and structure was a permanent presence in everything we did, so we could have gone to Mars or Venus and it wouldn't have made us any difference. The principles our leader articulated were ever present, and that is what made our team.
>
> Hank's basic comment to us all through the seasons was, "Letsgoboys." That meant at the time to focus, to challenge, go and win. It was like one word. Hank Stram was a very unusual personality, unusual coach. He could look you in the eye, encode where you should be, what he expected of you—all that without saying a word.

ED BUDDE: We had a great team, great athletes. That was what Hank Stram liked. He loved speed. One season when we came from an All-Star Game, Bobby Bell, Buck Buchanan, and myself, at our first practice, Hank called us all around him. He stood in the middle, and he says, "Okay, the three Bs: Buck Buchanan, Bobby Bell, and Ed Budde, we're going to have a race, a 40-yard race."

So just the three of us got out there and ran. You know who was last? Me! Bobby Bell was fast for a linebacker, and Buck Buchanan was fast for a defensive tackle. And believe me, I was fast for a guard, but nothing compared to these guys. They beat me by a couple yards. I wasn't blown out, but, still, I was last. Both of them are in the Hall of Fame.

Those were the kind of players we had in Long Beach getting ready for the Super Bowl. And Hank Stram loved it.

Hank Stram also loved Bobby Bell. "I can honestly say," the KC coach remarked, "that Bobby Bell had as much talent as anyone I ever coached."

JERRY MAGEE: I represented the *San Diego Union* and drove down to Long Beach. There was no need to make special arrangements, no pressure to show up with special credentials. No media hotel existed. I was an American Football League guy from the time the Chargers were in the AFL, so I stayed with the Chiefs in Long Beach where they were quartered. Never once did I go to Super Bowl headquarters in downtown LA.

The Chiefs, following Stram's and Hunt's lead, rather than seclude themselves, promoted their league at every turn, making themselves readily available to the media. Reporters interviewed players and coaches in the Edgewater bar after practice. It was standard operating procedure.

Johnny Robinson, one of the stars of the game, was interviewed under one of the goalposts at practice one day. That reporter was the only one who talked to him one-on-one that entire week in Long Beach.

Lamar Hunt made himself available in the middle of the bleachers during practice. He always had a lot to say. Open and caring, he shared whatever information he had. It was reported that the owner of the Chiefs had even offered to share with a reporter a peanut butter sandwich that he had brought along in a paper bag. It was not revealed whether the reporter took him up on the offer.

BILL ADAMS: Lamar was a realist. He was hopeful. He realized nobody else then could beat Green Bay. No one else was on the level of the Packers. They were all business. They were the epitome of champions of pro football at the time. Vince Lombardi was already legendary. It was an awesome experience to finally realize that an AFL team was going to play the giants of football. We were thrilled to see the AFL on a par with the NFL. There had been many years of bashing by people like George Halas and others.

But Lamar was a smart man. He had prevailed for this moment in time, this moment in sports history. He had no illusions, though. It would be tough to beat the machine that was the Packers of Green Bay. But he promoted the league he had created, the team he owned, at every turn. There was a lot of pride mixed into that.

MICKEY HERSKOWITZ: Coach Stram promoted the AFL, the Chiefs, and thought they had a hell of a chance to win the game. Just a sweetheart, Coach Stram cooperated fully with the efforts of the league to make the game a big success. He would have made commercials if we had done them. He took time out from his busy practices to make himself available. He accepted appearances. He had no beefs about anything.

DALE STRAM: My dad felt that outside of the AFL cities, they didn't know much about the AFL. Since Lombardi wouldn't give anybody any attention, all of the media converged on Long Beach and my dad. He granted interviews to everybody. He told the players, "Look, whatever we can do to accommodate these people we want to do it, it's gonna be great to put a face to this league." And that's what they did.

LEN DAWSON: The media had to find a way to get something to report back on. So they'd catch us in the coffee shop or knock on our door to get some kind of information. Hank Stram wanted to cooperate and get publicity because we were the new league on the block, the "other league."

JERRY MAGEE: I knew Hank Stram well. He did a marvelous job of selling the AFL that week. He made it his business to memorize the first names of all the writers there. And he spoke very kindly of his league every chance he got.

DALE STRAM: Lombardi holed himself up in Santa Barbara, and dad opened himself up in Long Beach. All day, every day my dad was doing some kind of interview, making himself available.

CHRIS BURFORD: It was a little different experience being in Long Beach, getting ready for the Super Bowl. It was several weeks since we'd played. Normally you'd play every week and you have that high of the game day, and then you would recover, and then you would build up for the next game.

This game was really a sequel to our championship game up in Buffalo. The preparation for this game was a little bit different because we'd worked out some at home, but then we went out to California and worked out. You did a little more hotel living than you ever did before.

HANK STRAM: No sooner had we begun workouts in Long Beach, about 30 miles south of the Los Angeles Coliseum, than we found ourselves engaged in controversy because of Fred Williamson, our left cornerback. Freddy, like me, came from Gary, Indiana, and was no stranger to controversy. He had broken into football with the Pittsburgh Steelers in 1960 and over the years had earned a reputation for being outspoken.

His nickname was "The Hammer," earned because of a characteristic tackle he made by hitting the pass receiver in the head with his forearm. Before the 1965 season, I had traded another good pass defender, Dave Grayson, to Oakland for Fred Williamson because I felt he would give our team a new dimension it never had before. Freddy was confident, cocky, and a bit arrogant. And this was something we needed at that point in our history. He did a lot of talking, but he backed up what he said most of the time.

Freddy began to describe how he was going to lower his hammer on the Green Bay Packers. He had numerous remarks to make about their ability and the relative ability of the other league. It seemed as though every sportswriter in the country had arrived for what some considered would be the greatest battle since the Spanish Armada, and they lapped it up. A lot of people assumed that the Packers would blow us out of the stadium, so it made good copy, and it helped with promotion of the game, for the Chiefs to come on talking big. But I certainly wasn't interested in making good copy or promoting the game; I wanted to win it.

Lured by Fred Williamson's outrageous commentaries, reporters asked him how he would compare himself to his opposite numbers on Green Bay, like Herb Adderley and Willie Wood.

Williamson was quick with the quip: "Willie and Herb who?"

I'm sure Freddy, in his own way, was trying to create a feeling of confidence on our squad, but football is a game you win on

Green Bay Packers cornerback Herb Adderley.

Photofest

grass. You don't win it on paper. Why give Vince Lombardi any kind of ammunition by which he could stimulate his squad? I expected the Packers to go into the ball game feeling they were playing the Mickey Mouse league and that our players were not as good as their players. That was the attitude I wanted them to have.

I came close to sending Freddy home because of his comments, but at that point it wouldn't have proved anything. From a practical standpoint, we didn't have anybody else at the time who could substitute for him at cornerback. I wanted to win the game, so Fred Williamson stayed. But that taught me a lesson.

LEN DAWSON: The Chiefs generally respected opponents. But then Freddy went and opened his mouth. I think Fred Williamson probably did that trash-talking to spur up some of our guys.

DAVE HILL: Yeah, Fred was a different kind of person. He was a good football player, but he wasn't nearly as good as he thought he was. He did a lot of that trash-talking in Long Beach, but he wasn't "The Hammer," put it that way.

BOYD DOWLER: We kind of chuckled about it. We didn't particularly dislike him for doing it or anything like that, but in those years, at least on our team and in our league, players weren't very outspoken.

CURT MERZ: Freddy Williamson thought he was better than he was. He played for Oakland before. And he was that way then. I couldn't for the life of me understand why we traded for him straight up for David Grayson, who was a good cornerback. I wondered a lot about that. David was an outspoken kind of guy—not a trash-talker—but he was kind of like an antiestablishment kind of a guy. David had an attitude. His attitude, however, wasn't like a Freddy Williamson attitude.

When Kansas City made the trade, I think all the guys said, "What the hell is this all about?" Because we all knew that Grayson was better than Freddy.

When he started mouthing off before the game in Long Beach, no one was real happy about it. We knew we would have a hell of a time playing these guys from Wisconsin, and now we couldn't sneak up on them. Now we just gave them an extra incentive. Well, there was no need for it. Things like that were not done like that back then.

FRED ARBANAS: As a team we were always kind of quiet type guys, and we knew we had some work to do and mentally we were prepared for it. Back then, guys didn't talk too much. They did what they were supposed to do.

CURTIS MCCLINTON: Our team was not much on demonstrating or trash-talking. The Hammer was an anomaly, more of an actor than a player. What made Fred Williamson was not that he was an outstanding player. What made him was that he was a stage show. He had a flash and a bombasity that got the attention of the press. It also got the attention of the Green Bay Packers.

Flamboyant Fred "The Hammer" Williamson, a wearer of turtle necks, bragged about his black belt in karate and garnered considerable publicity. That was his main goal, since he had dreams of a career as a movie star. He boasted he would use his "hammer"—forearm blows to the head—to destroy the Packers' receivers.

"I've cracked open 30 helmets since I've been in the pros," he claimed.

Annoyed with the Williamson boasts, one of the KC players quipped, "If he broke 30 helmets he must have taken them outside in an alley and stomped on them."

Amused with the Williamson bragging, during Green Bay practices Jim Taylor would shout, "Run, it's the Hammer."

BART STARR: We respected Williamson's skills—he was intelligent and strong—but we could see even from film that he gambled a little too often, making himself vulnerable to the big play.

At one of the Green Bay film sessions, Lombardi told his team that Williamson was the dirtiest player he had ever seen, saying, "If he hits one of our men in the back or head or throws one dirty elbow, he's out of there."

Most of the Kansas City Chiefs had gone through high school and college watching and respecting the Packers, who had won four NFL championships in the 1960s. The Lombardi Packers were like the Yankees of football; they had a magic and mystique about them.

LEN DAWSON: In Long Beach before the game, we tried to say all the right things, like if we played our best game and the Packers didn't, then we had a chance. To me that indicated we weren't all that confident. You had to understand we were a young football team, and a lot of our heroes were playing on the Packers. That was something to overcome.

BILL MCNUTT III: The pressure on these young men on the Chiefs getting ready for the Super Bowl in Long Beach was enormous. They were absolutely the other league and the underdog. And they took it so personally. The people who took it the most personally were the players that had been on the Dallas Texans' roster in '60, '61, and '62. People like Jerry Mays and Johnny Robinson and all those kinds of guys, because they felt like the National Football League drove them from their homes. They loved Dallas, they loved playing there.

CURT MERZ: The thing about the first Super Bowl, it was an unknown. It was the first time they ever did that, so you didn't know what to expect. We knew it was big, we knew it was something the AFL had fought for years to get on par with the NFL, to be respected. I don't think there was any extra, extra pressure.

Oh no, I had no idea; I don't think anybody knew what the game would become. My first indication that it was going to be different was one of the days before the game. We were in the hotel down in Long Beach and were told they wanted all the offensive linemen for interviews.

I said, "What? They're interviewing offensive linemen? Now that's different! They're either running out of things to print or this is a bigger game than we thought."

Yeah, we very rarely got interviewed. What're you going to ask an offensive lineman? The only interview that made sense to me was one I did for the *Newark Star-Ledger* because I'm a Jersey guy. I was born and grew up in Jersey. The crux of the article was "the only guy in the first Super Bowl that's from New Jersey."

JERRY MAGEE: To us, it was like a crusade. You couldn't be involved with the AFL and not feel it. We were the little guys tilting against the mighty monolith that was the National Football League.

"Objectivity went out the window when it came to this game," said *Buffalo News* columnist and sports editor Larry Felser, who covered the Bills and the AFL from the start. "The old NFL beat guys," Felser said, "most of whom were really third-string baseball writers, I might add, they looked at us as if we were a bunch of young punks."

JERRY IZENBERG: I wrote more about this game and the events leading up to it than probably anyone else. I had been a newspaper guy for 16 years by that time. I realized it was going to be a game of strangers going against strangers. The leagues had never played each other, neither had the teams in those leagues. Some of the players may have played against each other, but that would have been back in their college days.

I decided to talk to Fuzzy Thurston and Buck Buchanan. They would be going at each other a lot in the game.

I asked Fuzzy, "What do you know about these guys on the Chiefs?"

He told me, "I don't know anything about them. I don't want to know anything about them. I don't need to know anything about them. We are going to win the game so what are we talkin' about?"

I asked, "Why are you so sure?"

"We are going to win the game because we have the best coach in the history of football," he answered.

Later I spoke to Buck Buchanan in his hotel room in Long Beach. I asked if he was confident.

"We got a good team and they are not going to intimidate us, that's what makes us confident," he said.

I saw a copy of Vince Lombardi's *Run to Daylight* laying on Buck's bed. It was open. I had heard that in Kansas City, Junious "Buck" Buchanan had purchased that $5.95 copy of Vince Lombardi's *Run to Daylight*. It was reported that he had read it page by page, even taking some notes.

I went over and picked it up and put it down. All I wanted was the page number. On that page, Forrest Gregg, who had to come across the line in a game, was describing in detail the Lombardi power sweep and what it was like: "I hit the guy in front of me and then I go for the linebacker, and when he sees us coming around the corner you can see his eyes pop."

That was what Junious Buchanan was reading.

JERRY MAGEE: Yes, Buck Buchanan read Lombardi's book thinking it would help him, and it did. He went on to have a hell of a game.

CURTIS MCCLINTON: To me, as a fullback and someone who had to block him from time to time in practices, it wasn't Buck Buchanan's size. It was what he did with his size. And he sure knew what to do with his size. What he did with it mesmerized me.

The common talk, the norm of how to deal with a big player like Buck, was that he did not have the mobility, the speed, he wasn't a quick thinker. He did not have good hands. None of that applied to Buck Buchanan. He was an awesome football player. And beside his awesomeness, his size and dominance was critical to his team. Every player on the Chiefs respected Buck Buchanan. The only ass kicking on the team was going to come from Buck.

The 227-pound fullback Curtis McClinton, like the 270-pound Buck Buchanan, spent time reading in Long Beach. It was reported that McClinton went to bed each night with a copy of the Green Bay roster and studied his opponents until he fell asleep.

JERRY KRAMER: Watching film, Fuzzy Thurston saw tackle Buck Buchanan toss people around like rag dolls. Fuzzy wasn't laughing. He was thinking and saying "Uh-ohhh," because he knew he was going to be into a fight and would have to find a way to block that big horse.

FORREST GREGG: Fuzzy Thurston said, "I am six-foot-one and weigh 240 pounds. I will be playing against a guy six-foot-six or whatever and 290 pounds. Not likely I am going to be overconfident."

JERRY IZENBERG: Fuzzy Thurston tried to make light of the impending matchup: "Buchanan is about the biggest guy I ever played against. His big trouble is going to be finding me when we line up against each other. Maybe he'll trip over me."

CHRIS BURFORD: Buck was a load. And in Long Beach he and the other big boys and talent on our team gave us some confidence. We had weapons, strength. So those guys in green and yellow uniforms weren't a big deal or that much of a challenge the way we looked at it. People made more out of that than there really was. I didn't have any great mystique in my mind about the Packers.

Hell no! I'd seen them enough on film and on television, and they had some really great players, they had some average players. They had a great coach, too. But both teams had great coaches.

In Long Beach, I and my teammates didn't feel tight as we got ready for the game in Los Angeles. I frankly thought we were going to beat Green Bay. People tried to make a lot about the "Packer mystique." There was no mystique for me, probably not for most of my teammates.

We had as much size, if not more, and as much speed, if not more. To my mind they were a good, solid football team. They were not a spectacular team. I mean as far as their offense, I would fear the Chargers more than Green Bay just because the Chargers had Alworth and Lincoln and Lowe. They were guys that could really score from further out than the Packers did. What was the glue and the force of the Packers was the Lombardi Way though. It was a solid system he had put in place that really worked time and time again. That was a big challenge that we faced.

SMOKEY STOVER: Of course I'd always heard of the Green Bay Packers and their playing abilities and the people that they had. But I felt that we were just as big and tough as they were and really didn't have a problem of being scared of them or anything. I felt all along like we had the personnel to stand toe-to-toe with them.

JIM TAYLOR: We trained away in Santa Barbara and got the news that quite a few of the Chiefs training in Long Beach predicted victory for their team. The Chiefs were a little bit more talkative than our players. And Hank Stram always could be counted on for some quotes for the media. We were, I think, a very reserved team under Vince Lombardi, a matter-of-fact bunch of guys.

The press may have been making a big deal out of predictions about Green Bay winning that game in the Coliseum by three touchdowns. We were not making predictions like that.

HANK STRAM: Before the Super Bowl we had our choice of any three Green Bay movies we wished. I had a reason for picking each one. I wanted a broad view. I wanted to see Green Bay early in the season, at midseason, and in their championship game, which they won over the Dallas Cowboys, 34 to 27.

The first one was a contest against the Cleveland Browns. Another was against the Minnesota Vikings, which the Packers lost by three points to scrambling quarterback Fran Tarkenton, a player not unlike our Lenny Dawson. The third film was of the championship game Green Bay versus Dallas, in many ways a somewhat bigger and quicker version of the Chiefs. The rationale for the choice of these games was to view any changes in the Packers' play as the season ran its course. It was a way to see how Green Bay personnel either improved or declined and what changes were necessary.

It didn't take long to realize that the Packers played sound, fundamental football. Green Bay, under Vince Lombardi, was the team of the 60s. They didn't attempt to dazzle you; they had a few basic plays, which they executed extremely well. That was the key to their success: execution.

Watching film in Long Beach, Johnny Robinson said, "I've never seen that guy (Starr) throw a bad pass in the three films we've seen. He places the ball at just the right spot where the receiver has the advantage" (Devaney, 1971, 15).

DAVE HILL: Watching film of the Packers, I was an offensive tackle, and I'm looking at the guy that would play across from me and he wasn't no different than the guy that played at Oakland or the guy that played at Denver or Buffalo. AFL guys. The big, big difference was that the Packers had a lot more experience and had been doing the same things on a football field for years. In the films, we could see that experience at work. There were guys on Green Bay that had been playing 10, 12 years. Most of us had two, three, four years in. The more you play, the more experience you have, the better you're gonna be.

But also watching film in Long Beach we realized a lot of their starters were at the end of their careers—Bart Starr, wide receivers, and some of the offensive lineman and all. So we thought about that. We never went into that game thinking we were going to lose, but to be honest about it, they had Vince Lombardi as coach. That meant a great deal.

I don't think that the Green Bay Packers had any more talent than we did at that time, but they were more seasoned, had been through a lot together.

On our team, Lenny Dawson was the exception, you know, he had played in the NFL.

Called "Daddy Cool Breeze" by his teammates, usually when not playing with a king-size cigarette in his hand or mouth, Len Dawson was a leader and one of the most popular and respected players on the Chiefs. He was 31 years old, the oldest Chief, a senior citizen on a roster of players in their 20s. It was a group KC linebacker E. J. Holub referred to as the "snotty-nosed kids."

Hank Stram explained in Long Beach, "I had someone keep a chart of every pass that Lenny threw in practice over the season. He was the most accurate passer in pro football."

LEN DAWSON: Getting ready in Long Beach, I didn't care where the game was or who the team was. There was a lot being said and written. I knew my job, a quarterback's job, was to throw the ball to the receiver when he is open. That's what I had to do against Green Bay. It was as simple as that.

BILL MCNUTT III: Leadership on that team really came from Leonard Dawson on offense and Jerry Mays on defense. But the team was blessed with a lot of leaders.

Mr. Dawson and my dad were good friends. He was definitely a leader, you know. He had played five years in the NFL before he joined the AFL. He played a leadership position. He always called Hank Stram "Henry," and he was the only player that could get away with that. He was "Coach Stram" to everyone else, but to Lenny he

Kansas City Chiefs quarterback Len Dawson.
Photofest

was "Henry." I guess it went back to when Hank Stram coached him at Purdue and that there was only a 12-year age difference. But they always called each other "Henry" and "Leonard."

Jerry Mays, the defensive end, was like Captain America. He came from a very wealthy family in Dallas. They owned a construction company. He was the hardest-working person at practice on any football team on which he ever played. He motivated those around him with the phrase, "Huzza, huzza, huzza." We always thought that he was saying, "Hustle, hustle, hustle" in a raspy voice. He worked his tail off in Long Beach, getting ready for the world championship football game.

Mays had a tough time in Long Beach. "I lost 15 pounds the week of the game," he said. "It was absolutely the most nerve-wracking experience of my life. I despised the NFL for putting us down. The NFL was my enemy."

LEN DAWSON: My Purdue team played Notre Dame every year, and Paul Hornung was the quarterback in two of those games. And Jerry Kramer, I was quite familiar with him at Idaho. There were other players that I knew and knew about mostly just on a "Hi" basis.

We were thrilled to be in it, to be going to the Coliseum for the matchup when no other professional teams were playing football. Just the two of us representing our leagues and still standing. It was one of those deals where this and that has to happen to beat these people.

But the younger guys on the Chiefs, who did they watch on television? The Green Bay Packers! You know, they were very well-acquainted with the talent on that football team. And the Lombardi story was something mythic. The team was down when he went there to Green Bay, and he turned them around to what they were.

DAVE HILL: We knew our average age was two years younger than the Packers. It does make a lot of difference in maturity, being a football player, being a complete football player. The more you play, the more experience you have, the better you're gonna be. That's what happens; however, once you get to a certain stage, a certain age, you start going the other way and you know it's time to retire. That's the cycle. We talked about that getting ready for the game, and some made the point that was especially true of some of the players on the Packers.

They had a great defense. We had a great defense, too. To be honest with you, if you were to line up person-to-person, we had a more talented defense than they did, but they had a lot more experience. And a lot of people don't realize how much that means.

You know, a guy could be playing 10 years and playing against a guy that's been playing 2 years, the guy that's been playing 2 years may have more talent, but he ain't got near as much knowledge, and normally the guy that's been playing 10 years is going to get the best of him.

Most of the Green Bay Packers had more tenure and played together longer than most of the Chiefs had been in pro football. Several Packers had played pro football long before the American Football League came into existence. In fact, various Packers and players on other teams declined big-time contracts to play in the AFL. They chose to play for the Packers and other legendary franchises in an established league.

In Long Beach, 30 miles south of Los Angeles, some Chiefs had a sense of awe about the Packers, while others were honed in on getting ready and playing the game well and winning. Although the Chiefs were made to feel their responsibility of representing the AFL, they did not seem as aware of their potential place in history. To many it was just a game, even though there was a lot of hype.

CHRIS BURFORD: I'd seen Green Bay play before. They had a good, solid football team. I had no awe. I was really looking forward to playing! I thought it was a great opportunity.

JOHNNY ROBINSON: After seeing a lot of film in Long Beach and after doing a lot of talking about the Packers, we knew that we were just going to have to hang tough in there. I didn't see how we could stop them from getting maybe four, five yards at a crack, so we'd just have to wait and hope for the breaks and take advantage of them.

MICKEY HERSKOWITZ: A dreamer, Hank Stram was a guy who had nothing to lose. He was not the least bit timid or fearful about going into that game. He had some tricks he could put into play. He felt his Chiefs had more speed, more in them, than Green Bay realized. He was all into the big game ahead and ready to roll the dice. He thought his team was so underrated, so taken for granted. True, his team had talent, but I don't remember among the AFL insiders anybody picking Kansas City to win.

Focused, carefully organized, and doing all he could do in Long Beach to ensure a triumph for his team in the January 15 matchup, Hank Stram was also being sucked into the rivalry frenzy of the moment. "We are playing this game," he told his team, "for every player, coach, and official in the AFL."

Their time in Long Beach coming to an end and their football machine fine-tuned, the Kansas City Chiefs took leave of the Edgewater Inn. It was almost game time.

> **JERRY MAGEE:** Finally, getting all set to leave Long Beach, it was really, really foggy. I stood there as the players boarded the buses to take them to Los Angeles. It was like they were going to war. Hugging wives, intense.

The decision to have his players check into a Los Angeles hotel and be ready the next day when the bell rang was made by Coach Stram. Only five members of the Kansas City Chiefs had ever played in the Coliseum. It pleased the KC pilot that his team lacked familiarity with the stadium. He felt there was nothing to gain going there the day before the game to loosen up and have some final practices. Mike Mercer traveled alone the Saturday before the game to practice his placekicking.

> **FRED ARBANAS:** Being in that game meant a lot more exposure for us at that time. It was a pride deal because we were going to be able to have the opportunity to beat the best. The best was the Packers. Some of them were guys I had idolized in college. To play against them was a big thrill.
>
> The word that was passed out was that the Chiefs were awed by the legend of the Packers. That was newspaper talk. Not true. We knew they were a heck of a good team, and we thought we had a good team too. I think you played for the team and you played for your own pride. You know, when you stepped on a football field, it's usually man against man, and I was ready to take anybody that wanted to step in front of me. I was ready to go.

> **MICHAEL MACCAMBRIDGE:** Green Bay was power and execution. The Packers playbook was not a thick one. It was not as if the Packers were tricking anybody. Bart Starr could have called the plays at the line of scrimmage. From that Packer mindset, shifting, men in motion, moving pocket, the tight I formation, some of those things were looked at by the NFL as smoke and mirrors, gimmickry, and, to a certain NFL mindset, it was dishonest. It was a refutation of what pro football was all about. When, in fact, if you take a longer view, it

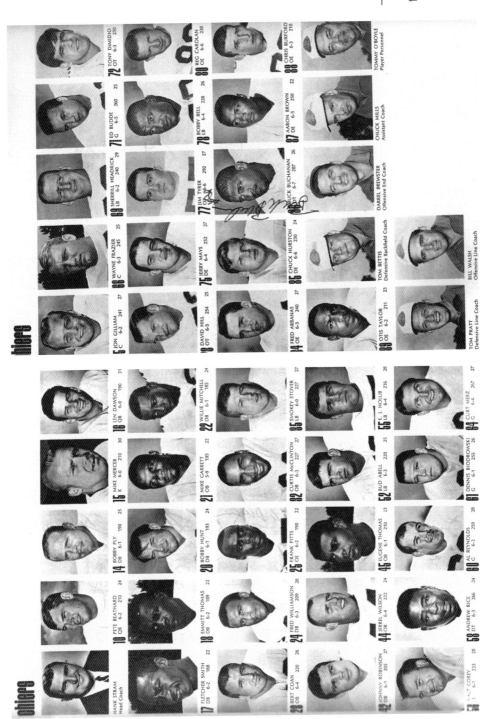

chiefs

TONY DIMIDIO OT 6-3 250 72

REG CAROLAN OE 6-6 230 80

CHRIS BURFORD OE 6-3 210 88

TOMMY O'BOYLE Player Personnel

ED BUDDE G 6-5 260 71

BOBBY BELL LB 6-4 228 78

AARON BROWN DE 6-5 250 87

CHUCK MILLS Assistant Coach

SHERRILL HEADRICK LB 6-2 240 69

JIM TYRER OT 6-6 292 77

CHUCK BUCHANAN DT 6-7 287

DARREL BREWSTER Offensive End Coach

WAYNE FRAZIER C 6-3 245 60

JERRY MAYS DE 6-4 252 75

CHUCK HURSTON DE 6-6 230 85

TOM BETTIS Defensive Backfield Coach

BILL WALSH Offensive Line Coach

JON GILLIAM C 6-2 241 50

DAVID HILL OT 6-5 254 76

FRED ARBANAS OE 6-3 240 84

OTIS TAYLOR OE 6-2 211 88

TOM PRATT Defensive Line Coach

chiefs

LEN DAWSON QB 6-0 190 16

WILLIE MITCHELL DB 6-1 185 22

SMOKEY STOVER LB 6-0 227 85

E. J. HOLUB LB 6-4 236 55

CURT MERZ G 6-4 267 64

MIKE MERCER K 6-0 210 16

MIKE GARRETT QB 5-9 195 21

CURTIS McCLINTON QB 6-3 227 32

BUD ABELL LB 6-3 220 52

DENNIS BIODROWSKI G 6-1 255 61

BOBBY PLY DB 6-1 190 14

BOBBY HUNT DB 6-1 193 20

FRANK PITTS OE 6-2 190 25

EUGENE THOMAS QB 6-1 210 46

AL REYNOLDS G 6-3 250 60

PETE BEATHARD QB 6-2 210 10

EMMITT THOMAS DB 6-2 189 18

FRED WILLIAMSON DB 6-3 209 24

JERREL WILSON QB 6-4 222 44

ANDREW RICE DT 6-3 266 58

HANK STRAM Head Coach

FLETCHER SMITH DB 6-2 185 17

BERT COAN DB 6-4 220 19

JOHNNY ROBINSON DB 6-1 205 42

WALT COREY LB 6-1 233

was part of the game, and it always had been. And some of the elements of what the Chiefs employed went back into parts of the package of football in the 30s and 40s.

The old Lombardi playbook worked, but history passed it by. In 1967, Lombardi's view of the football world was the conventional wisdom. And it worked; however, if you take a look at both styles of play, of playbooks, there is a lot more in pro football today that is similar to what the Chiefs did in Super Bowl I than what the Packers did.

HANK STRAM: On the bus heading to the Coliseum, the team was quiet and preoccupied. They were afraid of the game, of coming into the presence of greatness—the Green Bay Packers.

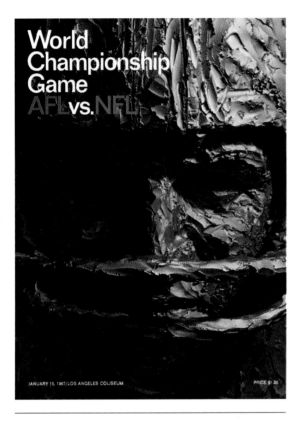

The official program of the "World Championship Game,"
later to be known as Super Bowl I.
Courtesy of the NFL

Chapter
FOUR

Pregame

Our goal was to make it more than a game, to make it an event. The initial perception was that the champion of the AFL wouldn't match up to the champion of the NFL, so we wanted people to have fun.

—Pete Rozelle

The funny thing is that when it all started, the league had no idea where it would go.

—Jerry Izenberg

THE NATIONAL Football League Championship Game, matching up the champions of the Eastern Division and the Western Division at the home stadium of one of the teams, had been taking place in the United States for 33 years. It was an exclamation point, a tradition, an end to another sports year, a concluding of another professional football season with the crowning of a champion.

It was passionate, pure postseason football played more times than not in snow, sleet, ice, in below-zero temperatures on frozen ground that lacked traction and often made running difficult.

Now a new game would take its place—the AFL–NFL World Championship Game.

The Packers of Green Bay would be matched up against the Chiefs of Kansas City.

Vince Lombardi's team was football royalty, a fabled franchise. Stories and images about the Green Bay coach and his players had appeared thousands of times throughout the 1960s in newspapers and magazines, as well as on radio, newsreels, and television. Green Bay was "Titletown, USA."

Kansas City had not lost a game in two months. The highest-scoring team in pro football at that time, and one that had bragging rights to a bunch of big boys well-versed in using grit and girth, the Chiefs outweighed the Packers by 15 pounds a player.

On November 9, 1966, the National Football League had signed the contract for the AFL—NFL World Championship Game to be played at Los Angeles Memorial Coliseum. There had been little time to get things in order.

BUD LEA: This was a game arranged in 26 days by political and legal wrangling after the merger.

JERRY IZENBERG: The funny thing is that when it all started, the league had no idea where it would go.

MICHAEL MACCAMBRIDGE: When I was getting set to write *America's Game*, the thing I struggled to articulate was this weird dichotomy, the public perception of the game and the way the teams participating felt about it. Publicly there was the perception that sports fans had been told since 1960 that the AFL was a "Mickey Mouse" league and that the Packers were emissaries of God or at least Vince Lombardi. There was no doubt the Packers were going to crush the Chiefs.

There had never been a precedent for this game, a world football championship at a neutral site. Pro football fans were not used to traveling great distances to go watch their team.

There was a feeling of anticlimax externally about the game and among sportswriters and fans; however, within the Chiefs camp and the Packers camp and the insular world of the American Football League, the National Football League, the game had this quality of a religious crusade. There was a chance in this game for the AFL to disprove every insult, every dismissal, every criticism.

For the NFL, it was even more grave because the NFL had been claiming superiority since the beginning of the AFL. All of those claims rested on the Packers winning that game. If they didn't, everything else that had happened beforehand would also be called into question. So it was in that weird environment that the game was to be played.

It was also very difficult to stage the game and what a short time frame there was to get it up and running. It was well into 1966 before the approval for the merger came through.

MICKEY HERSKOWITZ: In the spring of 1966, I left the *Houston Post*, where I was the sports editor, and took a job with Al Davis, then American Football League commissioner.

Working for the AFL, I was given the assignment of taking *New York Post* columnist Jimmy Cannon to lunch. A colorful and irascible sort, a product of the Damon Runyon era, Cannon had been taking pot shots at Davis and the AFL. Davis had read Cannon as a kid growing up in Brooklyn, read him every day, and considered himself a fan. Now it wounded him each time he picked up Jimmy's column and found another slam.

Dutifully, but with no joy, I would phone Jimmy at his apartment each morning and renew my offer to have lunch. In return, he would chew my head off. He was not an establishment guy, but he resented, I believe, what he considered an intrusion by strangers— the AFL owners—who wanted a piece of something other people— the NFL owners—had spent a lifetime earning.

"Nothing personal, kid," Cannon would bark at me. "Just tell Davis I don't understand your kind of hustlers."

I had a nice relationship with Pete Rozelle, and after the merger he drafted me off the AFL staff to work on that first Super Bowl. I happened to know him better than anybody in the AFL office. He wanted me to go out to California and set up and supervise all the arrangements. I was there really to see that the AFL had a presence in the management of the game. I was given a 22-page "to-do" list and a $250,000 budget to spend on supporting and promoting all elements of the game.

"Spend every single penny of it," Pete said. His single focus was for people to wind up believing how much better this game experience was than the World Series.

I was also given three pages of instructions about how to get the tickets printed, how to set up the halftime show.

The legislation to have the game played was passed in August. No one even started thinking about the game until September, October.

The game did not have tradition. It didn't have a buildup. It wasn't on people's minds for a year. Two Midwest teams were playing, and Kansas City was not a draw in California. There was no excitement about the matchups. Everybody assumed it would be a massacre by Green Bay. There was no sense of drama. There was nothing else to compare it to. The game was like a brand new baby left on a doorstep.

The game came so late into the historical football season, the 15th of January, a long time after the traditional professional championship games. There was lots of hustle and bustle in the league office in New York City. No one was really talking much about it in Los Angeles. The two major newspapers there and surrounding area papers had no daily stories. There was no real sense of excitement, drama, or newness. It was just being dropped into a period leading up to the New Year's bowl games and the Pro Bowl.

And since it was not a primary item on the Los Angeles agenda, ticket prices were thought to be high, ticket sales were slow. Many people thought they were being gouged.

I was not the first guy on the scene. Bert Rose Jr. was. A former Los Angeles Rams public relations director, the first general manager of the Minnesota Vikings, the one who gave them their nickname, making the point that it fit well with the Nordic tradition of the area they played in, had been hired for the league office by Pete Rozelle. Bert had set up his office in the bar of the Statler Hilton. I did not hear from him for about two weeks.

I went out there with a big list of what to do: get tickets printed and arrange for souvenirs, media entertainment, fashion shows for wives, excursions for the media, the pregame party. I had to get a press workroom set up, press box seating, phone lines, parties, half-time entertainment.

I was to provide cars for coaches, owners, general managers, press, and get hotel rooms arranged, take care of special suites, set up practice fields for the two teams. All of this had to be accomplished in less than three weeks.

In addition to a Friday night party at the Statler Hilton in Los Angeles, there was a field trip to Disneyland and the Santa Anita racetrack the Saturday before the game. The theme "Let me entertain you" held center stage, just as Commissioner Rozelle wanted it to.

MICHAEL MACCAMBRIDGE: Pete Rozelle wanted his staff to make the hospitality bigger and better than the World Series. He wanted the Super Bowl to be something better to experience if you were part of the audience, better to cover if you were a member of the media.

MICKEY HERSKOWITZ: Pete told me that I had one 11th commandment—I was not to do anything for one league that I did not do for the other one.

There was a rivalry between the TV networks and the two big sponsors, Ford and Chrysler. This brought an interesting dynamic to the game, since Ford was the sponsor of the NFL and Chrysler was the sponsor of the AFL. Each side would require 60 cars to cover team owners, general managers, and coaches, along with media from all over the country.

Before I headed out to California, I had gone out to Young & Rubicam offices in New York City, not far from the National Football League offices. I met with the man who handled the Ford account and made my little appeal.

He said, "I can't give you a damn thing. Not one single car."

I really didn't understand him. So I asked him again and told him, "It's the world championship football game. It makes sense. You are a major sponsor."

He said, "I can't give you anything, not a single car. Our big game is the Rose Bowl, and we use our cars for the Rose Bowl. I cannot get them back washed and serviced for you."

For the number-one item on Pete's list of 23 things to do, I came up empty. It was not a good feeling. I didn't tell Pete what happened. I wanted to salvage something. I left New York City and flew to Detroit and met with executive Jack Barlow of Chrysler and told him what had happened.

I said, "If you want total sponsorship—120 cars—you can have that."

"That's a deal," he said. "Tell me what you want." He was really lit up.

I was able to get 40 top-of-the-line Chrysler Imperial LeBarons for the owners, officials, VIPs, and 40 Dodges and 40 Plymouths for media and those connected to the media.

The Chrysler Imperial LeBaron he gave to me to use was not even available to the public. The one I was given featured a desk in the back seat that folded out. You could type on it, play cards. When you had no use for it, it folded back under the seat. The side of every Chrysler automobile we had bore the logo of the NFL–AFL Championship Game on it. Even Ford executives got to drive them. No problem.

The Chrysler people were ecstatic. Rozelle was pleased. He knew the game was not a top priority for some advertisers, but he also was convinced that someday it would be.

It was too bad that there was indifference from some big players towards that first game. It was too bad because the game from the start had a lot of glamour, aura, color, legend to it.

I stayed at the Statler Hilton in downtown Los Angeles. When I got out there, I don't know what Pete Rozelle had told the management of the Hilton, but they must have gotten the impression that I was one of the owners of one of the teams. I was provided with a three-bedroom suite with three bathrooms. I had never seen anything like it. There was a television set in every room, including the bathroom. And this was in the 1960s.

My first impulse was to ask for a smaller room, but I had my wife and three little kids all under the age of eight. They were at home in Houston. I had them fly out. They stayed with me the entire week before the game. The whole situation made me feel like some wealthy prince.

I went on almost every radio sports show in town, spreading the word about what Pete liked to call the "World Championship Football Game."

"Super Bowl" was already being used; however, that was mostly among the media. Fans did not know what to make of the upcoming game, what to call it. It was such a new event.

The game, set for January 15th—Packers versus Chiefs—for the world football championship, might have become a top story the day of the game and a few days later. In the weeks leading up to it, however, we had to scratch and claw just to let the people know it was coming. It was like the circus was coming to town, but nobody knew about it 'til they saw the tents going up.

For me, it was a big, big job. I was spending a lot of time on radio shows. I was doing a lot of talking about the game, selling. People kept calling in complaining that a family of four at $12 a ticket would cost $48.00 and then hot dogs, popcorn, soda. The line I was constantly getting was that a family could not go to the game at those prices. I sort of agreed with them.

And since the "World Championship Game" was not a primary item on the Los Angeles agenda, ticket sales were slow. Compared to a ticket to the Rose Bowl, which sat at about $6 a ticket, the price for the game at the Coliseum was a significant jump. The top ticket price of $12 was viewed as gouging by many people.

Critics pointed out that a capacity crowd of 75,000 was in attendance for the Green Bay–Dallas NFL Championship Game, which had a $10 top price ticket—two dollars less than the Super Bowl. The issue became more than a side bar. It became a big story in the media, a big story for fans to debate.

> MICKEY HERSKOWITZ: I spoke with Pete. I told him there were all these complaints about ticket prices. I told him the average working guy says he cannot afford the price.
>
> Pete said, "Well, tell them if they come to New York City and want to go to a Broadway play they won't be able to afford to take their kids either unless they find a way to spend more money."
>
> That was the answer I started giving, and it softened the blow somewhat.

The Packers and Chiefs were each allotted five thousand tickets to sell. Other NFL and AFL teams each received two hundred tickets to offer for sale. Remaining tickets were made available to the host city of Los Angeles and the public.

There were two thousand tickets in the safe of the Kansas City Chiefs. It was burglarized and money stolen, but the tickets for the game remained. Someone said the robbers were making a statement. Maybe it was not a statement. Maybe they were not football fans.

Less than two weeks before the big game, a Los Angeles newspaper headline announced, "47,000 SEATS STILL UNSOLD FOR BIG GAME."

Pete Rozelle had predicted a 93,000-seat sellout. His estimate was later decreased to 70,000.

Rozelle's rebuttal to criticism of sluggish ticket sales was, "After all, we've just been going through the holidays for one thing, and fans have been preoccupied with the college bowl games."

Since the game was not a sellout, according to NFL rules, by order of Commissioner Rozelle, a TV blackout for Los Angeles and a 75-mile area around it would be put in place. The television networks would black out 15 million viewers. Rozelle's office announced that it was the "fair thing to do for the people who bought tickets on the promise there would be no local TV."

The "blackout" was viewed by many, especially the local newspapers, as a slap in the face to fans in Los Angeles. Stories appeared in newspapers explaining how to pirate signals from television stations outside LA. Disc jockeys on the rock station KRLA on the AM band and "Boss Radio" station KHJ provided instructions for making a "Super Bowl antenna" from coat hangers.

Angelinos who couldn't afford a ticket to the game were strongly encouraged to purchase a newfangled contraption called a super aerial. More than 15,000 requests for a set of instructions were filled by a Los Angeles radio station. Explained were the steps for building a super aerial to defeat the super blackout. Interestingly enough, the main props of the instructions were five wire coat hangers and a broomstick.

Caught up in the swirl of criticism, Commissioner Rozelle defended the blackout as necessary. Years later, he was still defending it. In a statement before a Senate communications subcommittee in Washington, D.C., on October 4, 1972, he underscored the importance of the blackout policy for professional football: "We all remember the Friday Night Fights, but how about the Wednesday Night Fights, the Saturday and the two Mondays? This is correct. At the peak of TV boxing popularity from January 1953 to January 1955, there were two, by September 1964 there were zero. The sport simply ate itself with overexposure."

> **HOWARD COSELL: Along with the blackout, the pooling of television money helped save the game.**

The environment that the next big game operated in was underscored by a conversation on a Los Angeles local television newscast.

"Are you going to the World Championship Game?" a newscaster asked a guy on the street.

The guy responded, "The world what?"

The top $12 tickets could be gotten for $2 on the street. More than 30,000 seats were empty. The final announced official attendance would be 63,036.

> **CHRIS BURFORD: I really wasn't concerned how many people would come to the game. I was just glad that we were in there playing.**

The big game was a thrown-together affair, hastily organized. It was, in some ways, an afterthought to the merger agreement. Against its better instincts, the established 46-year-old league was matched up against the AFL, just seven years old.

> **MICKEY HERSKOWITZ: Creating the AFL–NFL World Championship Game was the peak of Pete Rozelle's being commissioner. He was committed to making it work. He knew the problems we had. There wasn't very much time to promote the game. It was a start-up venture. You were competing with all the bowl games. He also knew the game would catch fire very soon.**

The NFL commissioner had done everything in his power to attract a full house for the game. His secretary even sold tickets out of her hotel room until the night before kickoff.

Decades later, Rozelle, still dissatisfied with the turnout, said, "All I can remember is 30,000 empty seats."

MICKEY HERSKOWITZ: There was so much naiveté that it was refreshing. Barron Hilton gave a "unity party" for the owners of both leagues about five days before the game. It was at a mansion with large grounds and all kinds of attractive landscaping. There was an orchestra, entertainers. Barron Hilton had access to a lot of showbiz people, so they were there, including Clint Eastwood and Jane Mansfield.

A gigantic cake attracted a lot of attention. Some thought of it as a wedding cake for the "shotgun" marriage that had been created through the merger.

During a break from the band playing, a couple of the owners made the obligatory statements about how grand everything was. Then the wife of one of the American Football League owners, one of the younger wives, very attractive, in her 30s, probably had too much to drink, she got up and made a little impromptu speech and ended up with, "Go, Chiefs, go!!"

It was the first inkling I had that among the NFL crowd there was a concern that bordered on terror. I looked at the faces of three or four NFL owners. They had been scoffing and in kind of contempt at the college cheerleading of this AFL wife. But you could also most feel their reaction: "Oh, my God—what if we lose the game to the AFL?"

Cleveland Browns owner Art Modell said, "Some of our owners were petty in their distaste for the American Football League. A few of those petty owners, miffed more than a little bit at the comments of the young woman, walked out."

At the party in the Beverly Hilton ballroom in Los Angeles the Friday night before the big game, two uniformed policemen spent their time guarding an attractive trophy. It had been created as an award for the winner of the AFL–NFL World Championship Game.

As the story goes, during a luncheon meeting in Manhattan, Tiffany vice preisdent Oscar Reidner made a rough sketch of the trophy's design on a cocktail napkin. Pete Rozelle was approving. Instead of an urn or a cup, the traditional trophy envisioned by Oscar Reidner consisted of a regulation-size football in kicking position on a pyramid-shaped pedestal. That first trophy was manufactured in Newark, New Jersey.

It has remained the same throughout the years, made of sterling silver, weighing seven pounds, and standing 22 inches high. The original trophy contained the logos of the NFL and AFL on the sides of the pedestal. It was not until Super Bowl III that the Tiffany Trophy was renamed the Vince Lombardi Trophy.

Awarding that trophy to the winner of the game became a tradition from the start, as did the Super Bowl party staged before the big game. In 1967, many more people showed up than were expected. Almost 700 were in attendance, mostly writers in town to cover the game. Drinks and a buffet dinner were served to the assembled throng.

One attendee remembered, in particular, how well Les Brown and His Band of Renown played "I've Got the World on a String."

"But it was not that festive because of the bidding wars that had taken place. Acrimony was served up with cold cuts" (Rappaport, 2010, 178).

There were cold cuts aplenty, but also lots of sizzling steak and lobster on platters. And the liquor flowed freely.

> GEORGE MITROVICH: I was there and got into a rather nasty argument with Jim Finks, the general manager of the Minnesota Vikings, about why the AFL was better than the NFL. Later, my wife, LaVerle, made it quite clear she was embarrassed by my lack of decorum. (She must have been right, because later *Sports Illustrated* threatened to sue me for my attacks upon Tex Maule, their legendary pro football writer. I had repeatedly said he was an extension of the NFL's publicity department; a view I held then—and now.)

> JERRY MAGEE: Tex Maule went a bit overboard and predicted that the Packers would win, 58–6. So I picked the Chiefs, 58–6, or something like that, a big score.

Magee's blown out of proportion prediction was in response to some writers with NFL allegiance. They had predicted a Packer victory by incredulously outrageous scores, like 36–0, 58–6, and 76–0. Annoyed AFL writers like Magee simply sniped back, attempting to defend the Chiefs' credibility. There whole thing was a major disconnect from the old maxim, "No cheering in the press box."

> MICKEY HERSKOWITZ: Things in the press box were pretty primitive. We had play-by-plays run off on a mimeograph machine, no game quotes or things like that. We did have player notes and things of that sort.

> BILL CURRY: That day before the game, Coach Lombardi got us on a knee there in the Coliseum and he said, "Now, I want to make a couple of things clear. If you sneak out . . . if you're caught after curfew tonight, your fine will be $2,500." Previously it had been $100. My salary was $13,500.
>
> "I want you to know," he continued, "that if you are guilty of that transgression, or any transgression, you will never play another down in the National Football League."
>
> So for a second-year guy like me, that was heavy stuff. Our always-volatile head coach was even more so.

BUD LEA: A couple of the players remembered that the intense coach took a hard look at the 34-year-old veteran Max McGee when he made the announcement about punishment and fines.

The free-spirited Max McGee told his roommate, Paul Hornung, that he had met a couple of American Airlines stewardesses in the hotel bar, and they had agreed to meet later that night. He wanted his roommate to join him.

"He had met someone and had fallen hopelessly in love. I didn't go because I was getting married," Hornung later said. "I didn't want to get caught three days before I got married."

Their hotel room was checked at 11:00 p.m. by former Packer Dave "Hawg" Hanner, an assistant coach in charge of curfew bed check that night. McGee, under the covers with his coat and tie on, asked his old teammate if he was going to check his room again.

Straight-faced, Hanner said he was going to check every hour.

Then, closing the door, Hawg looked back one last time and said, "No."

"I told these two young ladies that Hornung and I would come back," McGee said. "Neither of us figured to play in the game. Then Hornung backed out because he had more value of money. The fine was something like $15,000. Hell, that's what we were going to get if we won the game. So I snuck out the back door of the hotel, got a cab, and went to the bar, where I met these young ladies. After the bar closed around 2:30, we all went to their room. I got back to my room at 7:30. I asked Hornung if they had caught me going out, and he said they did. He was lying."

An ace in the hole all season long, Max McGee, known as "Night Owl" to many on the Packers, seemed to have a way with words, with the ladies, and with Coach Lombardi. Even though he had caught only four passes all season, McGee was a clutch performer and an excellent athlete. The consensus was that the tough Lombardi looked away most times at McGee's after-hour's adventures, his breaking curfew to party in whatever town the Packers were visiting.

PAUL HORNUNG: Max McGee told this story years later at some banquet. Max said, "You know there have been a lot of stories about me going around and being out after curfew and being out with some broad until 2:00 in the morning. I'll tell you right now, that's a bunch of hooey. I wasn't out with some broad until 2:00 in the morning. I was out with two broads until 6:00." That was classic Max.

Paul Hornung.
Photofest

CHUCK LANE: I still question whether McGee was really out that night. I think that that might have been a convenient story that got a lot of traction. And all it did was to increase his legend, and he never did say much to contradict it. I think he (enhanced it). Max certainly looked—you'd see pictures of him on the cover of *Sports Illustrated*—and he looked like he was just *dying* out there on the field . . . and he probably was!

But that was typical of Max, he'd have big games in the big games. He was a punter at one time. He was a great receiver. He didn't look like an athlete but sure as heck was.

I'm sure McGee was out, but I'm not sure he was out after curfew. I can't believe they would have gotten away with it in that type of atmosphere, with that type of scrutiny. I can't disprove his stories, nor can he prove his, so who knows? But I think it was convenient to the legend.

Sports Illustrated and some newspapers called it the "Supergame." Both NBC and CBS promoted the game using the same slogan: "Super Sunday: Watch Our Broadcast."

On Christmas Eve 1966, the television networks' publicity and marketing machines set in motion the game within a game. Curt Gowdy and Paul Christman, who had both signed on with NBC after being with ABC and the AFL from 1962 to 1964, became tag ons to most NBC evening programs. CBS paraded out Frank Gifford and Ray Scott on their shows. Like tag teams, both sets of announcers made the rounds, seemingly getting face time everywhere. Gowdy and Christman, skilled and veteran sports jocks, even made appearances on the *Tonight* and *Today* shows. Both traced their AFL broadcasting tenure back to 1962. Gowdy made it clear that he "wanted to see how the American Football League would do against the NFL."

"Hank Stram," Gowdy reported, "was cocky with us before the game. He said Green Bay could be beat. Lombardi didn't meet with us. But his line coach, Phil Bengtson, sat with us and told us they wouldn't be doing anything complicated" (Stan Isaacs, *Newsday*, January 7, 1991).

MICHAEL MACCAMBRIDGE: Pete Rozelle knew this was going to be a huge sports event. He knew that the TV ratings would be wonderful. He knew there was going to be a lot of media interest. But what he was fighting was that all the other sports events of commensurate scope and draw had decades and decades of tradition.

The newness, the lack of tradition, the fact that things seemed to be being made up as the event was looming—all of this made for uncertainty, misdirection, snafus, and hazards.

JERRY IZENBERG: A good thing about it all was that you could see anybody. You could interview them in their room. The access was just wonderful. I had lunch with Chiefs player E. J. Holub at the team hotel the day before Super Bowl I, something that wouldn't happen today.

All of a sudden, Holub put his hands out; they were soaking with sweat.

I was a kid, so I asked the romantic question: "Is it because now you're going to get a chance to play against a team whose bosses said you were too small?"

He looked at me like I was from Mars. He said, "You don't get it. If the Kansas City Chiefs win this game, I make $15,000." That's tip money for these guys today. Thinking back to Holub and that conversation, that was amazing.

Controversy and intrigue, as well as hustle, hype, and hoopla, were on parade pregame in many different ways. It was almost naïve, primitive stuff.

In the *New York Times*, there were lineups and matchups for NBC versus CBS. Resembling the tale of the tape for a championship boxing match—well, not exactly—each network's announcer, director, and producer was listed by height, weight, and collegiate affiliation.

The Saturday night before the game, even chubby Jackie Gleason, one of the famed comedians of that era, got into the act. "The Great One" ended his black-and-white CBS television variety show *The Honeymooners* the usual way—by graciously acknowledging his fellow stars, Audrey Meadows, Art Carney, and Joyce Randolph. Then the boisterous Gleason urged his loyal and huge audience to make sure to tune in the next day to CBS and watch the Packers and Chiefs compete in the world championship football game.

"It's gonna be murder!" Gleason bellowed.

There were those who thought "The Great One" went a bit too far, that he was too much of a shill for his CBS network, which carried the NFL broadcasts.

The larger-than-life comic had moved *The Jackie Gleason Show* to Miami Beach in 1964 and set up residence in a mansion on Alton Road that measured almost 8,000 square feet. It had a grand staircase that led up to the second floor, affording its owner a nifty view of the Miami Beach Country Club. That special home was mostly used for parties.

It is not known whether the gregarious Gleason staged a Super Bowl party in his Miami Beach home or even watched the contest, as he had extorted his fans to do.

BILL MCNUTT III: Just before the game got underway, Coach Hank Stram had arranged for Mickey Mouse ears and music to be brought into the Kansas City locker room. The guy that procured all of that was Bobby Yarborough, the only equipment man the Chiefs had from 1960 to 1990. But he was more than an equipment man because he was also a qualified trainer. He was also a confidante, a protector of players and their possessions.

Bobby Bell would never let anybody tape his ankles but Bobby Yarborough. You know, players are so superstitious. During the 1966 season, Otis Taylor would give his wedding ring to Bobby Yarborough, who would tie it to his shoelaces.

And Bobby Yarborough, breaking some champagne after the American Football League Championship Game, made the mistake of saying something about that: "Oh, this is our good luck charm: I tie Otis' wedding ring to my shoe." And as the story goes, at Super Bowl I, somebody would steal the ring!

CURT MERZ: Entering the clubhouse that January 15, 1967, we heard the music of the Mickey Mouse Club. We also found Mouseketeer ears by every locker. My pants were getting taped pregame, and trainer Bobby Yarborough was wearing the Mickey Mouse ears. We had been called the "Mickey Mouse League" as a put down, and that was where that came from. I wasn't surprised by the Mickey Mouse theme in the locker room because it was in the press that we were being called the "Mickey Mouse League."

Nevertheless, we were surprised to see that stuff. I guess that was to motivate us. It didn't do anything for me. I don't know if it did anything for anybody else.

There was a lot of Mickey Mouse hats, music. Some of the players didn't want to wear them. Some of them did.

LEN DAWSON: Hank had a sense of humor. The guys were wearing those Mickey Mouse hats with the ears and parading around. A lot of the players were really uptight, that's for sure. And Hank was just trying to find a way maybe to loosen that up.

Infuriated that his league and the AFL had been characterized as the Mickey Mouse League and his Chiefs as a Mickey Mouse team, the KC skipper had arranged for trainer Wayne Rudy and equipment man Bobby Yarborough to embark on a shopping trip in Los Angeles the week before the game. Their mission: purchase as many sets of Mickey Mouse ears as they could. They were told to buy a record player and a recording of the Mickey Mouse Club theme song: "Who's the leader of the club that's made for you and me; M-I-C . . . K-E-Y . . ."

The ears and the song held center stage in the locker room of the Chiefs.

"I thought," Stram said, "it would either relax everybody enough so that they would play better or just maybe piss them off enough so that they would play harder."

HANK STRAM: A lot of people believed us to be awed by the Green Bay Packers in the first Super Bowl. I didn't feel that way at all. I believed we had a great chance to win the game.

There was no question that Packer coach Vince Lombardi had great material. Certainly, you don't win with mirrors. It's important to have talented football players, but in addition you need quality people. Look at the leaders they had on that club. On defense they had Henry Jordan and Willie Davis on the line, Ray Nitschke at middle linebacker, and Herb Adderley in the defensive secondary. On offense they had Bob Skoronski, Forrest Gregg, and Jerry Kramer in the line and Bart Starr the quarterback.

Green Bay had three major offensive weapons. They ran off tackle to the weak side with the halfback Elijah Pitts kicking out the linebacker. Depending on whether Pitts blocked the linebacker right or left, fullback Jimmy Taylor would run the other way. This was what Lombardi described as "run to daylight."

The second major weapon was the famous Green Bay Sweep, run to the strong side, with guards Jerry Kramer and Fuzzy Thurston pulling and leading Pitts around end. Green Bay's third offensive weapon was Bart Starr passing. Bart passed very well, and he also led his team with authority.

Few teams in the NFL had succeeded in halting the Packers' offensive unit, and I knew they probably would score on us. I felt we would have a very difficult time holding their offense to under three touchdowns. The question then became could we better that score?

Green Bay had a defense as strong and well-balanced as its offense. They gave yards grudgingly, mainly because they worked extremely well together as an 11-man squad. Football players often make the All-Star teams not only because of their own abilities, but because of the abilities of those playing around them, who make their job easier. Certainly this was true of the Green Bay Packers in the 60s. Their front four didn't dump the quarterback as often as some other teams, but they pressured him, while at the same time cutting off the run. Because of the consistency of the rush from the front four, the linebackers could play deep. Middle linebacker Ray Nitschke played so far off the line of scrimmage that the center rarely got a good block on him. Tackles Ron Kostelnik and Henry Jordan not only kept the blockers off Nitschke, but funneled the runners toward him. As a result, Nitschke could range up and down the line to always appear at the point of tackle. By playing deep, the Packer linebackers also could help guard against the short pass, which

Green Bay Packers offensive tackle Forrest Gregg.
Photofest

Green Bay Packers guard Jerry Kramer.
Photofest

enabled their defensive backs to similarly play deep to guard against long passes. You rarely got any easy touchdowns against the Packers. Nevertheless, I felt we could score on them. If we scored enough— maybe three touchdowns and a field goal—we would win. Football often is that simple.

MURRAY OLDERMAN: The Chiefs, on average, were bigger, slightly faster, and younger than the Packers. Of the 23 regulars on the offensive and defensive platoons of Green Bay, 11 were 30 years old or more. On offense, Green Bay averaged 29.1 years per man, with an average of 7.8 years' experience. The Chiefs offensively averaged 26.1 years per player. The Packers were more nimble, possessed more speed up front with Jerry Kramer, Forrest Gregg on offense and defenders Henry Jordan and Willie Davis on defense.

BILL MCNUTT III: Leadership on that Kansas City Chiefs team mainly came from Leonard Dawson on offense and Jerry Mays on defense. But the team was blessed with a lot of leaders.

The Chiefs entered the game after posting an 11–2–1 mark during the regular season. Their powerful offense paced the AFL in points scored and total rushing yards. Their running backs, Mike Garrett (801 yards), Bert Coan (521 yards), and Curtis McClinton (540 yards), finished in the top 10 runners in the AFL. Star wide receiver Otis Taylor gave KC a great deep threat at any time. He had 58 receptions, good for 1,297 yards and eight touchdowns in 1966. Tight end Fred Arbanas recorded 22 catches, while running for 305 yards and four touchdowns. He was one of six Chief offensive players named to the All-AFL team. Receiver Chris Burford added 58 receptions, for 758 yards and eight touchdowns.

On defense, the Chiefs featured All-AFL players Jerry Mays and Buck Buchanan. Another All-AFL pick was linebacker Bobby Bell, skilled at pass coverage and stopping the run. Bragging rights to the best on defense belonged to their secondary, which featured All-AFL safeties Johnny Robinson and Bobby Hunt. Both were credited with 10 interceptions. Defensive back Fred Williamson had four interceptions.

Green Bay's Bart Starr was the top-rated quarterback in the NFL for 1966, winning the league's Most Valuable Player Award and completing 156 of 251 (62.2 percent) passes for 2,257 yards, 14 touchdowns, and only three interceptions. His top targets were wide receivers Boyd Dowler and Carroll Dale, who combined for 63 receptions and 1,336 yards.

A consensus and summary of scouting reports on the two quarterbacks would prove to be right on target: Intercepted but three times the entire 1966 season, Bart Starr never threw a ball unless he was sure where it would wind up. Almost always honed in, never one to call a bad play, like a surgeon with the ball in his hand, the Green Bay quarterback was able to cut up, carve out the defense of the opponent.

Len Dawson was the top-rated passer in the AFL, completing 159 of 284 (56 percent) passes, for 2,527 yards and 26 touchdowns. He was a tremendous offensive weapon.

There was a feeling that Dawson's arm was very good, and he had the ability to make big plays. There was also a feeling that hesitation, at times, forced him into being boxed in. A slow Kansas City offensive line and an average secondary were deemed liabilities against a team of the championship caliber of the Green Bay Packers.

> **SMOKEY STOVER: Len Dawson was a good scrambler, and he wasn't a long-ball thrower. He'd just drive them on down the field. They criticized him about that, but he was very accurate and very elusive and a good quarterback. A lot of the guys called him "Ajax" or "Mr. Clean" because he never got dirty.**

The mighty Packers of Green Bay, who sat atop the world of professional football, had bragging rights to stars of stars. The celebrated Packers had also recorded four championship titles in six years, and their roster contained several future Hall of Famers. Depth was spread thickly throughout the team.

The offensive line, a major reason for the team's success, featured All-Pro guards Jerry Kramer and Fuzzy Thurston, as well as future Hall of Famer Forrest Gregg. Fullback Jim Taylor, a load, was the team's top rusher, with 705 yards, and he had also caught 41 passes for 331 yards. Paul Hornung was injured early in the season, but running back Elijah Pitts did a good job as a replacement, gaining 857 combined rushing and receiving yards.

Lionel Aldridge had replaced Bill Quinlan on defense, but Leroy Jordan and Willie Davis still anchored the line. Ray Nitschke excelled at run stopping and pass coverage, while the secondary was led by future Hall of Fame defensive backs Herb Adderley and Willie Wood.

Nine of 10 "experts" had picked the Packers to win big, with an average score of 33–18. Vince Lombardi, who had confessed to sportswriter Max Kaese of the *Boston Globe* that he was a bit tired of having football as a daily part of his life since July 10, 1966, was riveted into making sure his veteran team was poised, primed, and prepared.

Lombardi stressed paying careful attention to the fundamentals. His players knew that a defeat would besmirch all that Lombardi had built throughout the years. The entire Green Bay Packer organization was focused on settling for nothing less than a substantial victory over the Kansas City Chiefs.

Hank Stram, too, was swept up in the frenzy of the historical moment that awaited him and his Chiefs.

"We are playing this game for every player, coach, and official in the AFL," he told his team, many times.

> **BOBBY BELL: Buck and I were roommates. The guy was so big and strong most teams could not even block him. We also had some**

small guys that were quick and strong. We were a strong team, a physical team. We also had so much speed with Otis Taylor, Mike Garrett.

We were a different kind of football team, lots of individual talent blended. We were exciting and dynamic—typical AFL.

The Green Bay Packers were typical NFL—three yards and a cloud of dust. They ran the ball 80 percent of the time it seemed. The Green Bay Sweep off tackle, run it, run it.

Going into the game, we were confident, ready.

MICKEY HERSKOWITZ: Hank Stram was a guy who had nothing to lose. He was a dreamer and he had some tricks, and he felt his team had more speed than Green Bay realized. He was all in and ready to roll the dice. He thought his team was so underrated, so taken for granted. The Chiefs possessed talent, but I don't remember among the AFL insiders anybody picking Kansas City to win the game. And Coach Stram was not the least bit timid or fearful about going into that game.

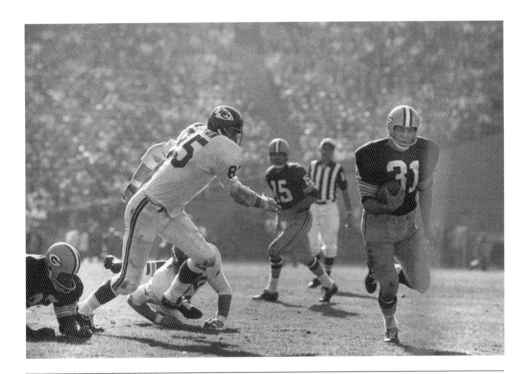

Jim Taylor rushes past the Kansas City defense.

Photofest

Game Time

When they brought the teams out and started introducing the starting lineups, I might have been the first guy, starting at left end, number 86. And I ran out on the Coliseum grass. Oh, wow.

—Boyd Dowler

The Packers themselves beat us in the first half, then the Packers and the Packer myth beat us in the second.

—Kansas City defensive lineman Jerry Mays

In fact, and to be brutally frank, this could wind up being labeled the "Stupor Bowl."

—Gene Ward, writing in the *New York Daily News*, January 11, 1967

The Super Bowl: Football's Day of Decision Stirs Nation.

—*New York Times* sports section headline, January 15, 1967

Super Sunday—Here At Last!

—*Los Angeles Times* headline

AT THE TIME of the first Super Bowl, the United States was involved in a bloody and unpopular war in Vietnam. During the game, an ad would feature President Lyndon B. Johnson encouraging the purchase of war bonds. On the home front there was protest against the war, and a surging civil rights movement. It was a time when the Louisville draft board turned back Cassius Clay's appeal for exemption from the service based on his plea that he was a Black Muslim minister.

In 1967, the Beatles, the Grateful Dead, and Jefferson Airplane made music. *Hair* opened on Broadway. The first issue of *Rolling Stone* was published, priced at 25 cents. The last *Milton Berle Show* aired on television. The National Transportation Safety Board was created. Seat belts were to finally become a staple in automobiles.

The median household income was a little more than $7,000. Unemployment was 3.8 percent. The average price for a gallon of gas was 33 cents. A home, on average, cost $7,300. For a nickel, one could purchase a first-class stamp. A ticket to a movie cost approximately $1.20. A gallon of milk was $1.03. A pack of cigarettes was about 30 cents. Life expectancy was 70.5 years.

On the Friday before the game, the Green Bay Packers arrived in Los Angeles. "If we lose it won't be because of our physical condition or the field. KC will just beat us," said Vince Lombardi.

The scene was finally set for a football game that many were calling the "Super Bowl" or "Super Game." After the historic announcement of the merger of the two football leagues, after months of bickering, backstabbing, bargaining, and ballyhoo, it was finally almost game time.

> **MICHAEL MACCAMBRIDGE: I think for Lamar Hunt, it must have been surreal to wake up on the morning of January 15, 1967, and get ready to go to a football game that he himself made necessary. Without Lamar's toughness and tenacity, you not only don't have the game, you also do not have the expansion in the 1960s where the number of pro football teams almost doubled.**

> **BART STARR: On the morning of our game, I woke up, took a quick shower, and headed downstairs to read the paper and have some breakfast. I walked by Max McGee and greeted him. He looked like he might need a shave and was wearing the same sports coat and slacks as the night before. Max said, "Hey, Bart," glanced at his watch, and headed for the elevators.**

At 11:00 a.m. sharp, the Packers, packed, poised, and feeling some pressure, although most would not admit it, took their seats on the chartered bus, taking leave of their Los Angeles Sheraton-West Hotel. All was in order for the trip to the Coliseum. There was a lot of hustling and bustling about by writers who were covering the team as they settled into seats.

A Murray Olderman tribute to Bart Starr. Starr's records have, of course, been eclipsed many times; Tom Brady of the New England Patriots holds the current record of consecutive passes without an interception, at 358.

Courtesy of the artist

Len Dawson à la Murray Olderman.
Courtesy of the artist

BUD LEA: Max McGee had returned to the hotel just in time for the team's breakfast. He napped for an hour and then boarded the team bus for the Coliseum.

"This is Super Morning of Super Sunday," an upbeat McGee shouted out. "We are all going out to the Super Bowl, and I am a Super End."

BILL CURRY: We didn't know at the time that he had been out all night, but he made that very clear later. McGee was hung over. There were some chuckles about that. There was some discussion.

The last one to come aboard the bus was Coach Lombardi. He settled in. He sat in the front seat, right side. The doors of the bus were shut. The bus began to slowly move out.

"Just a minute," the Packer head man told the driver.

Standing up, moving into the aisle, Lombardi called for the attention of his players. Then he slowly broke into a muted soft-shoe dance.

"Go coach, go!" some players encouraged him.

Lombardi later explained that he did what he did to loosen things up. "They were too tight," he said (Maraniss, 1999, 394).

> BILL CURRY: It was bright and sunny, and that seemed strange at that time of year. Getting on the bus it struck me: Everybody is behaving just like they always do. The players were not the least bit taken aback by all the stuff that went on. Nobody behaved any differently than normal. There was the regular, normal joshing by the ones who tended to be funny, like Hornung.
>
> A couple of guys on the bus were discussing the selections for the Pro Bowl, which was always a big deal to the players. Somebody was chosen, somebody wasn't. I remember Forrest Gregg saying, "Gosh, I never played very well in those things."
>
> And I wanted to say, "Yeah, but you've been in 10 in a row, Forrest!"
>
> I'm just sitting there listening to all of this.

> CHUCK LANE: Going to the game there were a couple of buses. In those days the local media were invited to travel with us. We had a number of people from our executive committee along. We were a very tight group. It was an awful lot riding on that game, and I think everybody had a great deal of confidence that we could win the ball game, but there was pressure.

> DAVE ROBINSON: I thought the game was never going to be that big. In fact, my wife wanted to come because she said some day it was going to be bigger than the World Series.
>
> I told her, "It's never going to be bigger than the World Series, but come on out to California anyway."

The Kansas City Chiefs players, who stood around their bus, some hugging their wives, were greeted by a foggy Sunday morning in Long Beach. The Chiefs were set to go directly from their Long Beach hotel to the Coliseum.

On the ride to Los Angeles, Hank Stram said, "the team was quiet and preoccupied. Each player was afraid of the game, of coming into the presence of greatness—the Green Bay Packers."

Stram had earlier made it a point of repeating to his players, "We're playing for every player, coach, official who has ever been in the AFL. We have a strong purpose." He repeated the same statement.

The *Los Angeles Times* assigned four of its top photographers to the contest. Art Rogers, Ben Olender, and Charles O'Rear were positioned on the sidelines, cameras at the ready, with 35-millimeter black-and-white film. Larry Sharkey, sequence camera in hand, was in the press box. He was shooting from an overhead location with 70-millimeter black-and-white film.

Ground for the impressive and gigantic Los Angeles Memorial Coliseum had been broken on December 21, 1921. Originally designed as a memorial to World War I veterans and built in the art moderne architectural style at a cost of $954,873, it opened on May 1, 1923, on 18 acres.

The Coliseum had a long history of playing host to all manner of events, including the 1932 Summer Olympics. In 1967, the USC Trojans began playing there and have used the facility ever since. After the Dodgers left Brooklyn at the end of the 1957 season, they played at the Coliseum as the Los Angeles Dodgers from 1958 to 1961.

It was now going to be the environment for the football game of all football games. Maximum effort had been expended to decorate the field of play. At the 50-yard line, a large brown football capped with a crown of gold was the central motif. The NFL insignia appeared in blue and the AFL logo in red on opposite sides of the football. "Packers" was spelled out in green on a gold background, with the NFL insignia on each side, in the west end zone. In the east end zone, "Chiefs" appeared in red on a gold background, with the AFL insignia on either side.

Members of the NFL since 1921, the Green Bay team was founded in 1919, by George Whitney Calhoun and Earl "Curly" Lambeau. The Indian Packing Company worked out a quid pro quo arrangement, providing $500 for uniforms and equipment, in return for the team being named for its sponsorship. Thus, the Packers have the oldest franchise name to continuously be used in the National Football League.

On that lovely California day, the team from Green Bay featured such players as Robinson and Starr, Taylor and Kramer, Hornung and Gregg, and Nitschke and Wood. They were the champions, the front-runners in the NFL since the first week of the season.

Wearing one of the most famous of uniforms in all of sports, the Packers, in their classic green jerseys, with gold piping on the sleeves and white numbers, gold helmets, and gold pants, had the look of gladiators as they amassed in front of their bench. Lombardi's team had given up the fewest points in the NFL that season.

The AFL Kansas City Chiefs, in their white road uniforms with red trim and red helmets and black shoes, looked resplendent assembling in front of their bench.

> **HOWARD MCHENRY:** It was a contrast, with Green Bay in green jerseys and gold pants, the Chiefs in white. I would rather have seen Kansas City in red, but they were designated the visitors and had to wear road uniforms.

> **BILL MCNUTT III:** The Packers wore the home colors. They were designated the home team. But the Kansas City uniform was fabulous, all white with the red helmets and the black shoes.

The Chiefs featured Dawson and Garrett, Holub and Bell and Buchanan, Stover and McClinton and Burford. The average age of their starters was 26. The Chiefs averaged 4.9 years of experience in professional football. There were players on Green Bay who had played together longer than the Kansas City franchise had been in professional football. Green Bay starters were, on average, 28.4 years old, with an average of seven years of experience in professional football.

Number 5, Bryan Bartlett Starr, was already a four-year veteran when the American Football League came into existence. Affable but totally business-like, the southerner was solidly in charge as the brilliant starting quarterback for Green Bay. He called the plays, not Vince Lombardi. He was the consummate pro.

In 1966, the Packers finished first in their NFL West Division, with a 12–2 record. Their defense had allowed a league low 163 points. Their offense had scored 335 points, fourth out of 15 teams in the NFL. They had eked out a tough win over Dallas in the NFL Championship Game. It was the second straight title for the Pack, their fourth in the era of Lombardi.

The Chiefs had posted an 11–2–1 record, finished first in the AFL West, scored 448 points in the nine-team AFL, allowed 276 points (second in the league), and shredded Buffalo (winner of the previous two AFL titles) in the league championship game. They were the best of the best in the AFL.

The Packers were the best football team in a generation. They were the crème de la crème, the top of the hill, a finely tuned machine that had much pride, much talent. In many quarters, Vince Lombardi was billed as the greatest coach there ever was.

The Chiefs were good, but would they be good enough in what was being promoted as the ultimate contest? Despite their proclamations of confidence, their belief in their youth and talent, their wonderful winning season and loyal fans, a "pedestal effect" was in place. Most Chiefs would never admit it, but to line up across from and be matched up against a Bart Starr, a Paul Hornung, a Ray Nitschke, a Dave Robinson, or a Willie Davis was challenging for some and weird for others.

> **WILLIE DAVIS:** The Chiefs were more talented than any other team we on the Packers had ever faced. Bigger, stronger, faster. We knew the game could have gone either way. But they were not experienced.

> **MICHAEL MACCAMBRIDGE:** It turned out that there were good football players on the Chiefs, but they were not as experienced, not quite as good as the players on the Packers.

Media mavens and self-proclaimed weather seers snidely referred to the ultimate game as "Super Bowl S." (for smog). How incorrect they were. No LA smog would darken the sky above the playing field. A soft haze dissipated as the sun came through into the Coliseum.

On January 15, 1967, Los Angeles was aglow in the warmth of a summer-like day, while much of the United States was feeling the sting of winter's cold. The warmth of the sun had convinced many men who had come wearing jackets to watch the contest in short sleeves on that inviting, windless afternoon.

Game time temperature was 72 degrees. Sun and haze intermingled. A slight breeze was in the air. It would be a Chamber of Commerce kind of day, with a high of 79 degrees and a low of 51.

"It's been a war of words for seven years. Now it's nice to have the war on grass, where it belongs," said Hank Stram (Devaney, 1971, 7).

> SMOKEY STOVER: It was a perfect day for football.

"The weather doesn't beat you. The other team does," said Vince Lombardi (Devaney, 1971, 11).

On the scene on that historic day, as he would be for every Super Bowl afterward, was George Toma, a son of a coal miner. A worker on fields of play since his teenage days, Toma grew up to become head groundskeeper for baseball's Kansas City Athletics. Pete Rozelle saw Toma's handiwork there. He dubbed the baseball field presided over by Toma the most beautiful he had ever seen. Then the NFL commissioner installed Toma as head groundskeeper for the AFL–NFL World Championship Game.

Toma cleverly made use of ice skating rink paint for the logos and names of the teams in the end zones. When he ran out of paint for the yard lines, he appropriated some of the white stuff from the ice rink. The creative Toma also came up with the idea to use a stencil to paint a football with a crown at midfield. But his specialty was grass. Toma expended maximum effort to make the turf at the Coliseum look luxurious.

> MICHAEL MACCAMBRIDGE: It was a beautiful game to watch and to play in—a sunny day at the Coliseum, natural grass. George Toma got his first NFL gig in that game, and they needed him because the LA Coliseum field was not in good shape.

> BILL MCNUTT III: Mr. Toma's job was to line and decorate the Super Bowl I field. It had a yellow logo at midfield, with 1967 and NFL and AFL on it. One end zone was yellow and green, the other yellow and red. My Dad, L. William McNutt Jr., gave Mr. Toma the idea to start putting a logo at midfield. Nobody had ever done that before they put it on the field in Kansas City. George went on to send my Dad a dollar a year as a royalty for his idea. Except one year he splurged and sent Dad a K.C. Royals bat autographed by Bo Jackson!

One hundred yards long and 53 and two-thirds inches wide, the field's grass was given a $3,000 green spray job the night before the game. It was well worth the price. Toma's terrific work and the field's gorgeous green sheen drew raves.

For this most novel of football games, celebrities in the privileged seats included famed movie and television stars Henry Fonda, Kirk Douglas, June Allyson, Janet Leigh, Chuck Connors, and Danny Thomas, as well as CBS television anchor Walter Cronkite, comedian and serious sports fan Bob Hope, and late-night television host Johnny Carson.

Ten astronauts were among the VIP guests invited to the game. Five were given seating behind the Green Bay bench. The other five had seats in back of the Kansas City bench.

Tickets and programs for the event read as follows:

World Championship Game AFL vs. NFL
Sunday, January 15, 1967
Los Angeles Memorial Coliseum
Kickoff One O'Clock PM

Game programs sold for $1 and contained an article entitled "A Day That Can Never Happen Again."

On this bright, clear day, a carnival-like atmosphere was on parade outside the venerable edifice. Lots of hawkers sold to a crowd that was well-dressed for the occasion. Many men wore suits with ties or came in sport jackets and slacks. Most women were bedecked in their Sunday best. Onlookers were wearing all manner of hats. There were even Kansas City zealots sporting caps and hats with feathers stuck in them—an acknowledgment of the team nickname: Chiefs.

That week, *TV Guide* carried just a listing of the game to be played, with no cover coverage. There was no big article. Television pregame festivities were simple. CBS showcased the Harlem Globetrotters playing basketball on an aircraft carrier. NBC carried a football year-in-review show broadcast on Armed Forces TV in Vietnam at 1 a.m. Beer, snacks, and rifles were at the ready as troops settled in to enjoy the game.

SHARRON HUNT: There was a sense that we were part of something new and history-making. We were seated just about halfway up, probably on about the 30- or 40-yard line, not real high or low in the stadium. It was a simpler time.

The name Super Bowl was freely used. It was something that a toy a child was playing with could have inspired. But the "AFL–NFL Championship Game" was just too cumbersome.

The multisyllabled official title was a mouthful. It was too long for newspaper headlines. "Super Bowl" was catchy, clever, and concise.

Those first two years, everything that was printed—the tickets, the programs—featured the words *AFL–NFL World Championship Game.* By the third year, "Super Bowl" would be the final and official name.

Less than a month prior at the Coliseum, a regular-season game between the Green Bay Packers and Los Angeles Rams had attracted 72,418 fans. The omnipresent and enthusiastic Pete Rozelle was initially convinced that for this championship game of championship games there would be a 93,000-seat sellout. His office later downsized the estimate to 70,000.

The day of the game, the official attendance was announced as 61,946, with lots of empty seats. It was reported that the NFL commissioner was taken aback when a stadium that had drawn 102,368 for a Los Angeles Ram–San Francisco 49er regular-season game in 1957, accommodated in excess of 92,000 for three 1959 World Series games, and could seat 93,000 for football was only two-thirds full on January 15, 1967.

> **MICKEY HERSKOWITZ:** The game drew over 60,000 but was considered a real box office bust. But even in today's new stadiums, 63,000 is considered respectable. We had only about a month of marketing to attract that.

> **LEN DAWSON:** They thought all they had to do was open up the Coliseum and people would come rushing in.

"The people in Los Angeles didn't attend because they didn't see it as a big game," explained cameraman Steve Sabol, who would go on to head NFL Films. "Super Bowl I was considered a sideshow, an afterthought. I had 10 tickets, and I couldn't give them away."

> **CHUCK LANE:** That day to start, there was almost like a maritime level atmosphere that was almost kind of misty. And then the sun came out, and it turned out to be a beautiful day. The Coliseum is a large, cavernous, historical building, and there was a considerable contingent from Green Bay present. We traveled well; that's kind of been a historical fact for the Packers.

> **FORREST GREGG:** The Coliseum, never gave it a thought. We could have played the game on the moon. It would have not made any difference.

> **FRANK GIFFORD:** I had played my college football in the Coliseum, so I was not awed by it. It was then and still is a pretty awesome place.

BILL MCNUTT III: I had never been to the Coliseum before. It was a magical place to a 12-year-old boy, second only to Disneyland. I remember the palm trees outside the stadium and a large number of TV trucks, since the game was being televised by both NBC and CBS. The entrances and exits were just tunneled into the stadium, and it was dark as you walked through them.

As you walked out, it just took your breath away because it was a beautiful vista with the end zone arches and the George Toma brightly painted football field of bright yellow, red, and green. If you were a sports fan, the Coliseum was a must.

The biggest deal was still Disneyland. We saw Lamar Hunt's personal lawyer when we went, Mr. Bill Adams, and his wife Molly. In those days you had a coupon book for the rides, and the most expensive was the E Coupon. And Mickey Mouse could still talk to you in 1967.

DALE STRAM: I recall my first sight of the Coliseum because I could compare it to the Cotton Bowl in Dallas, which I thought was big. My reaction to the Coliseum was like, "*Whoa*, it's really big."

BOYD DOWLER: We played in the Coliseum every year because we played the Rams out there every year, so it wasn't like our first visit to the Coliseum. Oh yeah, it was a special game. And we'd never seen those guys, we'd never lined up against those guys. The only thing was we had won the championship the year before, so we played against some of their young guys in the College All-Star Game. But that was different.

BILL CURRY: We arrive at the Coliseum. We get to the locker room, again, business as usual. Somebody had to get tape, another guy had to go meet with the trainer "for special reasons," meaning there was going to be an injection. I had my ankle injected, because that's what you did in the NFL. I had injured it in the game against Dallas two weeks prior.

CHRIS BURFORD: Compared to most of the places we'd played in, like the old War Memorial in Buffalo, the Coliseum was okay. I remember playing back in the day in Buffalo when we used to have to go to this little tiny locker room up these metal stairs that was right off the concourse, if you could call it that, where the hot dog stands were. And you'd have to dress in a little locker with a little tiny cage about one fect by three feet, put your stuff in it, walk down the stairs, go through the crowd by the hot dog stands, walk down through the stadium on, I guess, the third-base side of the old base-ball park there, and then go out on the field.

But we could have played in a school yard. It did not matter to me. The Coliseum was a nice place to play because they had nice locker rooms. The Coliseum was quite a bit different then. The Coliseum wasn't that old then. It wasn't any bigger as far as seating capacity than Stanford's stadium when I played there, about 90,000 also.

CURTIS MCCLINTON: For the American Football League, for our team and for all who supported us, that game was the first flight to the moon, momentous. That Coliseum stadium and any stadium for a player, it was how good is the grass and how good is the field. It was all about a bench that was not too close to the stands but close enough to the field so that we could observe it and not be close to fans and all the loud noise. That was the Coliseum to us.

The Green Bay Packers received the press box side, the shady side of the field. The Kansas City Chiefs, not too happy with it, were assigned the sunny side, the nonpress box side.

JERRY KRAMER: Stepping onto the field at the Coliseum, the place seemed half empty. The game was of less importance. I don`t think the public was ready for it. Our feeling was we'd beaten Dallas in the NFL championship, and that was our season. There were many more in attendance for the Dallas game. That was the big one. The Super Bowl was just another game.

BOYD DOWLER: There had been no preseason games between the leagues. This was the first exposure. We went down for pregame warm-ups and were looking at the Kansas City Chiefs.

"Good Lord," Max McGee said. "Big impressive looking bunch of guys!"

And I said, "Tell me about it!"

What he proceeded to tell me was about the events of the night before and the fact that he hadn't gotten too much sleep. He said he had missed curfew and had gotten in early in the morning. He said Bart saw him come in because Bart was always down real early in the morning. I never had a thought of what was to happen later.

"Are you okay?" I asked Max.

And he just said to me, "Don't go down today."

BILL MCNUTT III: Lamar Jr., me, and one of the Stram boys—sometimes it would be Dale and sometimes it would be Stu, sort of interchangeable—we could go anywhere we wanted. And I think that was just because our dads had passes. Of course, we were very comfortable going into the locker room and coming out. You know, having been ball boys and worked at exhibition games, we certainly knew everybody in the Chiefs' locker room.

I was completely in awe of Buck Buchanan's size and strength. He was the biggest man I had ever seen. Buck was a gentle giant and very kind to kids. Having gone to Grambling, he just wasn't used to the spotlight and all the attention. If Grambling played Southern, maybe you'd have 20,000 people there. Buck was very nervous before the game.

DALE STRAM: Each player had a stall in the Coliseum locker room. I went over to some of the stalls and spoke to players. I will never forget how wide receiver Frank Pitts was so concerned about playing against the Packers. He kept saying, "This is going to be a tough game. This is going to be a tough game."

After limbering up exercises were concluded, Sherrill Headrick of the Chiefs told his teammates, "I know we're the underdogs. But let's go out and play tough. This game is the biggest thing that's ever happened in sports, and this is our chance to be remembered because we played well in it" (Devaney, 1971, 19).

Bobby Bell and Buck Buchanan were so into it that they cried in the tunnel getting ready to go onto the field (MacCambridge, 2004, 240).

In the tunnel, Kansas City receiver Chris Burford told Jerry Mays to get a look at Buck Buchanan, all six feet, seven inches, and 290 pounds of him. The Kansas City defensive tackle's face was streaked with tears.

CHRIS BURFORD: I told Jerry, "I'd hate to play across from him at the start of this game. He is charged."

"Waiting in the tunnel to be introduced, guys were throwing up and wetting their pants," said Kansas City linebacker E. J. Holub.

CURT MERZ: We went in as a huge underdog. Pregame, I thought I was going to go over and see some guys I knew on the Packers and say, "Nice to see you again." To me that was the gentlemanly thing to do.

They were so tight they wouldn't even talk! I didn't know what was going on until I found out later all this stuff about the owners and everybody being just petrified that we just might have a chance to beat them.

BILL MCNUTT III: Pressure on these young men on the Kansas City Chiefs was enormous. They were absolutely the other league, the other league and the underdog, and they took it so personally. The people who took it the most personally were the players of 1966 that had been on the Dallas Texans' roster in '60, '61, and '62. People like Jerry Mays and Johnny Robinson and all those kinds of guys, because they felt like the National Football League drove them from their home. They loved Dallas, they loved living there and playing football there.

BART STARR: There were a lot of loud Packer fans there. I know they were very proud to be fans and be there for that team, and so we were extremely proud to see and hear that too. You'd be surprised at how many fans from an area back up in the Upper Midwest in a small community were at that ball game. And then I'm sure there were a lot of Packer fans from other parts of the country.

All things considered, there were two aspects about the crowd that were surprising. Its smallness was a surprise compared to the high hopes of the NFL office, especially Commissioner Rozelle. The other was the large number of fans at the Coliseum who, contrary to what was expected, seemed to be geared up to root for the underdog Chiefs.

BILL CURRY: The starting center was the first guy introduced. We ran out one at a time. So my concern was if I run out between the goalposts and trip and fall, that's the only thing I'm going to be remembered for the rest of my life! So I ran, watching my steps.

And I remember my wife asking me later, "Why did you prance? Why did you run so strangely?"

Coach Lombardi, the Packer legend, came out onto the field of play in a short-sleeved shirt, tie, and slacks. Hank Stram, proud and poised on the field of play, cut a dapper figure in a crisp white shirt, jacket, and tie.

DAVE ROBINSON: Vince and I happened to walk out on the field at the same time before the game, and Vince told me, "My, my, my, look how far football has come."

The field was all decorated with green, green grass. The big crown in the middle, the vivid colors in the end zones. Vince was really moved. He said jokingly, "I remember when football was played in cow pastures!"

BART STARR: There was very deep, embedded excitement coming out with my teammates onto the field. We were very, very anxious to begin. It wasn't just another game. More importantly, nothing like it had ever been done before. There was a sense for some of us that we were part of a historical event.

LEN DAWSON: I had a lot of incentive getting myself ready to play in that first Super Bowl. I was a cast-off from the NFL and was almost a Packer because they needed a quarterback while I was with the Browns. Paul Brown was thinking about sending me there, but he turned around and sent another quarterback who would and could do some punting as well. But to go against the Packers and all the players who were there, that were my vintage, a lot of the players I played against in college, it was special.

The groundbreaking game featured several unique public address announcements, including the following:

"After a touchdown, the teams will kick, run, or pass for one extra point. The AFL two-point option is not in effect."
"Remember the National Football League ball will be in use when the National Football League is on offense. The American League ball when the AFL team is on offense."
"Four thousand pigeons have been released here in the Los Angeles Coliseum."

Numerous unique features added to the culture of that first big game. The pitting of representatives from the two leagues against one another—who had never played against one another—for the world championship was trailblazing.

The disappointment in the empty seats at the Coliseum, the smallest crowd to ever attend a Super Bowl and the only Super Bowl that failed to sell out, was of note. The "newness" of it all made for a lack of tradition for the event. The playing of a championship game on a neutral site lacked a history. A neutral site made many fans neutral to the game.

DOUG KELLY: Two Midwestern teams, and LA is very into itself in terms of what they deem to be cool. The first time around, it wasn't cool! It was two relatively unknown teams playing in a huge facility, the Coliseum, and I think people looked at it somewhat askance.

A general view of Los Angeles Memorial Coliseum during Super Bowl I, January 15, 1967. The empty seats would be unheard-of today.

AP Photo

The AFL wanted its officials to wear the uniforms they wore in their league games—colorful, with red-orange stripes, black collars on shirts and black cuffs, and the logo of the AFL prominent on the front of their shirts, caps, and sleeves. The entire package was pretty easy to see; however, the sometimes surly and always assertive Mark Duncan, head of NFL officials, was downright dismissive. His opinion was that the AFL uniforms made the wearers resemble candy stripers in a hospital.

A compromise was reached. Wilson Sporting Goods designed "neutral" uniforms for the game. They had the familiar NFL look of black-and-white stripes, with the sleeves all black and bearing the official's uniform number. Hats were white with a black bill. That look would last until Super Bowl III, when uniforms sported by officials were standard fare in the NFL.

Another minor controversy centered on which league's football would be used in the game. It was decided that Green Bay would use the NFL Wilson "Duke" ball, and Kansas City would stay with its AFL-sanctioned Spalding J5-V. Little difference existed aside from the AFL ball being a little more pointed than the NFL one. A quarter of an inch longer and thinner than the Wilson model, some said the AFL ball was a bit easier to throw.

On offense, the football would be changed by game referee Norm Schachter, the NFL's top official. Sometimes the wrong ball would wind up in the hands of an irritated center or other player, who complained and insisted on having the "correct" football.

A Curt Gowdy malapropism underscored the excitement in the television booth: "And here come the captains, out for the toin coss."

> HANK STRAM: Our defensive captains, Jerry Mays and John Gilliam, met the Green Bay captains, Bob Skoronski and Willie Davis, in the center of the field to reenact the coin toss, which had been made earlier in the dressing room.

> JOE BROWNE: Teams used to meet regularly with the referee 30 to 60 minutes before the game in the dressing room to do the actual coin toss. The second one—minutes before the game—was just a simulation.

"There was a referee," famed photographer Neil Leifer told the *Huffington Post* in a story published February 3, 2013, "two captains from the Green Bay Packers—the offensive captain and the defensive captain—and two captains from the Kansas City Chiefs. . . . Five people and a coin toss. No NFL Films crew. No CBS television crew. No NBC television."

> BILL MCNUTT III: I was out on the field with my dad for the coin toss. He had passes. I was impressed with Mr. Schachter's biceps. He was a ripped guy, athletic guy. I remember thinking to myself, "Wow! He could play today if he had to."

Three officials from the NFL and three from the AFL would see duty that January day. There were six alternates as backups. That 1967 crew of a dozen officials is still a Super Bowl record.

When asked why there were so many alternates for the game, the quick-witted Schachter replied, "Who knows? Maybe they thought we would all get struck by lightning or something. I just didn't want them all to walk on the field at the same time. It might have scared somebody."

The Brooklyn-born Schachter began refereeing local football games in 1941, in California. He was a captain in the U.S. Marines in World War II. In 1954, he began working for the NFL as an official. He was paid $100 a game. Seven games were guaranteed.

Schachter tossed the coin. Willie Davis, captain of the Packers, called, "Heads!" Green Bay always called heads. Coach Lombardi believed that the eagle side of the silver dollar weighed more. Heads it was.

The captain of the Chiefs, Jerry Mays, asked Schachter to give him the coin as a souvenir. Schachter shook his head, adding, "No way. You lost the toss."

"Most teams," Schacter wrote in his book *Close Calls* (1981), "always take the ball unless it is a very windy day." Willie Davis, one of the two Green Bay captains, told Schachter his team wanted to receive the ball. He pointed to an end of the field. The experienced Schacter would not be fooled. "You don't have both options," he said. "You pick one or the other."

Schacter did not give Davis options, but in 1967, there were all kinds of options for the culture at large. One was technological advancement. New ways, new things, and new styles were au courant. And the NFL has never been an organization to lag behind in that respect.

Tex Schramm, general manager of the Dallas Cowboys, came up with the idea of using a remote control system for the Coliseum scoreboard clock for the first Super Bowl. That system had been successfully tested by his Cowboys during the just-concluded football season.

A primitive remote was attached to the huge wrought iron hands of the Coliseum clock. During the week before the game, test after test was conducted. The remote and the clock worked to perfection.

The time for the opening kickoff had arrived. An official on the field of play activated the system. Incredibly, one of the giant hands on the clock disengaged. As if in a scene from a horror movie, it fell more than 30 feet, like a gigantic dagger, into the stands below. It could have been a tragedy. Miraculously, however, that section of the Coliseum was empty, and no one was hurt.

In anguish, Pete Rozelle nevertheless asked, "What the hell happened to the goddamn clock?" (St. John, 2009, 76).

The "goddamn clock's" ancient hand had apparently been given such a testing and retesting workout that it just wore out and fell off.

The actual kickoff time was 1:16 p.m., Pacific Time, a little later than scheduled because of the "clock" issue. A NFL Films member gave a sound cue: "Super Bowl, reel one." It was a name that was catchy and seemed official and historical.

THE FIRST HALF

HANK STRAM: Fletcher Smith kicked off for us.

BILL MCNUTT III: With defensive back Fletcher Smith out of Tennessee State as the kickoff man in Super Bowl I, Hank Stram had another advantage. He had another sure tackler on the field.

Any edge was what Hank sought as a coach. Fletcher was one of the few African American kickers in pro football in the 1960s, perhaps the only one. Mike Mercer was an accurate straight-toed field goal kicker, but his kickoff distance was about the same as that of Fletcher Smith.

DALE STRAM: Mike Mercer was great at field goals that year for the Chiefs. Jerrill Wilson was our punter.

BUD LEA: As the game began, backup Max McGee, who caught only four passes all season, and Paul Hornung, sidelined much of the season with a serious neck injury, sat on the Packers' bench. The two were making plans for Hornung's wedding later that month in Hollywood. They were hardly paying any attention to the game.

KEN BOWMAN: Beginning of the '66 season I got a dislocated shoulder. I played periodically throughout that year. Shoulder would go out, and Coach Lombardi would go with Bill Curry. I sat on the bench next to Max McGee. He rolled up his pants' legs. "C'mon Ken, we can at least get a sun tan out here."

Fletcher, who many called by his nickname, "Duck," drove the ball to the Packer five-yard line.

HANK STRAM: Herb Adderley ran the kickoff back to the 25-yard line, and the game began.

The newness of this special championship game, the unfamiliarity of the teams with one another, and the desire to get a rhythm and a flow going would lead to much probing by both teams for the better part of the first nine minutes of play.

HANK STRAM: We started out with our triple stack defense, and Green Bay ran right into the strength of it by sending Jim Taylor into the line. Andy Rice made the tackle, but they still gained four yards. Elijah Pitts ran to the left side and made five yards. Then Taylor ran to the weak side, exactly what we expected them to do on short yardage situations. Green Bay rarely attempted to fool people. They executed well and took the attitude, "Here we come. Try and stop us." They were good enough at it to still ram it down the throat of a lot of teams. Taylor gained three yards, good enough for a first down on the 37-yard line.

Split end Boyd Dowler, who Green Bay scouting director Pat Peppler said "had size, speed, intelligence, and was totally loyal to Bart Starr," was injured. He was taken to the near sideline.

BOYD DOWLER: It was on the third play of the game. I blocked number 42, Johnny Robinson, and it was a bad idea because it didn't

Vince Lombardi having a word with a ref during the game.
Courtesy of the Los Angeles Public Library

work. And I hurt my shoulder and went out. In the NFL Championship Game against Dallas, defensive back Mike Gaechter's late hit
after a third-quarter touchdown injured my shoulder. So the hit in
the Super Bowl didn't do me any good.

On the sidelines, the 220-pound, six-foot, five-inch Dowler had his jersey and shoulder pads removed. Work on his shoulder began. No dice. The shoulder was wrapped.
Dowler would not—and could not—go back into the game.

Vince Lombardi called for number 85—Max McGee. At film sessions, the oldest
Packer had bragged that if his competition was Kansas City's Willie Mitchell or Fred
Williamson, he would have them for lunch.

BOB LONG: I was the guy playing behind Boyd Dowler, and if
he got hurt, I was supposed to go in, right? That's how things are

organized. McGee was behind me on the depth chart. I was the third receiver behind Boyd Dowler and Carroll Dale—he was in on the other side. He was a flanker with Max McGee then because he was second on the depth chart.

We start the game, and I realized that this game was on national TV, two networks, and as a young impressionable kid, I'm thinking to myself, "Wow, this would be a good time to play a lot. All my buddies from high school in Pennsylvania and all my friends from all over the place, they get a chance to see me play."

In the first series of play, Boyd Dowler hurts his shoulder. So I'm getting ready to put on my helmet and go in. In typical Vince Lombardi style, this is really typical of Coach Vince Lombardi, he was known for doing the unexpected, all at once, Lombardi yells out, "McGee!"

On the bench everybody's looking at each other. He's going to put Max McGee into this game? Max was also getting older. By the way, 34 years is old for a receiver. That's really old. So McGee goes to get his helmet to go into the game. I'm distraught.

McGee looks around for his helmet and cannot find it. One of the guys on the team yelled out, "Max! You left your helmet in the locker room!" He didn't expect to play at all, in fact so much so that he forgot his helmet.

I said, "Max, use my helmet. Take my helmet for the first series of plays, and we'll send someone into the locker room to get yours."

BUD LEA: McGee said later he had absolutely no idea why Lombardi called him to replace Dowler. "I hadn't played all year," McGee told me. "Let's put it this way," he said, "He had several guys he could have put in there. But I knew enough about Vince to know that he wasn't going to put in the younger guy if he could stick me in there for a game that meant more to him than any game he ever coached. And that is exactly what he did, and it worked out all right for the team, for him, for me."

BART STARR: I was just well aware that Max, being the quality player that he was, was now coming into the game to replace Dowler. We were grateful that we had someone like that. My concern was not knowing whether he had been out most of the night breaking curfew. My concern was the game.

HANK STRAM: Bart Starr next attempted to pass to McGee. The pass fell incomplete. As the game progressed, however, this approach would become better. On second down, Buck Buchanan burst through the line and dropped Starr for a 10-yard loss.

After Buck dropped Starr, Jerry Mays and Bobby Bell rushed him on third down, forcing a five-yard loss. We had pushed Green Bay back to their 22-yard line, forcing them to kick. Mike Garrett caught the punt on our 28 and ran it back to the 37. We had good field position for our opening drive.

I felt we could throw against the Green Bay defense, so on our first offensive play Dawson called a pass to Chris Burford on a square-out pattern. Green Bay's defensive secondary played man-for-man with very soft coverage on the outside. Their cornerbacks, Herb Adderley and Bob Jeter, protected against the deep pass by allowing a five-yard cushion between them and the receivers they had to cover. We would be able to throw in front of them, particularly if we could delay the linebackers so they wouldn't immediately drop back into pass coverage. We hoped to do this by running draw plays up the middle. Burford beat Jeter to the outside, but we missed a block on linebacker Lee Roy Caffey. Dawson had to hesitate a fraction of a second before throwing because Caffey got in the way. Burford caught the ball on the sidelines but couldn't keep both feet in bounds, so the pass was incomplete.

Garrett gained four yards on a draw play, which helped educate those linebackers to wait before dropping back.

Number 21 jitterbugged his way a few times during the first half, making the Packers miss. Garrett slipped tackles and showed the stuff that had made him the Heisman Trophy winner.

HANK STRAM: Then on third down, Burford ran a quick slant pattern across the middle. Fullback Curtis McClinton ran his pattern to the outside, and middle linebacker Ray Nitschke followed him. This opened the middle, and Dawson hit Burford for 11 yards and a first down. We would succeed with this pattern four or five times during the game.

Two plays later, we had Burford line up in the slot and sent Garrett in motion to the outside. The Packers failed to rotate with the shift. Jeter covered Garrett and left Packer safety Tom Brown to cover Burford, what we considered a mismatch. Burford beat Brown to the outside but again caught the ball out of bounds. We had located the gaps in the Green Bay pass defense but had failed to execute with sufficient precision to take advantage of them. A third-down pass intended for Otis Taylor fell incomplete, and we had to punt.

Jerrel Wilson kicked 47 yards, and after a five-yard runback by Donny Anderson, Green Bay took the ball on their own 20.

Green Bay came back quickly with passes to Marv Fleming, Elijah Pitts, and Carroll Dale for first downs. Then with the ball on the (Chiefs') 37-yard line, Starr underthrew Max McGee, who was being covered by Willie Mitchell. McGee reached back, made a fantastic catch, and ran for a 37-yard touchdown. That's football. Green Bay had us down 7 to 0.

BOB LONG: Max McGee is wearing my helmet. Max McGee scored the first touchdown in Super Bowl history. My kids and friends sometimes say, "Hey Long, did you play any in the first Super Bowl?"

I say, "Yeah. And let me tell you another thing: My helmet scored the first touchdown in Super Bowl history!"

BOB SCHNELKER: Max McGee was a good guy, a smart player, but he didn't train like the rest of them. He had other thoughts on his mind. You understood that. Even Vince understood that. He knew that Max and Paul Hornung would be out on certain occasions doing things they shouldn't be doing, but he didn't want to get rid of them. They were great players and fit into his system. I liked Max. He was easy to coach. He would listen to you. Maybe sometimes he would do it his own way.

When Dowler went down you hated to see a player that hurt. But you knew Max was good enough. He was a seasoned player. But you didn't expect him to do as great as he did. He knew the plays. Mentally he never screwed up. He was always into the game. Physically he trained enough that he could play the whole game. He worked hard on the practice field, just as hard as the rest of them.

He always felt he was as good, was better than the next guy. When he went into the game that showed. Even though he was near the end of his career, he could still play.

I was watching the game from up in the press box, and that first pass from Bart that Max caught was not a great pass, but Max was in the right place and caught it with one hand. Max had been making great plays like that since college and through pro ball. Vince kept people like Max around who knew what they were doing, who knew what they had to do.

KEN BOWMAN: Bart didn't throw the ball very well on that play to Max. He threw it about two yards behind Max. And here's Max reaching way back and kind of playing the flute throwing it up in the air and finally catching it. He didn't have much for speed, but Max had fantastic hands. If the ball was anywhere close to him, he would catch it.

Attempting to find a rhythm, searching for a way to go, and gauging the competition, quarterback Bart Starr seemed tentative, a bit disconnected in the opening minutes of the game. Then, at eight minutes and 56 seconds into the first quarter, the catch by McGee changed everything. It underscored a play that the great Packer quarterback would go to again and again. It also revealed serious weaknesses for the Chiefs at the corners. On an afternoon without wind, with welcome January warmth, it also foreshadowed what was to come as the game moved forward.

The brash McGee's catch came on his inside move on Kansas City cornerback Willie Mitchell, who valiantly tried to knock the ball away. The catch was an incredible one-hander, with McGee pressing the football to his chest and taking off.

BART STARR: The pass across the middle to McGee was thrown behind him because I was hit by Buck Buchanan just as I released the ball. Max still caught it with one hand. Willie Mitchell, the defender, couldn't intercept it because Max stuck his hand way behind his back and grabbed it and outran Fred Williamson for the first score of the game.

"I think Bart saw the player on the Chiefs moving over," said McGee, "and wanted to be sure he wasn't interrupted. I reached my right hand back, and it stuck. I was so surprised that I expected to open my left hand and find a silver dollar" (Horrigan and Rathet, 1970, 150).

BOB SCHNELKER: Bart Starr was very into everything, very serious. He was not a great physical specimen, but he could get the job done, mostly on his smarts, his experience, knowing that he was well prepared by Vince Lombardi. Mentally, emotionally, he was way beyond most quarterbacks. Bart more or less called his own plays. Vince, in between series or during a time-out, would give him ideas. Once in a while Vince would call a play for him.

BILL CURRY: Bart really got drilled, his arm got nailed. But he got the ball off, and he threw it behind Max McGee, who plucked it with one hand and ran it in for a score. Everybody else was excited, but I was not because I had missed my block.

The center's job is to hike the ball and be run over slowly, and I didn't get run over slowly enough in that game. The attitude on the team with Bart Starr was that we would die before we let anybody hit him; that was the attitude we all shared. If we did get beat and he did get hit, first of all it was hell to pay from your peers, and then from Coach Lombardi after the game.

BOB LONG: Bart really never said a word; if your guy drilled him, he'd just get back in the huddle and call the next play. That was part of his great strength and magic. That was Hall of Fame stuff. And if he did make a mistake, he'd take full responsibility.

KEN BOWMAN: A little after Max had gone in, Curry went out. He said he had a sprained ankle. And Lombardi was a man who did not believe in sprained ankles. You had to have a bone sticking out of your ankle or something. He used to tell players, "We don't have sprained ankles around here." Just tape it up and go, that was Lombardi.

So Coach came up to me and said, "Curry said he can't go. You go in."

I said, "I'll give you what I got until the shoulder goes." As luck would have it, I stayed in and played a pretty good game.

"When it's third-and-10, you can take the milk-drinkers and I'll take the whiskey-drinkers every time," was a favorite saying of McGee. Lombardi was tested a lot by the free-spirited veteran, but he tolerated and respected him, especially for clutch play-making moments. This January 15th day at the Coliseum would showcase classic clutch catches by the McGee who made no secret of how much he lived for the moment and the spotlight.

FORREST GREGG: I had no idea McGee had broken curfew. He had the game of his life. When Max got in the game he did what he always did—when the ball was thrown to him he caught it. I had high regard for him as a player. And he was a tremendous athlete.

BOYD DOWLER: Out of the game, I am standing there on the sidelines watching everything. Fuzzy Thurston was matched up quite a bit against Buck Buchanan, who was about six-foot-seven and 300 pounds.

I looked down and Fuzzy's face mask was bent.

I gave Fuzzy a look and said, "Fuzzy, your face mask is all bent out of shape!"

Green Bay Packers wide receiver and "free spirit" Max McGee (85)
makes a juggling touchdown catch during Super Bowl I.
AP Photo/NFL Photos

He said, "Well for God's sake! If you were blockin' that big son
of a bitch, your face mask would be torn up!"

I said, "Okay, how are you doing against him?"

He just looked up at me and smiled.

"I'm kicking his ass!"

And I think he thought he might have been.

CHRIS BURFORD: They had no answer for Buck Buchanan. Hell, no!
Buck was a man among boys. Not that the Packers were boys, because
they were big guys too. But I don't think they'd seen a player like Buck,
you know? Fuzzy Thurston must have had some respect for Buchanan.
I don't doubt it. I mean Green Bay had some of the great players that
ever played, all of those guys in the Hall of Fame. But frankly, with
guys like Buck and others, I think that our talent was better.

BILL CURRY: Buck Buchanan was the one who gave me the most
trouble. Gigantic size, great quickness, great intensity, outstanding
intelligence in the way he played. He was a dominant figure and gave
us all a hard time.

JERRY KRAMER: They lined up one time in an odd-man line, with Buck over the center, and Buck was 300 and change. Kenny Bowman was on him, and I was checking the outside linebacker for a blitz and coming back to help on the middle. I got out just two or three steps and I heard, "Jerry!"

I looked back and Buck was coming free. He surprised a lot of us, not only with his size and strength, but also with his move, his quickness. He was a much better ballplayer than we had seen in the films. Of course, I hadn't studied him. He played on the other side of the field.

CURT MERZ: We were a younger team, but we were pretty big and strong; we were not undersized. That play that stood out at the beginning of the game was when number 86 Buck Buchanan ran all over Fuzzy Thurston and sacked Bart Starr. Oh yeah, Buck was a real specimen. Until they had to double-team him, they were trying to single-team him. He went through Fuzzy Thurston a few times, so they strapped him with double team. That helped them some.

ED BUDDE: I had to handle Henry Jordan. Oh yeah, it was a tough job. He was quick. He wasn't big, but he was quick. He was one of the best defensive guys that I ever faced too.

You know, they always ask, "Who's the best defensive tackle that you've faced?"

And I say, "Buck Buchanan." Because in practices I'd have to block him in scrimmages and workouts all the time. I knew what he was made of.

FRED ARBANAS: I remember Buck picking up Jim Taylor and wheeling him around in the air like a little doll. It was probably early on in the game.

At that time I came down and really got a nice block on their right defensive end, Lionel Aldridge. And I mentioned to him, "This is just the first time you're gonna see me all day." And he laughed at me.

At the end of the game he was doing a little bit more chuckling. But I hardly ever said anything to anybody ever, but that was one time I did talk my mouth off a little bit, probably when I shouldn't have. I guess I was happy with the block I had on him. I think I could handle anybody. Aldridge was good. But you know, I played against a lot of good defenses. The AFL was loaded with them.

Buck Buchanan, arguably the most feared Kansas City Chiefs player, slams into Jim Taylor during the first half of Super Bowl I.

Photofest

SMOKEY STOVER: A specific play that stays with me from that game was when Green Bay's Thurston pulled out of the line. He hit me so hard with his helmet in the stomach, I mean, my feet were off the ground, and my arms were out extended, and it looked like he had just cut me in two. I remember that to this day! Lombardi trained him and them to be that way. They did well with it.

HANK STRAM: Our defensive backs, particularly Willie Mitchell and Fred Williamson, received considerable criticism for failing to contain Green Bay's receivers. But frequently when an individual, or team, fails, it is less a matter of him or it doing poorly as it is a matter of the opposite player or other team playing extremely well. When you examine the films of the game, you see that Williamson and Mitchell did not let down, nor did our two safeties, Johnny Robinson and Bobby Hunt.

CHRIS BURFORD: A lot of people got on our defender Willie Mitchell's case, and it really wasn't Willie's fault as much as Willie was doing what he was supposed to be doing, but the inside wasn't taken away. People didn't really know exactly what was going on as far as I'm concerned. Willie took a lot of abuse he probably didn't deserve.

HANK STRAM: On most plays, our players covered their men as anticipated. But Bart Starr that day possessed an uncanny ability to hit his receivers right on the numbers at the instant they made their break. There is no way to defend against a perfectly thrown ball.

CHUCK LANE: It was amazing. Nowadays, you know, with the helmet radios and all that, and the signaling from the sidelines, that is one thing. But Bart would study the game plan with Lombardi and backup quarterback Bratkowski, and they would put in the game plan. And after that Lombardi would just basically turn him loose, and Bart would call the game.

I was not in the planning and strategy meetings, but I am told that Bart would follow that up just impeccably, just right to the letter. The guy had a Howard Cosell memory. He called his own plays. Exactly.

FORREST GREGG: Bart was flawless. He knew the game plan. He spent the time being ready for the ball game. He never beat himself. I had his life in my hands. I was acutely aware of that all the time. We had a lot of pride. We had a relationship, of course. He knew what his job was, and I knew what mine was.

Despite the early scoring strike by the Packers, Kansas City hung in. The team's stacked defense created some challenges for Green Bay on running plays, and play-action passing by Dawson that first half also pushed the Packer defense into a somewhat cautious mode.

Early in the second quarter, the six-foot, 190-pound Dawson, AFL pass leader that 1966 season, with a 56 percent completion percentage, cheered Kansas City fans as he got into the flow. The Green Bay defense was still adjusting to the Kansas City offense.

Aided by the "moving pocket," with blockers in motion, the determined Dawson connected on three straight passes. One of the throws was a 31-yarder to Otis Taylor. Another was a seven-yarder to Curtis McClinton for a touchdown. In six plays, the AFL champs efficiently moved the ball 66 yards.

HANK STRAM: Because we had proved our ability to run up the middle, the Packers assumed we would do the same near the goal line. Dawson took the ball from center, spun, and seemed to hand

Green Bay Packers Hall of Fame safety Willie Wood (24)
leaps over fallen players during Super Bowl I.
AP Photo/NFL Photos

off to Mike Garrett. Three Packer defenders pounced on Garrett,
who didn't have the ball. The play-action fake had worked perfectly,
freezing the linebackers. He connected with McClinton. A lot of
NFL boosters up in the stands and in the press box suddenly became
very nervous.

The curdling celebration call of the Kansas City trumpeter revved up the KC faithful,
but the noise irritated most everyone else. Chief banners and Packer pennants created a
sea of red and green.

CURTIS MCCLINTON: I felt like a champion to be crowned. It
was a matter of straightening up the tie and straightening the hat.
The play "54 Mike Backs O." It was something that we practiced
from the first practice in summer training. It was our standard play
because it was a difficult play for defenses to read. The first part
of that comes from the "54," which is a mountain, because that is
where we made most of our running touchdowns. We'd kick out the
ends, bring down the tackle, and run through that hole, making the
linebacker come up. And if they came up enough we would fake that

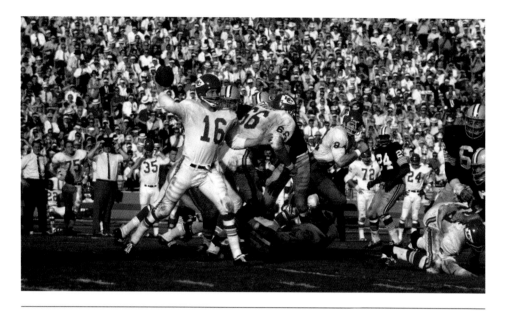

Kansas City Chiefs Hall of Fame quarterback Len Dawson (16) fires a pass during Super Bowl I.
AP Photo/NFL Photos

we were running and send the back out into the backfield and the end down the field. It was a very tough play for linebackers, middle linebackers, and the cornerbacks because we would run that play successfully as a run, successfully as a pass in the flat, and successfully as a pass to the other side. It was the meat and butter of our game because either one of those plays could hurt you. And we had the personnel to do it.

Mercer's kick for the extra point was true. The score was tied, seven up.

BUD LEA: The Chiefs had success sending five receivers (including backs) out on most of the passing plays, leaving unprotected quarterback Len Dawson throwing on the run.

FORREST GREGG: You didn't really know what you were up against. We were used to going up against a basic four-man line. We went to the line of scrimmage, and Kansas City showed a defensive front we had not seen before. It was puzzling, out of our realm of experience on a football field.

Jerry Kramer was playing right guard. I looked over at Jerry. He looked over at me and threw his hands up and shrugged his shoulders like, "I don't know."

During their next possession, still early in the second quarter, like a veteran fighter in a boxing match, the machine-like Packers counterpunched. Directed by Starr, they drove down the field in 13 plays for 73 yards. The drive was highlighted by Starr's clutch third-down passing. He passed to McGee for 10 yards on third-and-six, Carroll Dale for 15 yards on third-and-10, and Marv Fleming for 11 yards on third-and-five.

Starr then gave the ball to fullback Jim Taylor, number 31, in the "power sweep," a weapon not used as often by Green Bay as it had been in the recent past against NFL opponents, who had great familiarity with it. Behind tackle Bob Skoronski's powerful and precise blocking, the burly Taylor carried the ball in as guards Thurston and Kramer did some mopping up. The score was now 14–7, Packers.

> HANK STRAM: Although we proved we could move the ball on Green Bay, we again found ourselves unable to contain them. On that series, Pitts ran six yards. Taylor got three more, bringing up a third-and-one situation. Then Bart Starr just plain fooled us. Instead of running safely for a first down, he sent Carroll Dale deep. Dale had a two-stride lead before our defense realized it was a pass, not a run.
>
> Had George Plimpton been playing quarterback for the Packers, he might have thrown to Dale for a touchdown, so Bart Starr had no trouble completing that pass. But one of the Packer interior linemen had moved. Even super teams are human. Illegal procedure nullified the play, costing the Packers five yards and seven points.
>
> But with it now third-and-six, Starr completed a pass to McGee to keep the drive going. Then on the next series, at third-and-10, Starr found Carroll Dale open again. On the next series, at third-and-five, he hit Marv Fleming. On the next series, at third-and-seven, the pass went to Elijah Pitts. Finally Jim Taylor ran the ball in.
>
> If you look at each play in that drive, you realize that our defense was succeeding quite well—on first and second downs. But on four third-down situations, Bart Starr had thrown perfect passes.
>
> Dawson, on the next series, proved almost the equal of Starr. On first down, Green Bay smothered him for an eight-yard loss. But he got up and completed three straight passes to Arbanas, Taylor, and Burford to move us into Green Bay territory. But a third-down pass to Garrett was two yards short of a first down, and we had to settle for a Mike Mercer field goal. We had played the Packers to a near standstill.

The day before the game, Mike Mercer had spent time practicing his placekicking in the empty confines of the Coliseum. It paid off. His 31-yard field goal attempt with just 54 seconds left in the first half was good and buoyed the Chiefs and their supporters.

So did the play of Len Dawson, who glittered on the field of play that first half. Razzle dazzle, sleight of hand, play action, moving in the floating pocket, firing into passing lanes that opened up—he was a magician. But despite this, his Chiefs were trailing the talented team from Wisconsin, 14–10. Nevertheless, they were still very much in the game.

"The gun sounded, ending the half. The Packers roared into their dressing room, clapping each other on the back. Lombardi's raw voice cut through the bedlam, demanding silence. He told the players they had much to be thankful for: They had won, no one had been seriously hurt" (Devaney, 1971, 32).

> GEORGE MITROVICH: So competitive was the game's first 30 minutes the NFL brass, along with Las Vegas gamblers, were on suicide watch.

> LAMAR HUNT JR.: My father was really a low-key person. He was not a braggart, he was not a chest-pumper. He was, I think, humble, but I'm sure for any 30-something-year-old man he was puffed up with a little pride. What I remember is his energy and enthusiasm. But I also know that there was a real, I wouldn't call it dread, but concern that the Packers were really gonna just kill us, and just really steamroll us.
>
> And there was great relief at halftime of the game that we were only down 14–10 and that we had played actually reasonably well. We hung in there.

On the field of play at the Coliseum, there was a battle being waged. There was also a battle going on between the rival television networks. Each strained to out-do the other, and there was a struggle to show the game to its best advantage.

During a two-week span, CBS had devoted 75 percent of its nighttime promos and 50 percent of its daytime spots to what was being called "Super Week." CBS transmitted "living-color" promotions that ran anywhere from 16 to 60 seconds. CBS also provided special closed-circuit television color tapes to its affiliates, making available four different-color films, slides, mats, and glossy photos. CBS bragged that only its television cameras would be used inside the Coliseum and that 11 "Norelco Plumbicon cameras" were poised and ready for action. The cost of all this high-tech stuff, the network made clear, would top $1 million.

> JERRY IZENBERG: By the new year of 1967, NBC had devoted 505 of its evening spots to gushing over the glory and goodness of Gowdy–Christman. Special mailings had been sent out to 1,400 TV–newspaper editors. The stream of radio and newspaper ads seemed to never end.

A sign of the times: Len Dawson relaxes with a smoke and a Fresca at halftime.

Photo by Bill Ray/LIFE Premium Collection/Getty Images

The price war for one-minute ads was won by CBS over NBC, $85,000 a minute to $75,000. Thirty 30-second ads were the same price—$42,500.

Ford and Chrysler were major advertisers. Others included McDonald's, making its point about "Over Two Billion Served." Muriel Cigars exclaimed, "So much more cigar for just 10 cents." Coca-Cola boasted, "Coke Has the Taste You Never Get Tired Of." And "Tang," an energy drink of that time, urged everyone to "Start off your team with vitamin C."

CBS Sports president Bill MacPhail set out to make a point, stating, "We wanted exclusivity of the Super Bowl. You always want things you cannot get. This thing is extremely complicated; however, we wouldn't have agreed to this Super Bowl arrangement if we weren't satisfied" (Fortunato, 2006, 81).

"I have never been a rooting broadcaster," Curt Gowdy said before the game. "I went down the middle on the game. But inside myself I wanted the AFL to make a good appearance in the game. I just wanted the Chiefs to make it close. I did not think they could beat the Packers."

Daily meetings were staged between CBS and NBC before the big game was played. It was the first instance of a pool feed in sports television history, the first time the two networks had worked together in a major way on a sports event. In the words of one who was there, "It was hysterical. Grown men and women scheming on both sides to screw the other network."

> **FRANK GIFFORD: To me it was a joke, all these guys running around talking about ratings.**

The disadvantaged NBC was forced to broadcast the game over the CBS feed and cameras. Little control existed for the NBC crew as to how the game would be telecast. As a result, NBC attempted to be inventive wherever it could. Boasting a veteran crew, with Curt Gowdy handling play-by-play, Paul Christman doing analysis, Charlie Jones handling sideline comments, and George Ratterman serving as interviewer at large, the network was primed with a big lineup in the battle for viewers with CBS.

Ray Scott was the CBS play-by-play announcer for the first half of the game, while Jack Whitaker took over in the second half. Frank Gifford and Pat Summerall rotated roles for CBS. Summerall worked the first half of the game in the booth as color commentator and switched places with Gifford as sideline reporter in the second half.

The contest between NBC and CBS was a high-stakes and tremendously pressurized event, with a payoff, in the minds of many, as high as the one that would be awarded to the winner of the Green Bay–Kansas City matchup. A tale of the tape, which resembled the practice normally followed for a boxing match, appeared in newspapers throughout the United States. It compared features of the two broadcasts, for instance, personnel on each side, equipment, number of cameras, and number of tape machines. It also evaluated weird matchups, for example, Gowdy against Scott, Christman against Gifford, Jones against Summerall, and George Ratterman against Jack Whitaker.

FRANK GIFFORD: Since both networks were telecasting the game, we at CBS had to make the pregame different. That's where we were going to get our scoop. Since I had played for Lombardi with the New York Giants and was a friend of his, he agreed the night before to go on TV with me just before the kickoff. It was going to be a great scoop.

Just before the game, he brought his team out of the locker room, and I'm there holding my microphone in front of a camera. I made a motion for him to come over. Just as he came out of the tunnel, Vince shook his head to me. It was, "No. No."

I dropped my mike and ran over to him. He was trembling, scared to death, which wasn't anything new. He did that when he was with the New York Giants. I talked to him in hushed tones, telling him he had to do this interview, that millions had tuned in to watch history be made. Vince was unsettled, but he agreed to do it.

I began the interview, putting my arm around him. Then I can remember seeing NBC's Paul Christman out of the corner of my eye running across the field. He stuck his microphone in front of Vince. So we didn't get our scoop after all.

I touched the arm of my sports jacket afterward. It was soaking wet because Vince had been sweating so profusely.

Pregame maneuverings between CBS and NBC had been a week-long occurrence. Snubs, slights, shouts, and screwing took center stage, a prelude to the big battles that would take up most of the afternoon at the Coliseum. Competition and ego fueled everything that happened as network battled network.

"CBS was mad that NBC was involved," said Curt Gowdy. "They argued that they'd been in the NFL all these years, who are these new guys? NBC said they'd put money into the AFL and so deserved to be there."

NBC was upset with the televising philosophy. It believed that the best seat was on the 50-yard line. All 11 cameras were positioned at different levels of that spot. To give its presentation a contrasting look, NBC placed a camera in its mobile unit to enable a tight shot to be taken of the shot and put on the monitor. NBC planned to punch it in replaying it as their close-up shot—something different.

"NBC felt it had a chance to grow into something more than the new kid on the football block," observed Gowdy. "All during the game the late Carl Lindemann (head of NBC Sports) was in the truck calling the ratings services. Those guys were really something."

Different unions, allegiances, agendas, and ways of doing things were part of the mix. Tension ruled the day.

BUD LEA: The pregame tensions between the technical crews of CBS and NBC were almost ludicrous. Both belonged to different unions. Harsh words and some physical gesturing highlighted the rivalry. It got so heated that a 10-foot chain-link fence was erected between the two network trailers. That kept the peace, sort of.

The game within the game, the war between the two rival networks, was symbolized by the erection of that chain-link fence. It was set up in an attempt to keep the peace after there was cursing, pushing, and shoving by engineers from both networks.

"Animosity between tech people was unbelievable," recalled CBS's Pat Summerall. "It would make for one of the most memorable broadcasts I'd ever done."

> BILL MCNUTT III: Being kids, we were fascinated by television cameras and ran around taking it in. The networks didn't share cameras for the game. Basically wherever you had a NBC camera you also had a CBS camera next to it.
>
> I think clearly there was an AFL bias, as there should have been in the NBC coverage, and very much a NFL bias in the CBS coverage, but the coverage of NBC had a lot more pizzazz. CBS covered the game, but their announcers would speak like it was a radio broadcast, whereas the NBC announcers were much more animated, colorful.

Transmission was fairly primitive—a pool of 10 cameras for game coverage. The television cameras were positioned in such a way that shots were framed to avoid showing empty seats; however, it would prove nearly impossible to track the football through punts and field goals without showing the Coliseum's largely vacant upper stretches.

The NFL network, CBS, was persuaded to go along with the dual telecasting with NBC because it had been paying the AFL $1 million a year for television rights. Executives at NBC, whose network paid big bucks for the rights to broadcast the game, were not happy campers. They were of the opinion that they had been relegated to a disrespected and subordinate role by CBS.

"For all we were given to do we could have phoned it in," griped Chet Simmons, second in charge at NBC Sports. "The NFL had to have us there but did everything possible to keep us under their heel."

NBC director Harry Coyle tried technological upsmanship on CBS. He advocated employing his network's "X" camera. It was disassembled, put into the pockets of NBC personnel, and brought to the production truck. The grand plan was for the camera to be put back together into working order. Unfortunately, like the best-laid plans of mice and men and media types, the idea never came to fruition.

There were concerns by many that the game would delay the start of the *Ed Sullivan Show* on CBS. Some viewers even called their local television stations to explore the possibilities of watching an *Ed Sullivan* rerun instead of a football game. Some callers were unable to provide the name of the game they did not want to watch. For many, the name was too long for them to remember precisely. They just knew they had no interest in watching it.

Despite the bickering and bad blood, and the newness of the game, the drawing power of the event on television proved more successful than the live game on the playing field. It attracted the biggest television sports audience in history. More than 65 million viewers tuned in to either CBS or NBC. The game was fed to 365 television stations by CBS, while 225 stations broadcast the game via the NBC feed. Audiences in all time zones in the United States, Canada, Mexico and Puerto Rico, and South Vietnam watched the new sporting event. It was estimated that 71 percent of Americans watched all or part of the game.

But there were few television watchers in the Los Angeles area because of the blackout. Football fans in the Los Angeles area were frustrated and angry, and their frustration and anger was fueled by the media and capitalized on by enterprising hotels, motels, inns, and even rooming houses throughout the California Southland, from San Diego and Orange Country to Palm Springs and Bakersfield.

Newspaper ads appeared in the *Los Angeles Times* and other publications, saying such things as, "Enjoy the game and get a winter suntan too," or "See the Super Bowl Game on TV Jan 15 at San Clemente Inn." Another ad read, "The Super Bowl's in Palm Springs! See the Super Bowl on Palm Springs TV. Come Friday Night for the weekend. Come Saturday night only. Or rent a suite with your friends just for Sunday. Call HO 6-1626."

That summery January 15, 1967, when history was made, was a long time ago, but some can still vividly remember watching the game on television or at the Coliseum.

GEORGE MITROVICH: Being there on a sunny Sunday in mid-winter in 40-yard line $12 seats on the Coliseum's north side, looking down on the historic oval's field of green and past its peristyle end to the snowcapped San Gabriel Mountains rising to the east, thrilled to witness a greatly anticipated football game between champions of two leagues, Green Bay against Kansas City, was a magical, magical moment.

Later, I would learn that half the homes in America were watching on television, a game I was privileged to see in person.

ANN BUSSEL: At that time I was living with my husband in New Jersey, and he was in the scrap iron and metal business. We were attending in Los Angeles a convention, a meeting between dealers in that industry. A gentleman had extra tickets that he could not sell to the Super Bowl. That was hard to believe. So he offered them for free to men attending the convention. My husband was a big football fan, a fan of the New York Giants. He was thrilled to go.

This gentleman rented a bus and offered free transportation to and from the game. That is how I had the privilege to attend the first Super Bowl. We got on the bus that he chartered. It was loaded up with about 30 or 40 people, all in a happy and party mood.

Lo and behold, we arrived at the Coliseum, and wow, the tickets were on the 50-yard line. I really did not know anything about the Kansas City Chiefs and not much about Green Bay aside from Bart Starr. Out of gratitude for the man who gave us the tickets, we rooted for Kansas City. Their fans there were pretty happy the first half of the game.

It was a pleasant day. It was a plus-plus day. And when I tell my children and especially my grandchildren that their grandmother attended the first Super Bowl, they say "What?"

I did not think to save my program or my ticket.

FRED WALLIN: We were among a minority that watched the game on television in the Los Angeles area. We had a directional antenna on the roof to get reception from San Diego. We had 30 friends over to the house. Everyone had a good time. In the second half, the picture became fuzzy. Dad asked me to go up onto the roof to move the antenna. It was quite a day. The next week we attached a rotor so that could adjust the antenna electronically.

DOUG KELLY: I was a senior in high school. We were living in Menlo Park, California. The television set was in the living room, and it was in color, which had recently come into vogue. We had to get up from time to time and adjust the color. We watched on CBS. My Dad loved Ray Scott. Looking at that first game and all the stuff that surrounded it, you would never guess in a million years that it would become what it is today.

Little did I realize that I would join the Kansas City Chiefs organization in 1974, working in public relations. There was still a pretty good core of players who had played in that first Super Bowl, but the problem was they were all seven years older.

LU VAUGHN: I'd never been on a junket before, but through the Meadowbrook Country Club in Kansas City, a group of guys got together, and we chartered a jet to go out to Los Angeles for the Super Bowl. The trip cost me about $200. I think the ticket was around $10 for the game. I was about 34 or 35 years old at that time.

We went to Las Vegas first, where we were comped food, beverages, and lodging. We were at the Sands Hotel, one of the earliest of the great places out there. We even were comped to see a show at the Flamingo. Bill Cosby was the celebrity.

Our flight from Vegas to LA did not happen—Los Angeles was souped in. So they woke us up at 5:00 in the morning at the hotel to bus us from Las Vegas to the LA Coliseum. We had three buses for about 100 of us, all Kansas City Chief fans.

After about a five-hour journey, we arrived. We missed the first quarter. Our seats were not really good, more to the end zone than anyplace else. We wore jackets and shirts and other things that let people know that we were Kansas City Chiefs fans. And we were harassed. People teased us and said Kansas City was going to be badly beaten. But of course we thought otherwise. We felt that we stood a good chance of being competitive in the ball game and maybe winning.

STEVE FOLVEN: I was about 19 years old and living at home in Lowell, Mass., and in my first year of college. The biggest game of the year at the Boston Garden was at 12:00—the Celtics versus Philadelphia. Bill Russell versus Wilt Chamberlain.

My two buddies, Billy Brooks and Charlie Gallagher, and I were going to the game. In those days you could go the day of the game and actually get a ticket. Billy Brooks had the car. He said we would all have to leave the Celtic game a bit early to get home in time to see the big football game between Kansas City and Green Bay. That was at 4:00.

We got to the Garden about 11:00 or so. I had attended early Mass. We tried to sneak in and pay the ushers some money, but there weren't any ushers around. We got in for six bucks or something like that. We had pretty good seats, and it was a great game. It was too bad we had to leave early in the fourth quarter.

I was a Boston Patriots fan in the AFL, but to me the AFL was a minor league compared to the NFL. I thought it was nice that finally the two leagues were meeting in a championship game. I felt the Chiefs were going to get creamed.

The first half I was surprised. The Chiefs looked okay. But I wanted the Packers to win. They had Lombardi and Starr and Hornung and Taylor and all that great talent. They were always winning, always on television.

Our only TV set was black and white, a small one, in the living room. I watched the entire game on NBC—Gowdy and Christman. The next day I read about the game in the newspapers—it didn't get that much play.

BILL GUTMAN: I followed the birth of the American Football League. In the New York City area and its surroundings, there was interest in the game, not only among fans, but also the media. I was living in Stamford, Connecticut, and was two years away from beginning my writing career.

The talk in the media and popular conversation was about the need of the NFL to win that game. A defeat in that game would have been crushing to the old league. There was also talk, "Thank God, it's Lombardi and the Packers who are there representing the National Football League."

My feeling was it was an unknown thing—two teams, two leagues that have never met before. You just did not know what to expect. At the first snap, however, when the two lines collided, then you realized it was just another football game and all the talk meant nothing.

I watched the game on both CBS Channel 2 and NBC 4 in my room alone at home. The set had a 13-inch black-and-white screen. The antenna was rabbit ears, but the reception was pretty good. I was a sports fan, not a fan of either league. I enjoyed the game.

SUSAN LOMBARDI: I was in Marymount College in Boca Raton. It was a finishing school, and there were a lot of politicians' daughters there. It was warm but I wanted to go to the game in California, but I knew my father being the teacher that he would never pull me out. He wanted me to be in school.

I watched the game on a 19-inch nothing TV in the middle of the community area in our dorm with my college girlfriends. The nuns, our teachers, wandered in and out. They let us have snacks. I was just another student. This was the first time I ever watched my father on TV. I had a difficult time watching it because I had always been at the game watching him live. At Lambeau, in Green Bay, we had A1 seats on the 50-yard line. When we went to away games, the seats were good but nothing like Lambeau. For me being in Boca in a community room watching my father and the Packers on TV—it was a strange experience.

TOMMY BROOKER: I was back in Tuscaloosa with my wife and a bunch of Alabama friends, and that was where I watched the game. It was a Super Bowl party, probably one of the original parties. We watched the game on a 25-inch television. It was in color. The set was in our dining room–den combination, one big room. It wasn't any fun watching at home, but I didn't have any choice because I was on injured reserve for the Kansas City Chiefs. That '66 season I was kicking in Boston, and somebody forgot to block. And they came into me, into my leg that was raised up.

Watching the first Super Bowl I always thought Kansas City had a chance to win that game, but that McGee was something else. When a guy catches one behind the back and fumbles it around and finally holds on, when a guy catches the football in the neck area, damn!

You can't expect the ball to tumble in the right direction every time.

I was not believing it as I watched, and neither were all the people in my house. There was a lot of shouting, a lot of "damns!"

PETER GOLENBOCK: I was the sports editor of the *Dartmouth*. I had predicted that the Packers would blow the Chiefs out. I was a serious New York Giants fan and was rooting for the NFL.

A married couple by the name of Ray and Velda owned the Midget Diner, a stone's throw from the Dartmouth Green. I would go there every morning to eat steak and eggs for a dollar. Ray and Velda had become part of my Dartmouth family, so when it was announced that the Green Bay Packers would play the AFL's Kansas City Chiefs, they invited me and my Fayerweather Hall roommate to their house for dinner and to watch the game on their Dumont TV.

I somehow knew that the biggest screen around then was a 25-inch console that featured one speaker. I also knew that there were color sets available, but adjusting the set while the game was in progress was part of the drill. My hosts did not have color, nor did they have a very big screen.

Everyone knew the game was important. The NFL was risking its reputation playing the game. My hosts didn't much care who won.

Ray and Velda served an interesting, unidentified meat dish, which I ate. "Delicious," I said. "What is it?"

"It's venison," Ray said. "I shot the deer myself."

It was all I could do to keep it down. The idea of eating Bambi really revolted me.

The game itself was rather anticlimactic. The Packer offense was as good as advertised. They only ran a few plays, but they ran them often and very well. Starr wasn't spectacular, but he was very efficient. His touchdown passes were elegantly thrown.

I thanked Ray and Velda profusely after the game was over. I never ate venison again.

With the first half of the super game of games, as one scribe not sparing the hype described it, in the record books, there was a regrouping, a taking stock, and a getting ready for a second half of football in the press box, stands, and locker rooms.

> BILL ADAMS: We had proved we could move the football. I was pretty excited about our chances. But it would turn out to be a Pollyanna thought that we could win the game.

With the Chiefs down by just four points, it appeared that the game was up for grabs, that the Chiefs were much better than most of the experts thought they were. Many people watching the game were surprised at how close the score was, how well the AFL's champions were playing. And Kansas City had a first-half edge in total yards over the Packers, 181–164, and an 11–9 edge in first downs.

Surprise, elation, disgust, annoyance, tension, pride—all were on display in the press box, depending on one's rooting interests or affiliations.

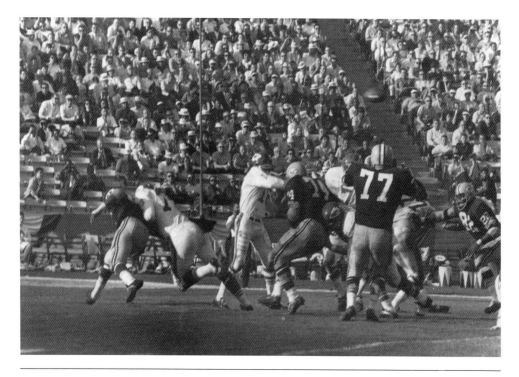

Len Dawson about to be swallowed up by the Green Bay defense.
Photofest

A number of pro AFL scribes were anxiously confident.

A number of NFL-oriented media were antsy.

In his loud-mouthed prime, broadcaster Howard Cosell was not even at the game. He was three thousand miles away, filming his *Speaking of Sports* show. An AFL zealot at that point in his career, Cosell announced the following at halftime: "The whole country has been served notice that the American Football League is far from a minor league. The Packers may win, but they are scared. I picked Green Bay by 17 points. I think I may have been a fool. Time will tell."

Former NFL star running back Buddy Young, who had moved on to work for the league, was up in the press box and warned, "Old age and heat will get the Packers in the second half."

JOE BROWNE: Buddy Young was hired full-time by Commissioner Pete Rozelle in early 1966 to be the first African American front office executive in all of sports. Young was one of the earliest babysitters who got their name because they watched over the drafted collegians and "held their hand" until they signed with a NFL club.

Satisfied overall with their performance in the first half, in the KC locker room the Chiefs showed some exuberance, even confidence. They sat around resting, regrouping, reflecting. Number 16, Lenny Dawson, dirtied uniform still on, solitary and seated on a chair, was taking drags on a cigarette.

> LEN DAWSON: The attitude before we started playing the game was reflected in things we were saying, like, "We can do this, we can do that." But those comments were not confident statements.
>
> It was like, "If this happens, and that happens, and this doesn't happen, and that doesn't happen, we've got a good shot at these guys."
>
> But at halftime it was completely different. We felt we could win that football game.

"We felt we were doing the things we had to," Hank Stram said, "and doing them well. We were only four points behind and were confident we could get that back and more" (Horrigan and Rathet, 1970, 150).

> HANK STRAM: I saw no reason to alter our game plan going into the second half. We had proved we could score against the Green Bay Packers and also had discovered, as expected, that we would have a difficult time holding their offense.
>
> On several instances in the first half, they had run right into the strength of our defense, yet still gained four or five yards. They just blew us off the line of scrimmage. We had several breakdowns in execution, but overall when you play a great team like the Green Bay Packers you have to realize they're out there playing too. They don't give up anything easily.
>
> SUSAN LOMBARDI: The Packers were not winning by much at the half, but I was not worried about Green Bay losing. I knew my father. I knew he would instill something in the minds of the players and get it done.
>
> PAT COCHRAN: We were so used to winning. I thought we would win. Vince would get it done.

In the Packer locker room, there was a calm, but also some anxiety. Many Packers were sitting on the dressing room floor, sucking the juice of oranges. On one side was the defense; on the other side sat the offensive players. They were listening to their coaches, hanging on every word.

Lombardi walked over to the defense and said, "Stop grabbing and start tackling" (Devaney, 1971, 27).

FORREST GREGG: It was anybody's ball game. I was not surprised they played that well. They had talent.

JIM TAYLOR: Lombardi gave just a regular pep talk at halftime, no changes. We had played so many games with him, and we were so established and had so much confidence. We'd been there and done that. They were like the new kids on the block. I was 31 at that time, and I had already played nine seasons in pro football.

WILLIE DAVIS: The coach was concerned.

BUD LEA: The Packers' defense was all worked up. The players didn't like the way defensive coach Phil Bengtson's game plan was working to the Chiefs' advantage.

DAVE ROBINSON: We kept complaining the whole first half that the Chiefs were getting too many guys open on passes. They were running five-man patterns. There was nobody back there to block for Dawson. We didn't blitz at all in the first half.

"We weren't getting a real good pass rush in the first half," Phil Bengtson explained later. "When we got at Dawson, we grabbed instead of tackled. So it resulted in a bit of uncertainty on the part of our individuals."

PAT PEPPLER: I was to be on the field the whole game but not near Lombardi if I could help it. I did not have that much to do, but if the team needed me in any way, I sure was there to help. I was proud of the fact that on that team about 50 percent of the players were ones that I had scouted. I knew them very well. I had very good relationships with them. And I kept an eye on them especially.

During a game, Coach Lombardi would do very little on the sidelines but praise and scold. Some of the Packers called him the "most useless guy on the sidelines." But the consensus was he always prepared his team very well for all types of game situations.

BOB SCHNELKER: At halftime, Vince always spoke. We coaches never attempted to do anything. He was in complete charge. In that day and age the head coach did most of the talking because there weren't that many coaches.

PAT PEPPLER: Vince was highly intelligent, flexible, too, able to change in any way necessary to fit in with the game situation.

At halftime he made a short speech about the need to tweak some things, execute better. He did not do a lot of hollering. He had a key to what he wanted to say. His speeches were thought out, planned carefully. Players always reacted well.

Vince told them, "Win, lose, or draw, you are my football team. You are the Packers. You have your pride. Let's re-group and get out there. We are representing the entire National Football League."

DAVE ROBINSON: They were giving us trouble in the first half running that five-man pattern. I found out much later on from Lenny Dawson that he and Hank Stram had analyzed our defense, made note that we only blitzed the quarterback three times per game.

Lenny told me they decided that if that happened to them, they would either throw the ball away or take a sack for those three downs, and they'd run five-man patterns and really tax our defense as far as coverage was concerned.

And that was the only play that they ran that was effective for the whole first half. We stopped the run, but they had these little passes. Everybody was coming free, and there was no help. I couldn't get to everyone who needed help because I had a man of my own to cover. Our defense was set on us helping each other, and we couldn't do it. They were very much still in the game at halftime. They had their confidence up.

Vince was upset. I guess he was giving (defensive coach) Phil Bengtson some trouble. So Phil calls our defense together and asked, "What's going on with that play that they're killing us with?"

So he diagrams it on the board, and he says, "That's a five-man pattern."

We said, "Yeah Coach, we've been trying to tell you. They're running five-man patterns out there! And we don't have anything to stop them."

He said, "Well, what do they do when we blitz?"

We said, "Coach. We didn't blitz the whole first half."

And he said, "Well, we'll correct that."

BART STARR: Coach Lombardi also told us at halftime, "You can understand now why we were getting you so well-prepared in Santa Barbara, because you can sense and feel and see the strength that this team has. They are very, very good, and that's why we're having to play as well as we are, and we'll continue too in this second half. We have to press this so that we win this. And that is exactly what we're going to do."

WILLIE DAVIS: Typically what you do at halftime is kind of freshen up. And Coach said, "I want you to sit down because there's something I want to share. You know, we played 30 minutes of football adjusting to the Kansas City Chiefs, and we're probably okay, but what I want you to do is go out and play 30 minutes of Green Bay Packer football and see how the Chiefs adjust to you."

It was kind of interesting. Coach Lombardi said we had played 30 minutes adjusting to the Chiefs, and we were not where we needed to be. "Now, I want you to go out there and play 30 minutes of tackle football and see if they can adjust to you." We all looked at each other, and it was like, "Wow!"

That was so meaningful from a man who said meaningful things to his team. We had, as he said, spent the first half being very conservative and being very cautious. And the second half, from the first series on defense, we were going to go after Kansas City unlike we had ever been before. Yep, yep, yep.

Highly businesslike and tremendously focused on the situation in hand, the Packer leader, who had been through all kinds of situations in his years of coaching, ended his comments by clapping his hands and shouting, "All right, defense. Let's take control of the game, defense. Let's get more pressure on Dawson and create some opportunities for the offense."

Then Coach Lombardi knelt and led his players in the Lord's Prayer.

MICHAEL MACCAMBRIDGE: To Lombardi's credit, the most overrated thing in football is the halftime adjustment, but Lombardi truly did make some halftime adjustments that changed everything. What did take place in that second half was that the Packers were able to exploit their physical superiority they had on their offense versus what the Chiefs had in their defense. Other than Bobby Bell, the linebacking core of Kansas City was undersized. It was also not as effective as they needed it to be, especially to deal with the Packers' power sweep. To Lombardi and the Packers' credit, they found the holes, and they made the most of it.

On the field getting ready to play the second half, number 7, defensive back Willie Wood, in what would prove to be a prophetic statement, told a teammate, "What we need is one big play to wake us up" (Devaney, 1971, 27).

CURT MERZ: Sure there was talk of winning during halftime, but not any more than there was before the game. We knew we had a good chance—we played well. We had been behind before, and there was no panic.

ED LOTHAMER: I was starting tackle that year up until late in November. I had a chronic shoulder injury, and it finally got so bad that they had to operate on it. So actually I flew out with all the fans from Kansas City. I was basically more or less a fan for the whole situation!

I went down to the locker room, and everybody was normal, seemed confident, but they were really nervous. Everybody was serious, everybody was just resting and drinking.

I think we were drinking Gatorade back then—we were the first team in the NFL, I think, to have Gatorade. Everybody was getting their tape redone or whatever. The mood was confident; the mood was, "We're going to win this game." They were working on offensive and defensive formations. There wasn't any foreboding feeling in there at all. Everybody I think realized we were in the game, only behind by four points. We were playing well. Lenny was doing well, so here we go. If not for that 14-yard touchdown run by (Jim) Taylor, who knows?

For the first quarter and the second quarter, we did pretty well. Dawson was moving the ball. (Otis) Taylor was catching the ball. And Burford and our line was holding up against them. Garrett was able to run a little bit. We were in the ball game.

"We're going to win this thing." Hank was running around as he always was, pumping people up. And they were pumped up by him—you know, everybody was just pumped up.

CHUCK LANE: I was not in the locker room for the halftime commentary. I was standing on the press box roof at the Coliseum. I believe I was up there with broadcaster Jack Whitaker, really a gentleman. Here I was, all of 23 years old, standing shoulder-to-shoulder with Jack Whitaker, and he's assuring me that, "This is nothing to worry about."

And I tell you what, I was just nervous as a cat in a room full of rockers. Watching the game unfold, you know, I was scared to death. It was my first year with Lombardi, and I sure as hell didn't want to be part of a losing effort.

In the Kansas City and Green Bay locker rooms, there was a pause in the action. On the field of play during the break there was action everywhere. The first Super Bowl halftime show in history was on.

It featured six-foot, 300-pound jazz trumpeter Al Hirt in the first of his five Super Bowl appearances, playing the national anthem. Organized by Jack Lee, director of the Pride of Arizona marching band, the show was a salute to American music and dubbed "Super Sights and Sounds." The band entered the field playing "The Sound of Music." That fabulous song from the acclaimed 1965 film was still a big part of the public consciousness.

The band performed about a dozen pieces. With each new song, the orchestra moved about the field, creating different displays, from the O.K. Corral gun fight to a cracking Liberty Bell. Orchestra members even formed two giant football players running to kick a giant football. In addition, Lee brought in a local high school band just to have more bodies available for forming a map of the United States from end zone to end zone.

The University of Arizona's symphonic marching band, Anaheim High School's drill team, and Grambling College's Tiger Band from Louisiana provided entertaining musical sounds for the program. Sizzling with style, energy, and jazz, Grambling's band stole the show. Its spirited marchers, uniform capes flying behind them, jerked their instruments from side to side in synch with Sam & Dave's "Knock on Wood." The Tiger band stamped its feet, and the crowd at the Coliseum roared with approval.

> WILLIE DAVIS: I probably couldn't have felt more sense of pride than that my old college Grambling had its band there. I was too involved in the game to watch them. I did see them going on and off the field, but that was about my full extent.

On the field, there was a hustle and bustle, with all kinds of noise and people in motion—a drill team, dancing girls in Indian costumes. The Los Angeles Ramettes, who performed in the LA Coliseum for Ram home games, were well-prepared to strut, march, and twirl. They did their thing pregame and after each of the quarters.

Climax upon climax on the field ended with the release of ten thousand helium-filled balloons and four thousand pigeons. Before the pigeons could be released, Dr. Ralph Walter Emerson Jones, grandson of a slave and president of Grambling College, had to be convinced to move from his comfortable perch on the field on a very large crate.

"Hey, you've got to get up," a Coliseum spear-carrier shouted. "You're sitting on our pigeons."

After their release, the pigeons whirred and flapped their wings in flight. They were a sight. Some of them left a mess, causing a few problems for people like Brent Musburger, a young sportswriter from Chicago, who had the delicate and unpleasant chore of removing pigeon droppings from his typewriter.

Two men wearing jet packs landing at midfield was another highlight. This was two years before men would land on the moon. In 1967, it was science fiction.

> CHUCK LANE: That really was an amazing technological feat for that time period. Normally, all our halftime performances, and mostly around the NFL, were either a marching band from a local

Green Bay Packers defensive end Willie Davis.
Photofest

college or high school, and it was pretty conservative. But we had never seen anything like that. And Grambling was really the show band of all show bands.

ED LOTHAMER: I was with the play-by-play guys in the press box high above the field. So I had a marvelous view of the goings on. To see those guys with those packs on, their backs up in the air, that was just incredible! They then crossed in the air and then came back down. That was some big deal then.

It was a big deal back then and drew ooohs and ahhhhs from the crowd. The daring duo was referred to as the "Space Age Supermen." One of the high flyers was William P. Suitor. He would later be given featured parts in film and on televison. The other was Peter Kedzierski, dubbed "Bird Man" at the 1963 Paris Air Show. Both men sported James Bond jet packs. They flew for about 20 seconds—just long enough to allow sufficient hydrogen peroxide propellant into their Bell Rocket Belts to elevate them 100 feet and move them 300 yards. They landed at midfield in a gesture of peace.

DAVE ROBINSON: I wanted to see the Grambling marching band. We were inside, and all I got to see was the band leaving the field when we came out for the second half. And I never saw any film—there wasn't any videotape like we have now—and I've never seen the program they put on at halftime.

MICHAEL MACCAMBRIDGE: What they were trying to do with this game was to make it more than just a game. That was why you had all these various bells and whistles—guys in the jet packs, the sense of pomp and circumstance that wasn't part of a byproduct but was really part of the total mission.

Prior to the game, barbed wire had been strung as a barrier between the cheaper end zone seats and the pricier midfield seats. Undeterred, scores of enterprising fans used the halftime break as an opportunity to move into the high-rent district $12 seats for the second half and an enhanced view of the game.

THE SECOND HALF

Jack Whitaker told *Real Clear Sports* on May 12, 2012, "After an interminable halftime show, the second half was ready to begin, and I was on the air. Kansas City took the kickoff, and we were underway. But wait a minute. Officials were running around and blowing whistles and waving their arms. I had no idea what happened. There was no penalty flag on the ground. I was bewildered and scared to death."

An irritated Pat Summerall was questioned if he would ask Vince Lombardi to have his Packers kick off again. The dignified Summerall declined, stating, "They told me to ask Lombardi to kick off again because NBC had missed the second-half kickoff. I said, 'You've got the wrong guy. I am not doing that'" (Rand, 2008, 158).

> DAVE ROBINSON: There were those two kickoffs for the second half. I know NBC was still on commercial break and NBC complained, and the commissioner ruled for them to have another kickoff. Vince went crazy. Oh man, he was just screaming and hollering. He said he had made an official announcement to the commissioner—he was playing the game under protest.

> CURT MERZ: They screwed up one of the kickoffs. So I bust my ass going down on the kickoff and then get over to the sidelines. I was not a very happy football player. And an official says, "We're going to have to do it again."
> I asked, "What for?"

"What for" was because NBC's sideline reporter, Charlie Jones, had become too engrossed during halftime in interviewing famed comic Bob Hope, who loved to talk. The interview ran over.

Jones later attempted to explain what had transpired. NBC went to commercial, he said. "I was just shocked."

The signal had been relayed to the field that both networks were set to telecast the second half. Green Bay's Don Chandler kicked off. CBS viewers watched the game action. NBC viewers watched commercials. Referee Norm Schachter blew the ball dead while it was still in the air.

"We didn't know what was going on," Curt Gowdy recalled. "We thought it was a mistake in the booth."

"It comes under the question of your guess is as good as mine," was the immediate explanation given to the announcers.

Green Bay's Don Chandler kicked off again. Kansas City received the ball and moved it to their 49-yard line.

> DAVE ROBINSON: The second kick was really five, six yards different than the first one. No big deal. And then we held them for the first two plays.

Not enamored with blitzing, looking at it as a sign of weakness, never really scripting it as part of his game plan, Vince Lombardi nevertheless made up his mind to unleash its full force on the Chiefs in the second half. The idea was simple, basic football, what St. Vincent liked—send six rushers against five blockers.

> SCOUTING REPORT: A Packer blitz could hurt KC. Len Dawson is accurate when he has time to throw. Chiefs, however, may not be able to buy him time. A retreating Dawson can be a quarterback in interception mode. Feints and fakes and hesitation part of Dawson's game. Packers not too vulnerable to that. The KC quarterback is vulnerable, especially with a slow offensive line and KC secondary problems.

To argue the point that Lombardi opposed blitzing was to understate the case. Most of the time he was opposed to it, deeming it the "weapon of weaklings" (MacCambridge, 2004, 244).

> WILLIE DAVIS: Our winning and our preparation, our desire, every aspect that's important to winning, Coach Lombardi made that available. In that second half from the sidelines, he was into the game!

Lombardi was so into the game that the image of him in shirt sleeves, a tie hanging limply from his neck, a sun visor on his head that it was clear he did not own but put on to shield himself from the sun that came over the field still remains in the memory of many who saw that game. On his head, the visor made him look like anything but what a leader of men would wear. It looked like something somebody bought for him at a concession stand in the Coliseum.

> WILLIE DAVIS: More than anything, all week long, Coach had talked to us about what we probably had to do to survive in this game. And I think that's why we were so cautious the first half. But then we were ready to throw that away the second half and go after a team the way we historically had gone after the other teams we had played against.
>
> We did practice for Dawson's moving pocket, but the surprises Stram would pull, I think, that concerned Coach Lombardi more than anything. There was a feeling that if we didn't play with some caution in that first half, Kansas City would get a couple of plays that would work big time. And then all at once we'd have a tiger by the tail! That's how Coach Lombardi described it. The one reason he thought best to avoid the tiger by the tail was to play conservative in the first half.
>
> I knew I had not attacked the guy in front of me with the best efforts I could put in the pass rush.

And then second half, all at once I'm saying, "Hey. Hey buddy, it's over, because now I'm coming!"

It was a game with the entire tradition of the NFL on the line. All at once it had been put in the hands of the Green Bay Packers. We were much looser in the second half. I was playing against Dave Hill, Kansas City right tackle.

And by the second half I said to myself, "Now Dave Hill, you're going to have to cope with everything I can do." That second half I was in charge.

Yes, I was proud to be a Packer. It was players like Bart Starr and other players on the offensive unit that gave great reinforcement to this. There's no question in my mind, the last three or four years before Super Bowl I, the defense truly probably carried the Packers. After a while, we'd go into a game, and the offense was struggling. You know, my first attitude was, "That's okay, we'll win the game." We really strongly felt that. We believed that.

BUD LEA: On the third play of the second half, the Packers came with their first blitz of the game. Lee Roy Caffey, Dave Robinson, and Henry Jordan just bull rushed Len Dawson.

DAVE ROBINSON: Phil (Bengtson) called "blitz 3." I was lined up on Fred Arbanas, the tight end. My job was to jam him to hold him up temporarily at the line of scrimmage. So I jammed him and headed towards the backfield, towards Dawson. By the time I got there, Lee Roy Caffey was almost to Dawson. I was the third one coming. I was in about less than five yards from Dawson. And he threw the ball up trying to get rid of it. I was the last one to reach him. Lenny's eyes were as wide as saucers.

CURT MERZ: They never blitzed, and then all of a sudden they started to blitz because they couldn't stop our little runs, counters. We really hadn't prepared for them to blitz. We had played against blitzing teams, but because they'd never blitzed before they had the element of surprise.

The stumpy rookie Kansas City halfback Mike Garrett, seeing what was unfolding, yelled out to Dawson, "Don't do it! Don't do it!"

FRED ARBANAS: I was man-to-man with Wood. I gave him a head fake to the inside. When Len threw, I cut to the outside. But the ball was not there.

What was there was Willie Wood, standing five feet, 10 inches tall and weighing in at 190 pounds, in his seventh season with the Packers and one of the most exceptional backs in professional football history. Intent, alert, and always prowling, he was at the top of his game and totally involved. He would not miss a single game in his 12-year NFL career.

> WILLIE WOOD: I had slipped away a bit from Arbanas. I was ready and watching quarterback Dawson. He threw. The ball seemed to be hanging. I stepped in and stretched out to the fluttering ball. I caught it. I took off towards the sideline.

> MICHAEL MACCAMBRIDGE: Lamar Hunt Jr. recalled he had heard his father curse just a couple of times in his life. One of those times was when Len Dawson threw that interception in the second half. And Lamar Jr. remembered his father saying "Damn" when he saw the football picked off.

Showing off his great speed and agility, Wood ran with the ball, the AFL ball, as he remembered. It was a foot race. Blinding speed versus blinding speed. Mike Garrett caught Wood from behind, dropping him at the five-yard line.

> HANK STRAM: Wood would have gone all the way in for the touchdown except Mike Garrett, who had been running a pattern on the far side of the field and sprinted diagonally across through the middle and caught Wood on the five. It was a demonstration of fantastic desire on Mike's part, but it was typical of the effort he constantly displayed as a Chief.

> CHRIS BURFORD: Well, the pass wasn't wobbly, it got tipped. That was the problem. Mike Garrett makes one of the great plays I've ever seen, running the guy down. Willie Wood had great speed, but so did Mike have great speed.

> BILL MCNUTT III: Mike Garrett made the best tackle in the game. If you'll look at the Willie Wood interception, I think he intercepted the ball at about midfield, and Mike Garrett just weaved in and out of a Packer convoy to tackle him.

> FRED ARBANAS: The nightmare I have to relive once in a while was when I was in the flat and Dawson went to throw the ball to me, and the Packers hardly ever blitzed, and they blitzed that play and

they tipped the ball, and I could see the ball sort of fluttering my way instead of getting out there quick. Oh my! Had I caught that ball, I would've made some decent yardage on it.

Willie Wood stepped in there and the ball flopped around, and all I can see is Willie running with the ball. His cleats on the bottom of his feet is all I can see. Yeah, because I was open, and I was ready for a nice play, and all of a sudden here comes the ball, which just sort of looked like a wounded duck coming through the air.

Well, when they started to blitz in the second half, I think that surprised us. They hadn't done that in any games we had seen. That was the biggest play of the game.

It wasn't Lenny's fault, just one of those plays. I always thought the ball got tipped by the blitzing linebacker. I wouldn't swear to it, but that's what I thought happened.

ED BUDDE: Lenny was "Mr. Cool." He never got excited when we got in the huddle after he was smashed by anybody; he just shook it off. He was our leader, and he didn't have to say too much, just his looks. He would just look at you and you'd know that you screwed up! No, he didn't make any comment after the interception.

It seemed that Lenny Dawson never got angry. But he did. He was an expert at doing his stare down. A couple of the Chiefs were quick to point out that when Lenny gave the "look," you never forgot it.

BOYD DOWLER: When you've got Dave Robinson and Lee Roy Caffey and Ray Nitschke, who were all really good athletes, big and strong and fast, and you start blitzing along with the four guys up front we had rushing the passer, it is a lot of trouble for any quarterback. They just put a lot of pressure on Dawson. I think that hurt. That led to the interception that Willie made.

LEN DAWSON: We sent five receivers downfield, and they blitzed. The blitz was the big play of the ball game, the interception that I threw. We knew they were not a blitzing team. It just so happened that the call that I had, the pass that I had, if it had been to the other side, that interception would not have happened. The tight end was going to drag out into the flat, and he was going to be my first option. But they came with people, and we didn't have enough people to block them.

The pressure bothered me. I didn't have any zing on the pass. They hit my arm or something, or the ball, when I threw it, and it was just floating out there. If we had had a running play called the other way or something like that, but who knows?

Lombardi happened to guess right at the right time. I gave them seven points. And then we had to play catch up. You can't imagine how many times I wanted to have that pass back.

CHRIS BURFORD: If you go back and look at the film, when that ball got tipped, which really took the score up another notch, we were moving the ball prior to that. And we were moving the ball the very first time we got it, and then we got a bad sideline call. I'd caught a pass, and they called it out of bounds. It was a tough call for the official, but it actually was good. But they called it out of bounds. It knocked us off from a first down, which would've been around midfield or past.

LAMAR HUNT JR.: The interception in the second half really turned the game. There are a handful of plays that can literally change a football game, and that was one of them. It was dramatic. My dad had an entourage of friends that were there sitting and watching the game. That play really took the wind out of everybody's sails.

As a kid you might feed off of what's going on around you a little bit, you know, pick up on the adult anxiety or sadness or whatever. But there was definitely a feeling that the wind was blown out of the sails. A game changer. They really had a ball-control type of offense. They could run the ball. From then on it was kind of "game on" for them.

SMOKEY STOVER: Lenny kind of threw a little wobbly pass. He had lots of pressure coming in. They blitzed him. He just got off on the wrong foot when he threw that ball, and the Packers intercepted. They caught on fire, and that was it.

I was on the bench when it happened. No, it wasn't that loud on the bench. I don't think there was a lot of hootin' and hollerin' going on, I really don't.

On the next play, Bob Skoronski, the gritty Green Bay left tackle, opened a big hole. Elijah Pitts, eluding Buck Buchanan's grasp, busted through on a five-yard run. Touchdown! Numbers 75, Green Bay's Forrest Gregg, and Kansas City's Jerry Mays trailed the play. It was the first of what would be three unanswered Green Bay touchdowns in the second half. The Packers led, 21–10.

JERRY KRAMER: That first half we got a feel about who they were and what they could do, and we sobered up pretty quickly. We were in a ball game. We were like surprised, what the hell's going on? The Chiefs did play their heads off for a half, but Willie's interception broke their backs.

Years later I talked to Len Dawson about that. We were bullshitting and having a beer. I told him we came out for the second half ready for a tough game, and it seemed like you guys just mailed it in.

He said, "What do you mean, Jerry?"

I mentioned the interception and Pitts taking it in for the touchdown. And my blocking on the extra point and their defensive tackle lined up against me with all the strength of a feather duster. He leaned on me with no force and let out a groan.

And Lenny responded, "Jerry, you may be on to something. You guys were our heroes. We watched you on TV. We watched you for years, and we were in our first really big game."

CURT MERZ: They just didn't make any mistakes. The whole Packer team was very disciplined. That was, I think, the key to Lombardi's success. They ran the sweep time and time again. And

The beginning of the end: These side-by-side photos diagram the interception that doomed the Chiefs. The three Packers closing in on Len Dawson demonstrate just how intense the pressure on the quarterback was.

Courtesy of the Los Angeles Public Library

they ran it perfectly. Whatever they did, they didn't do that much. But it was enough. I played against teams that were more physical that beat you up more. These guys, however, weren't that physical. But they were where they were supposed to be at most all the time—just a very good team. Lombardi had that military coaching background, and it showed in the way the Packers conducted themselves.

CHUCK LANE: Wood had the interception, and the rest was kind of a cakewalk after that.

The game changer truly was number 24—Willie Wood and his immaculate interception. Up to that point, Hank Stram's team had picked up 201 yards in 32 plays, holding their own.

"It was over then," remarked All-AFL Kansas City lineman Jim Tyrer. "They wouldn't respect our run again. Our play fakes were useless, and they just flew to the quarterback" (MacCambridge, 2004, 241).

Buoyed by their 11-point lead, the Pack, playing pressure defense, took charge. Their eyes were constantly on the prize: quarterback Len Dawson. Control him. Win the game. He became the Green Bay target.

That second half for the Packers was a mix of running to daylight and using the entire field against a demoralized and exhausted Kansas City defense. As the game moved on to its conclusion, there was ferocious blocking by the Packer offensive line. They seemed more mobile, fueled by a second wind, bigger as the game moved on. The Green Bay front four was driven, dogged, and determined.

After that magnificent (for the Packers) interception, the Kansas City team had the ball half a dozen times, and half a dozen times Lombardi's defense was so strong, so honed in, so full of fury that the Chiefs managed just 38 yards and five first downs in 25 plays.

ED LOTHAMER: We went into the game confident, but, I mean, everybody knew how great the Green Bay Packers were. They had excellent people at every position. I really believe that somewhere deep down in the back of your mind or heart, we maybe knew that they were really, really, really great. And that we were good.

When they got the interception, I think then that the confidence on the Chiefs' side started to ebb a little bit.

The third quarter was just a completely dismal time for us. I think we only had the ball for a few minutes. And they started picking up the pace and were scoring touchdowns.

Green Bay Packers safety Willie Wood.
Photofest

DAVE ROBINSON: From a defensive standpoint, for two weeks Kansas City had analyzed our defense and was running five-man patterns. They practiced them for two weeks until they got them down pat. Now, all of a sudden, in 20 minutes, they had to go to the sideline and refresh their memories about three-, two-, four-man patterns because they had to keep somebody in to protect the quarterback. Keep him from getting killed.

While they knew their assignments, they hadn't practiced those plays for two weeks. And they looked like it. When they came outside to run pass patterns, the timing was off. It was just disastrous for them.

To me, the key to winning that game was our blitz on third-and-eight. That was the key, because after that we had complete control of them. Once we neutralized their five-man patterns in the third quarter, they didn't score another point.

LEN DAWSON: You don't like to think that one play can make that much difference, but in that case it most certainly did. Play actions and rolls are what we did best, but when we got that far behind, we had to deviate from our game plan, and we got in trouble.

It was a disheartening second half for Len Dawson and the rest of the Chiefs. Swarming Packers seemed to be everywhere. Stifling, shifting, shuffling, the team from Green Bay had amped up its defense, determined to short circuit the offense of the Chiefs. The pressure was unrelenting. Kansas City was unable to get beyond the Green Bay 44-yard line in the second half.

HANK STRAM: Hindsight analysis had the Packers timing their blitz for the third quarter to set us off balance. Maybe so, but again a statement like this is deceptive, since we were prepared to handle the blitz. Many AFL teams, particularly the Boston Patriots at this time, used the blitz extensively as a defensive weapon, so our players knew how to protect against it. It's feast or famine for the defense, and on that first play of the second half, it was famine.

After the game a number of reporters looked on that interception by Willie Wood as the key play on which the game turned. That interception certainly didn't improve our chances of winning, but perhaps a more critical play came in the following series of downs. We continued to move the ball. Dawson completed a pass to Taylor for a first down. Curtis McClinton gained four yards through the middle, and Bert Coan caught a pass on the 50-yard line that missed being a first down by only one yard.

Then with third-and-one, Coan started around left end, but Lee Roy Caffey shrugged off a block and dropped him for a four-yard loss. Instead of our cutting seven, or at least three, points off our deficit on that drive, we had to punt.

We held the Packers on the next series, but not on the one after that. Max McGee caught another pass from Starr, and the Packers led 28 to 10 near the end of the third quarter.

Late in the third quarter, the ground game of the Packers found its groove. Runners moved more easily against an opened up Kansas City defense. Still Starr preferred attack by air rather than on the ground. In a 10-play drive that covered 56-yards and ate up 5:25 minutes, the very composed quarterback hit McGee three times. One pass was good for 11 yards, another for 16 yards on third-and-11. Another went for 13 yards and a touchdown.

The red-hot Max McGee made the juggling catch in the middle of the end zone.

The Packer player who was not shy about strutting his stuff once again earned bragging rights. McGee danced by former Tennessee State standout Willie Mitchell one more time for that Green Bay TD.

All three Bart Starr passes leading to the touchdown were essentially the same: down-and-in patterns. The Packer lead was stretched. It was no longer a question of who would win the game. It was how many points would Green Bay win by?

The garrulous McGee reportedly told Packer broadcaster Ray Scott days before the big game, "I've been studying film, and I found me a cornerback. If I do get in there, I'm gonna have him for breakfast, lunch, dinner."

True to his word, McGee had a fantastic feast that January 15th.

CHRIS BURFORD: Max McGee had the game of his life. When the ball hits your wrist and trickles up your arm, there's just no way are you going to catch it.

CURT MERZ: Max McGee just played out of his butt. But he was a decent receiver. The story there is that I guess it's better if you play with a hangover! Either that or he took a couple extra pills to get ready.

JERRY MAGEE: Bart Starr had Max McGee catching the ball out of his asshole.

Green Bay Packers wide receiver Max McGee (85) leers down at Kansas City Chiefs cornerback Fred "The Hammer" Williamson (24) and Hall of Fame linebacker Bobby Bell (78).
AP Photo/Vernon Biever

An Associated Press story claimed that the Chiefs' defensive backs, and all others in the AFL, "have been criticized only slightly less than President Johnson's Vietnam policy." The claim would prove to have some truth to it.

> BART STARR: It was clear that spending all that time in Santa Barbara and watching the game movies of Kansas City had paid off. We realized how vulnerable the Chiefs seemed on the flanks. We attacked with our flanker and spread end.

That led to Max McGee and number 84, Carroll Dale, catching 11 passes for a total of 197 yards and two touchdowns.

> BOYD DOWLER: They didn't have a whole lot of answers. We got to a point where we ran it pretty well, and we certainly threw it pretty well. And of course, the defense kind of sparked us in the second half.

"They pick out a weak spot and stay with it better than any team I've seen," Mike Garrett would say later. "Which weak spot? Well, they were passing like mad on us and hitting those third-down plays, so there must have been a weakness somewhere. But they make mistakes. They are not superhuman."

> ED LOTHAMER: They got to Dawson several times in the second half. We did have good protectors for Dawson—Jim Tyrer, Ed Budde, were Pro-Bowlers. The guy who was center at that time wasn't. Right guard was Curt Merz. And Curt was a good guard. Our right tackle, David Hill, who would become a member of the Chiefs Hall of Fame, would always get all the good defensive ends on his side.

> WILLIE DAVIS: We were a little too cautious in the first half. We were concerned with that rolling pocket. It wasn't all that new, because Detroit used it against us some. But we were getting in and then not making tackles, and we weren't blitzing at all.
>
> They were spaced wider than we thought they would be. If you wanted to get any kind of inside rush you had to line up head up on your man. In the second half we did that and spread the linebackers a little wider to contain Dawson. I figured, forget Kansas City and the Super Bowl and do what you do best!

> HANK STRAM: We now needed to score three more times to win and only had 15 minutes to do so. To conserve time, we stopped shifting. We centered the ball on quick counts. We abandoned our running game and with it the play-action passes that had worked so well during the first half. Green Bay now knew we had to pass, and that made their blitz more effective toward the end of the game. If we could have scored quickly, we might have been able to revert to our original game plans, but we were clutching at straws.

> BOYD DOWLER: We went into the game knowing we could throw on them. We weren't a great big passing team. We were known as a running team, but we knew, just watching the tapes, that we could execute throwing the football against them, and we did.

Defensively, the Packers were at the top of their game. Offensively, they appeared unstoppable. And they were. They were pulling away, moving the ball wherever and whenever they wanted to.

HANK STRAM: The secret of pass defense then is to not permit the quarterback time to throw the ball perfectly. For this you need a consistent pass rush. Unfortunately our front four lacked both balance and depth. Buck Buchanan and Jerry Mays gave us two strong rushers, but right defensive end Chuck Hurston started the Super Bowl weighing 215 pounds. Our regular left tackle, Ed Lothamer, had undergone a shoulder operation after our seventh game, so we replaced him with rookie Andy Rice from Texas Southern, who had brief tryouts with the Houston Oilers and Chicago Bears before coming to us for what would prove to be his only year in professional football.

In all fairness to Andy, he played well during our championship season, but in the Super Bowl he had to face Green Bay's All-Pro guard Jerry Kramer. As for our linebacking corps, Bobby Bell was sound, but E. J. Holub was experiencing knee problems and middle linebacker Sherrill Headrick had reached the twilight of his career.

We just didn't pressure Bart Starr sufficiently, and when as good a quarterback as he has time to throw, he'll shoot your eyes out. The thing that kept Green Bay going all day was Bart Starr's uncanny ability to come up with the big third down play. Bart Starr shot our eyes out.

Number 15, Bart Starr, was the star of stars that sunny day. Throwing to multiple receivers, in rhythm more and more as the game progressed, using the entire field, he showed why he was, at that moment in time, the over-the-top, top-of-the-hill quarterback in the NFL.

BOB LONG: That Super Bowl I team, all those Lombardi teams, were known for their execution. They were matter-of-fact. This is the way it is. We're going to do our job. And we're going to beat you.

CHRIS BURFORD: Green Bay was frankly a team that you weren't going to come back on real easy because their defense was very, very sound. I mean, they had good players, and they knew what they were doing. But they did have some weak spots.

Their strong safety, Brown, was not a great cover guy. We tried to take advantage of that. We did on only one play, we ran a special slot play on him, beat him relatively easy, but then the pass was out of bounds, so it didn't count. We somehow never ran that again.

During the fourth quarter, Green Bay once again started from their 20-yard line. KC fans were encouraged when their team showed some fight with a Willie Mitchell interception of an underthrown Green Bay long pass from Starr to McGee.

Later, as if to show up Mitchell, Starr cocked his right arm and threw the ball from the Green Bay 20-yard line 25 yards to Carroll Dale. Mitchell was outmatched by the speed of Dale. The square-out pattern left him straddle-legged. Next came a 37-yard pass to McGee. Again, the victimized Chief was Mitchell. Taylor failed to gain from the Kansas City 18-yard line. Then Starr passed to Dale (against Mitchell) for another seven yards.

Number 22, Elijah Pitts, out of Philander Smith College in Little Rock, Arkansas, scored his second touchdown, the final one for the Packers, on a one-yard run, giving the Packers a 35–10 lead. Jerry Mays remembered well the extra point. The Chiefs were in a typical gap alignment, one where the offensive linemen would simply point and tell one another which defenders they intended to block.

> FORREST GREGG: I played offensive right tackle in the game. My first season, 1956, I was a guard. When Lombardi came along, he changed me to right tackle. I faced off against Jerry Mays, a tough opponent, but I had had lots of experience on him. We went back a long way. He was a SMU graduate who said I had been his hero when he played at SMU.
>
> Jerry Kramer said to me, "I will take number 58 and you take the hero, the guy whose idol you are."
>
> Jerry Mays heard Kramer's comments, laughed, and said, "You really know how to hurt a guy."

The Packers played that game as they played all their games, with toughness, ruggedness, and determination—hard football. Intentionally hurting a guy was not the Packer way.

> BOB LONG: Coach Lombardi's teams were never known to be dirty. They didn't talk much.

> ED BUDDE: But they really knew how to hurt a guy. Yeah, we all collapsed. They had a heck of a defense, and I can't blame it on Dawson, I can't blame it on Tyrer or David Hill or anybody else. Blame it on "The Hammer."

Fred "The Hammer" Williamson of the Kansas City Chiefs talked too much. He and his over-the-top comments were on Green Bay's radar.

Green Bay quarterback Bart Starr hands off to halfback Elijah Pitts.
Photofest

BOYD DOWLER: After being injured early in the game, I just kind of hung around the bench feeling sorry for myself. I'd walk up and down, sit down for a while. Before the game, Fred Williamson had bragged, "Two Hammers to Dowler and one to Dale should be enough."

I had a good seat and watched Carroll Dale and Max McGee abuse The Hammer as the game played out.

FORREST GREGG: The Hammer was the guy on our list. If you ever get a chance . . .

BOB LONG: "The Hammer" Williamson insulted our guys. Herb Adderley and Bob Jeter on our team were pretty good trash talkers too, especially Jeter, but nothing like Williamson. He was putting down our team and Lombardi to an extent and Green Bay, too.

BUD LEA: Cornerback Fred Williamson was the only player on the field wearing white shoes because he wanted to be seen. In fact, he was the first in pro football to wear white shoes.

BILL CURRY: The Hammer? Against those Packer teams, it was not a good time to shoot your mouth off.

WILLIE DAVIS: I knew Fred pretty well. I had met him in college, went to Northwestern. And he was just a trash-talking guy. He was big-time trash.

JERRY KRAMER: The Hammer? What he was saying was something that was not done at that time, especially by us. We were firmly, surely by the rules. Show up and do your job.

We talked about Freddy in practice. Coach Lombardi explained the "bootsie play" to us. He explained that if Freddy did anything dirty like he was threatening to do, the quarterback and one of our ball carriers or guards would go one way and the other guys would go after "The Hammer"—only if we needed it.

BOB LONG: The procedure for getting into a game for regulars, for players like me, was to be near Lombardi. This was not only for the Super Bowl, but all games. Coach would say, "Stay fairly close to me."

They would usually just call your name—"Long!" I have pictures of me standing right beside Vince Lombardi, or right behind him, usually behind him.

I go in, I'm playing flanker back. There was the great Green Bay Sweep right, left. Power sweep. That's what Lombardi was known for. No putzing around. He demanded of his players to be mentally tough. By that I'm saying, "You don't make mental mistakes at all, ever." Because if you did, he wouldn't keep you around, quite frankly.

My job as the flanker back, offensive guard, was to come down on the strong safety. But none of our receivers were known to be great blockers. So I figured out a way to go down there and use a screen like they use in basketball. If you put on a good screen, that's almost as good as a block. I came down on the strong safety.

The game almost over, Lombardi inserted high-paid rookie running back Donny Anderson and rookie guard Gale Gillingham, the latter of whom would go on to play a decade of football and become the final member of the Lombardi Packers to be active with the team.

BOB LONG: Gilly was a young, great pulling guard from the University of Minnesota. Let me tell you, he was so big and tough and strong, that's what he was known for. I get down to the safety, Gillingham was pulling out to the right on the Green Bay Sweep. Donny Anderson was running with the ball. All at once, kind of behind me, off my right shoulder, Gillingham hit "The Hammer" so hard his helmet popped off!

I might have heard a "thud." I knew it was a hard hit. I remember specifically a lot of the players that were in that play saying, "Take that Hammer! Take that Hammer!" That was a little bit of pride for us. Get even like you do with a bully.

Anderson stepped on him. This is really getting even with your opponent when you step on him. The guys got a big kick out of that.

BUD LEA: Williamson actually went into the Packers' rookie guard low and caught Anderson's left knee head on.

The force of the collision coldcocked the 29-year-old Williamson. He seemed down for the count. One of his teammates, Sherrill Headrick, who would later be inducted into the Chiefs Hall of Fame, fell on "The Hammer." Williamson's arm was broken.

ED LOTHAMER: A lot of the drama was over Fred Williamson. Green Bay was screaming on their sidelines, "Get the Hammer, get the Hammer! The Hammer's down, the Hammer's down!"

The Green Bay players were just thrilled. They were dancing on the sidelines. Fred was a good cornerback. I'm not saying he was great, but he was a good player. And he made some serious tackles for us during the season.

JERRY KRAMER: The highlight films showed our guys on the sidelines after it happened. They were yelling, "The Hammer is down. Somebody got the Hammer!"

Somebody came up to me. I guess it was Fuzz (Fuzzy Thurston). "You get him Jerry?"

"No I didn't get him. I was turned inside." I said. "Did you get him?"

"No I didn't get him. Who the hell got him?" Fuzz asked.

Donnie Anderson was our multimillionaire bonus baby. It probably was Fuzz who said, "Anderson must have hit him with his purse."

Surveying the pileup, with Williamson down and out, Fuzzy Thurston quietly hummed "If I Had a Hammer," a song of that era (MacCambridge, 2004, 241).

JERRY KRAMER: Williamson was hauled off on a stretcher, and that was poetic justice for a loudmouth. The reason he used his mouth so much was that he was not that good a player.

WILLIE DAVIS: It's kind of interesting because there was a sense in us, "Let's shut 'The Hammer' up!" I don't know whether I was one that ever got caught up in it, but I sure wanted to shut him up.

FRED ARBANAS: The Hammer, well, he liked to flap his gums a lot, there's no doubt about that. I was not shocked when Williamson got laid out in the third quarter. Guys get their bells rung all of the time.

In the Kansas City dressing room, a groggy Williamson asked, "I don't remember a thing. Did I make the tackle?"

Vince Lombardi was later asked why it took so long to hammer the Hammer. "Well," the Packer head man replied, "He never got close enough to anyone before that."

MICHAEL MACCAMBRIDGE: It was not a good game for Fred Williamson.

HANK STRAM: Toward the end of the contest I sent in backup quarterback Pete Beathard, hoping that perhaps he could scramble for some first downs and maybe turn the game around, but you never get anything easy from the Green Bay Packers—especially not when they have a lead.

Those three second-half touchdowns enabled the team from Wisconsin to whip KC, 35–10, besting the Chiefs in yardage, 358–239. A harried Dawson was 16-for-27 passing for 211 yards. The blitz and the Wood interception truly broke the back of the Chiefs. In their last half dozen possessions, they punted the ball away each time. The official time of the game was two hours and 37 minutes.

> **PETER GOLENBOCK:** The win by the Packers left my world intact. The AFL champs, it turned out, weren't all that good.

The man who had the game of his life, William Max McGee, out of Overton, Texas, bagged seven passes for two touchdowns and 138 yards. With just four receptions that season, McGee's seven catches almost doubled what he had accomplished the entire year.

A statistical oddity of the game was the scoring of five touchdowns by the Packers but no field goal attempts.

The Chiefs' bitter defeat, the entire experience of that mid-January day at the Los Angeles Coliseum, had a gut-wrenching effect on some of the players, for instance, Jerry Mays. His hair began to fall out in clumps every time he removed his helmet. He lost weight. "It was the end," he noted, "of playing for fun."

"It was almost," said Phil Bengtson, "as if we had played a cruel trick on the young AFL hopefuls, threatening them with Taylor, the ailing-but-ready Hornung, and a host of other players, then sending out an old man to humiliate them," referring to Max McGee (Povletich, 2012, 151).

> **ED BUDDE:** Max McGee, he curled those balls in unbelievably. But they had a great team! They beat other NFL teams just like they beat the AFL champions.

An enduring and poignant image of the sidelines during the final moments of the game for fans of Kansas City is that of a composed and strangely quiet Hank Stram, assistant coach Tom Bettis near him, head in hands, as well as Len Dawson, sun visor on his head, helmet hanging limply from the hand of his throwing arm.

> **LEN DAWSON:** In the KC locker room after the game, not much was said because we knew that it really wasn't a game for four quarters. It was a game for two quarters. You know, when you're playing an outstanding team like the Green Bay Packers, you better bring it all of the four quarters, and we just didn't.

> **MICHAL MACCAMBRIDGE:** It was a humbling experience for Hank Stram. As Tex Schramm of the Cowboys pointed out, nobody in the National Football League had been doing a very good job of beating the Packers for years, so it wasn't like the Chiefs humiliated themselves in any respect.

HANK STRAM: Green Bay carried their coach Vince Lombardi to the dressing room cheering and shouting, as they had every right to do. They had proved their superiority over us that day.

KEN BOWMAN: Game over. Coach Lombardi was carried on the shoulders of Jerry Kramer and Forrest Gregg. We all knew he was coming near the end of his coaching career. We did not know he was sick. I do not know if he knew he was sick.

JOHN FORTUNATO: Years later, Rozelle commented, "I was pleased that it was a close game for more than a half. I think we all feared that it might be a one-sided blowout. I was very happy with the 35–10 result."

DAVE ROBINSON: Everybody had taken sides. I'll tell you how bad it was. My barber in New Jersey, who I had known since the third or fourth grade, he bet on Kansas City. I asked him why.

And then he told me, "Well, they gave me 19 points."
I said, "They gave you 19 points? The score we beat them by was 35–10."

Vince Lombardi, of the Green Bay Packers, accepts the Super Bowl Trophy
from Commissioner Pete Rozelle after defeating the Kansas City Chiefs.

Chapter
SIX

After the Game Was Over

We didn't necessarily show it on the field, but we were a very emotional group. Winning was never a mundane thing.

—BART STARR

It was not so much that they were better. They guessed right on a particular play.

—LEN DAWSON

THAT JANUARY 15, 1967 NFL–AFL World Championship Game at the Los Angeles Memorial Coliseum passed into history. Opinions, stories, sidebars, commentary, statistics, and memories remained.

Despite the fact that the war within the war on the field of play was tremendously heated, the war between the television networks was, in some ways, more emotionally intense and significant than the game itself. Yet, oddly enough, neither CBS nor NBC retained a video of the game. And in the ratings battle, the network of the established league, CBS, bested NBC by only four points.

"Television had a lot to do with the success that was to come to the Super Bowl and pro football," said Steve Sabol, who would become president of NFL Films. "Once the networks realized that they had a ratings hit on their hands, that machine went into action."

Western Union announced that 582,334 words were filed by reporters covering the game—the most ever for a single sporting contest to that point in time.

Reactions to the event included the following:

"The contest was more ordinary than Super."—*New York Times*
"Too predictable to be memorable."—Heywood Hale Broun, television commentator
"Nothing will ever come of it."—*Atlanta Journal-Constitution* publisher to columnist Furman Bisher
"The advance buildup was more impressive than the show, and the script fell apart in the second half."—Jack Gould, television critic
"Like a stern parent chastising a mischievous child, the Green Bay Packers soundly thrashed the upstart Kansas City Chiefs. . . . The outstanding master of the whiplash . . . was Bryan Bartlett Starr, who had been playing in the NFL four years before the junior circuit was born."—*Los Angeles Times* sports editor Paul Zimmerman

The cover of *Sports Illustrated* carried the headline, "GREEN BAY ON TOP OF THE WORLD." An image of number 85 in full color was amplified by the caption, "Max McGee puts the Packers ahead of the Chiefs."

In the locker rooms of both the winners and the losers, souvenir $1 game programs were stacked up. Each featured the article "A Day That Can Never Happen Again." The programs were there for the taking; however, there were few takers.

Green Bay had won its fourth championship in six years. Its $15,000 winner's share per player represented the largest single-game payout in sports to that point in time. The $750,000 gate was the biggest ever for a football game. The total payout to Green Bay Packer players for winning the NFL Championship Game and the Super Bowl amounted to $24,813.63.

"It goes to show," Vince Lombardi said, "how far professional football has gone."

It also showed how far the man who had once considered the priesthood as a calling had come as a coach and general manager. During Lombardi's first year in those roles, the

Packers showed a team net profit of $75,203. The next year, Green Bay's profit jumped to $115,128. By 1966, when tallied up, net profit was $827,439.

HOWARD MCHENRY: Most players had second jobs back then, so the money from the championship games was much welcomed.

BOB SCHNELKER: As a player, the most I ever made—and I played in two Pro Bowls—was $15,500. That year I got a $15,000 share for the Super Bowl win and another $10,000 for the game with Dallas for the NFL championship. So I made $25,000 extra above my $18,500 salary. That was really, really a lot of money, especially for that time. We thought it was a big game at the time, but compared to what it is nowadays, it was very minor. They just didn't know what it was going to be like and how big it was going to get.

JERRY MAGEE: That first game was a true war of the worlds. To me, it is still the most memorable of the Super Bowls. It established a pattern and put professional football firmly on the map.

GEORGE MITROVICH: I hated Green Bay and the NFL winning. Hated it! The experts had been right; the Packers were too good for Kansas City. I was embarrassed and depressed. I stayed in a football funk until Matt Snell ran off left tackle into the end zone of the Orange Bowl in Super Bowl III, sealing what I knew would become a Jets win over the Colts—as Joe Namath predicted.

HOWARD MCHENRY: We were drained when the game ended. I felt like the game was closer than the score indicated. The Packers had a better team. It would take two more drafts for the Chiefs to really get strong.

WILLIE DAVIS: We didn't play any bush leaguers, and we were happy to accomplish what we did. You could probably hear the giant sigh of relief in the dressing room when the game was over.

BOBBY BELL: The Packers were a great team, a veteran team. We had a great team, a young team. We talked about it. We knew we could not make mistakes. We played a great game in the first half. We thought we could win the game. In the second half we turned that ball over twice. The two times we turned it over—that was 14 points against us. That basis was the game right there.

DALE STRAM: Dad and Lloyd Wells were walking together off the field after the game. Dad turned to Lloyd and said, "We are going to come back and win a Super Bowl."

BILL MCNUTT III: When the game was over, I was walking with my dad into the locker room. My dad, Bill McNutt Jr., who flew from Dallas to California in the summer of 1960 to see the Dallas Texans' first preseason game, put his arm around Coach Stram and told him, "Hank, they are going to play this game for years to come. Your day will come. Don't be down on yourself."

And then I walked behind Jerry Mays and Forrest Gregg up that steep ramp to the locker room, and I overheard their conversation. And, of course, it was a poignant moment for Jerry Mays because Forrest Gregg was literally his hero. They had both played at the same university but not at the same time, and Forrest Gregg was the greatest lineman in football and everybody knew it.

The conversation went something like this, "Forrest, you got me good on a couple of those plays, you really got me good," Jerry said to him.

Forrest said, "Well Jerry, you made some pretty good tackles today. And Buck Buchanan is just a pup, and he's going to be a great one."

I remember that. Buck was only in his fourth year in the league at that time and one of the hugest football players! And underestimated was his wing span, which was over and beyond even his big frame.

CURT MERZ: Nitschke was the only Packer I talked to after the game. He was just outside of the locker room, and most guys went up to talk to him. It was the first time I'd ever met him. I congratulated him. He was civil and decent. It was just, "Nice game."

DALE STRAM: By the time I was 20, I was still with some of the same guys that I had started with when I was five, so they knew me my whole life. I grew up around these guys. It really was a family.

Dad made the first interleague trade between the AFL and NFL. After the third game of the 1961 Dallas Texans' season, Vince Lombardi called Dad to inquire about the availability of Texan kicker "Bootin'" Ben Agajanian, who had been a placekicker in the NFL and had kicked for the New York Giants during the years that Vince had been the Giants' offensive back coach, 1954 to 1957.

Vince was in need of a kicker and thought that Ben could help the Packers win a championship, and in 1961, they did! Vince offered to trade to the Texans the Packer's 11th-round draft choice, quarterback Val Keckin, in exchange for Ben Agajanian. Keckin was a talented six-foot, four-inch, 215-pound quarterback who had played his collegiate years at Southern Mississippi. Dad agreed to the trade, but Val Keckin never reported to the Dallas Texans and later became a backup quarterback for Jack Kemp during the 1962 San Diego Charger season.

Shortly after the Chiefs arrived in Los Angeles for Super Bowl I, Ben Agajanian showed up at the Chiefs' hotel in Long Beach. Ben had retired from pro football as a member of the San Diego Chargers in 1964. He and Dad had stayed in contact and remained friends. Ben was having a party at his Beverly Hills home and invited my Dad, my Mom, my brother Henry, and myself to attend. Ben also asked if the Chiefs' 1965 USC Trojan graduate and Heisman Trophy winner Mike Garrett would come.

Dad was unavailable, but Mom, Henry, Mike Garrett, and I attended, and we all had a great time at Ben's house. The night was highlighted by meeting Jay North, the star of the *Dennis the Menace* TV series, which was very popular during the early 1960s. He was a huge football fan and a nice guy.

Upon entering our locker room after the disappointing Super Bowl loss, Ben Agajanian was the first person we saw. He went straight over to where Dad was standing and gave Dad his condolence on the loss. Afterward, he spotted me and asked if I would like to go into the Packer's locker room with him.

I agreed. I had a pen and a game program in hand. When we entered, Ben was congratulating many of his old teammates, all the while, introducing me as Hank Stram's son. Many of the players told me what a great coach my Dad was and that he had a good football team. I was gathering their autographs as we moved around the room.

In the center of the room, surrounded by the press, was Coach Lombardi. Ben cut right through the crowd straight to Coach Lombardi, where he introduced me.

Coach Lombardi said, "Kid, your Dad is a great coach."

I thanked him and asked what he thought of Len Dawson.

Lombardi said, "He is a real fine quarterback."

I asked him to sign my program. He did and, of course, I thanked him, and then went back to the Chiefs' locker room.

BILL MCNUTT III: I also was in the Packer dressing room. I got all kinds of good autographs. I wanted Forrest Gregg, because Forrest Gregg was from Texas. I got him to sign. I got Jim Taylor. Herb Adderley. I didn't get Bart Starr. I wish I had.

The Packer locker room was strangely quiet, with some beer drinking, some cigarette smoking, and some checking of bruises.

PAT PEPPLER: When the game ended, we were all greatly relieved. Lombardi always tried to keep the players controlled. There was not a great deal of hollering or anything like that. We felt pretty good about ourselves. There was a lot of pride in what was accomplished. There was no showing off.

DALE STRAM: And there may have been some relief on their part that they won the game and did what they had to do. There was no champagne. It wasn't that kind of environment. It was an environment, an atmosphere that they did what they were supposed to do—win and uphold the honor of the old league, the old guard.

FORREST GREGG: It felt good to be the first Super Bowl champion. All those years we were expected to win, and the pressure was on us to win. Pressure was never a problem. It was there, something we lived with, something we overcame.

The Green Bay Packers were a family, a team that worked and played for each other.

JERRY KRAMER: The Chiefs had some good players, as we suspected, but they didn't have the overall quality to stay with a top National Football League team at that time.

FORREST GREGG: There was not a lot of cheering. There was no bragging. Hell, no, there was no champagne. Most of the guys on our team dressed and the next day were getting set to go back to Green Bay. I stayed in LA with some others. I was going to the Pro Bowl the next week.

LAMAR HUNT JR.: We did go into the Kansas City locker room after the game, and it was very subdued, which you would expect. We also went over and congratulated the Packers in their locker room. Now, we were a little late getting over there, but there was no state of jubilation in their deal. They didn't brag in our face or do anything like that.

I was with my dad. I shook Vince Lombardi's hand. I was just kind of in awe of him because he was a legend. He was not haughty, not a braggart. Vince Lombardi was not that kind of a person. He was a devout Catholic. He did go to Mass every day. But with him and his players there was definitely a sense of, "We won."

KC linebacker E. J. Holub said, "I'm not gonna hang my head. We're embarrassed but not disgraced."

Defensive tackle Buck Buchanan said afterward, "Today they were a better team, but I'd like to play them again next year or next week or even tomorrow. I wish we were in the same conference with Green Bay. We have people in our league just as good or better. I don't think we got disgraced. We just got beat."

The powerful Buchanan explained how he had played in that game: "I cursed and screamed all day. I cussed everybody I possibly could. I'll never forget one time they ran a play for Elijah Pitts, and I laid a hit on him. 'You can't run this hole here, man,' I told him."

"'I'll be coming back,' he said."

"'Every time you come back, I'll be right here waitin' on you,' I shot back" (Connor, 1974, 37).

Captain Jerry Mays, KC defensive lineman par excellence, was more than a bit surprised at the way the game turned out. "It's impossible for me to believe those bald old men on the Packers could have handled us with such ridiculous ease."

In truth, 13 Packers were more than 30 years old.

CHRIS BURFORD: I think we were all disappointed. We probably felt a little bit like we had let the league down. I don't think we played our best game. I think the first half was a pretty good game for us. And I felt really pretty confident. And then I think we got away from what we really could do well. We didn't do some things that we could have done. I would have loved to play them again. I certainly never felt intimidated, or I never felt I was being shut down personally. Otis Taylor and I both could compare to any wide receivers in the NFL.

You're an All-American in college and you lead the nation in pass receiving, and you go to the AFL and all of a sudden you're no good? Ha, give me a break! I mean I never thought that way. That was always nonsense.

LEN DAWSON: We had won a championship—the championship of the American Football League—but not that world championship football game.

SMOKEY STOVER: After the game, coming into our locker room, it was very quiet. Nobody really talked. Everybody just kind of broke up and went their own way after that. We didn't fly back as a group. Everybody went home or to wherever they were going.

FRED ARBANAS: We were a bit angry, mostly dejected, but we didn't feel like we were embarrassed. The mood in our locker room afterward, we felt like hell. There was no doubt about it. We felt like we had let each other down. You got beat. And we didn't get beat often, but we got beat in our own league from time to time, too. You had to get ready for the next season.

I went into the game with a separated shoulder. I got in the championship game against Buffalo, so I played with my shoulder frozen and taped up, and it bothered me, but not that much once the game got going. But back then guys played with a lot of different aches and pains. We were treated like workhorses, and these guys now are treated like special racehorses of some kind. I think I did okay.

BUD LEA: In the Chiefs dressing room, running back Curtis McClinton was overwhelmed. "Never before had I felt like such a loser," he said. "There was no way we could tell ourselves we played a fine game; we hadn't. The Packers exposed our weaknesses to the world. They picked apart our defense, they stopped our offense, and they demoralized us. There was nothing in this game that indicated it could have gone either way."

CURTIS MCCLINTON: I remember how I felt. I felt like one of the losers at Pompeii. It was like being on a deathbed. Everything you've accomplished up to that point didn't mean a damn thing. No matter who we played, a loss was unacceptable. We were not losers.

CHRIS BURFORD: I felt if we played them again the next week, we'd have a good chance to beat them. They had a couple of breaks.

We'd seen enough of them on film. They had strengths and weaknesses, and we didn't take advantage enough of some of the weaknesses they did have. We did a little bit, but we had a couple of breaks that didn't help us. We had a couple of early calls in the game that I thought were somewhat instrumental that really kind of went the wrong way as far as my view of it.

Those guys in green and yellow uniforms weren't a big deal! I mean, people make more out of that than there really was. I didn't have any great mystique in my mind about the Packers. I'd seen them enough on film, and they had some really great players. They had some average players. They had a great coach, too. Both teams had great coaches. We take that for granted or neither one of us would have been there. But was there a mystique? Hell no!

These were guys who played football for a living. This was eight years after I'd been playing or seven years after playing in the pros. You'd played against these guys in college back eight, 10 years ago, and then, you know, they don't change.

There are a lot of little things that swing things in those kind of tough ball games. And Green Bay was . . . frankly, the kind of a team that you weren't going to come back on real easy because their defense was very, very sound. I mean, they had good players, and they knew what they were doing.

That said, they did have some weak spots. The linemen that they had, their strong safety, Brown, was not a great cover guy. We tried to take advantage of that.

One of the keys to winning the game was the Packers' ability to shut down star KC running back Mike Garrett. He managed just 17 yards on six carries.

Defensive halfback Willie Mitchell of the Chiefs, beaten by two touchdown passes from Starr to McGee, said, "I don't feel that they were working on me too much. And they can't make me believe that Green Bay is that much better than we are."

"They don't hit any harder than anyone else," linebacker Sherrill Headrick said. "The thing is, they never block the wrong man—they're always in your way. And their backs always hit the hole. On their sweeps I was getting blocked by a different guy each time— the tight end, the pulling guard, the back. I don't know where they all came from" ("Bread and Butter Packers," 4).

PHYLLIS STRAM: I was used to the routine, having done it many, many times. We stood outside the locker room after the game. That's what most wives always did, huddle up outside and wait for their interviews to be over and their getting dressed and so forth.

I kissed and hugged Hank when he finally came out. There was nothing I could do about soothing the hurt. Of course he was disappointed. It just wasn't in the cards that we'd win.

HANK STRAM: After the game at least one of the Packer assistant coaches, operating on hindsight, remarked that they had played conservatively against us during the first half, planning to lower the boom in the second half.

I find this difficult to believe. You don't pace yourself through a football game like you might for a long distance race. You go hard on every play. You get what you can when you get it, because later you may not have the chance.

With the game over, postgame theatrics and ceremony on tap, and a new world of professional football on the horizon, zany and awkward, poignant and dramatic, controversial and historic moments took center stage.

> **BUD LEA:** Pete Rozelle was very pleased with the outcome. He confessed later that he was rooting—silently, of course—for the Packers because his NFL loyalties were still strong.

A man who had experienced much glory and accomplishments as a player, the late and great Pat Summerall, coped with a couple of challenging experiences while handling his television assignments.

The former New York Giant star, who at one time had been coached by Vince Lombardi, asked Pete Rozelle, "Are you the commissioner of the one league, the two? What is your title now?"

Rozelle politely responded, "Well, I'm the commissioner of two leagues."

> **FRANK GIFFORD:** The arrangement for the postgame was Pat Summerall was to be the host and control the microphone for CBS. NBC's George Ratterman was to be allowed into the locker room with permission to ask questions. Summerall, following the agreement, would be the one to allow Ratterman to ask a question. But Ratterman grabbed the microphone away from Summerall at one point.
>
> Summerall vividly remembered hearing Lee MacPhail, our boss, screaming from the truck into his headset, "We didn't say give him the microphone. We said let him ask a question. You were to be in charge of the microphone. Now get that freaking microphone back."

Summerall and Ratterman almost engaged in a tug of war on national television.

The next blip involved Packer fullback Jim Taylor, who characterized the outcome of the game with the phrase, "We mangled them a bit."

Getting set for his postgame television interview, Taylor stood next to Summerall, who was sweating profusely because of the hot lights. The television lighting was not as sophisticated as today. Taylor offered the CBS announcer a swig from his can of Coca-Cola.

An annoyed and agitated voice came through Summerall's headset. It was sports director Bob Dailey: "Tell him to get rid of that Coke can."

In a way, Summerall followed the suggestion. Taking the can of Coke from Jim Taylor, he took a big swallow and wound up choking and gagging. The Packer had filled the can half full of whiskey. It went down like firewater. The pro that he was, the suave and affable Summerall coped with the on-air pressures.

Vince Lombardi had also coped with the pressures he faced leading up to the Super Bowl and during the game itself. He finally looked relaxed but also seemed a bit uncomfortable. Through the ebb and flow of his coaching that day, the Windsor knot on his tie had become tighter and tighter on his neck. No matter how many tugs he gave it, the tie would not loosen. At long last, Packer trainer Dad Brazier came to the rescue. Armed with a tape cutter, he sliced the tie off. Even a legend needed some help once in a while.

BUD LEA: Pete Rozelle presented the legend Lombardi with the trophy as the coach of the winning team.

From the beginning, the plan had been to create a simple trophy to be awarded to the victor of the final game. Its inscription would read, "World Professional Football Championship," and on it would be the location of the game and the final score. It was reported that Vice President Oscar Riedner of Tiffany & Company had sketched the trophy's basic design on a napkin during a luncheon meeting at a Manhattan restaurant with Pete Rozelle.

Twenty-two inches high, the trophy featured, as it does today, a sterling silver regulation-sized replica football on a pyramid-shaped pedestal. The plan was always to return the trophy to Tiffany's New Jersey workshop, where the name of the winning team would be hand engraved on the base before being returned to the victors.

In 1967, however, Vince Lombardi was so smitten with the trophy that he insisted it be sent to Green Bay to be immediately enjoyed by Packer fans. The champs had their charter flight back to Green Bay delayed by fog and smog. Thus, the team spent another night in the welcome warmth of Los Angeles. When the club returned to Wisconsin with the trophy, it was taken to the local ABC television station. Jim Irwin, sports director, made the decision to use it as a prop on the set that evening.

After a time and after being viewed by many, that first trophy was sent back to Tiffany. Unfortunately, it was shipped back in an ordinary cardboard box and arrived crushed. Another trophy was created in its place. The second time around, the pack job was peerless; however, it was never revealed who paid the bill for the new version. The Packers were moved by their silver football trophy, which would be renamed the Vince Lombardi Trophy in 1970, at the suggestion of Lamar Hunt, according to Green Bay Packer historian Cliff Christl.

The star of stars in the game was number 15, Bart Starr, who completed 16-of-23 passes for 250 yards and two touchdowns. Performing like the big-time pro he was, Starr felt the pressure but remained in control. He was brilliant.

Starr was named the Super Bowl's first MVP. In the locker room, as part of the postgame activities, Al Silverman, *Sport* magazine editor, gave the Green Bay quarterback a set of keys to a brand new Corvette. The Green Bay star never drove the car. Raffling it off, he used the money to cofound Rawhide Boys Ranch in Wisconsin for at-risk youths. Rawhide Boys Ranch still exists. And years later, Max McGee was still grousing about not being named MVP.

Super Bowl I MVP Bart Starr.
Photofest

One who was especially impressed with the brilliant play of the Green Bay quarterback was the Kansas City coach.

> HANK STRAM: It took exceptional timing between Starr and his receivers. The thing that kept Green Bay going all day was Starr's uncanny ability to come up with the big third-down play. It also took great pass blocking, and they got it. We had a variety of coverages, but they were able to isolate our corner men one-on-one. It was imperative not to give them anything easy. We did, and it cost us.

> BART STARR: There was no one to help a defensive back stop a receiver. We isolated our wide receivers on their cornerbacks.

"I think their defense hurt them," said Lombardi at the postgame press conference in the Green Bay locker room. "The KC secondary played very loose. They seemed to be daring us to throw against them. We were glad to accommodate them."

> HANK STRAM: One game is not a true test of the abilities of both leagues.

The articulate and diplomatic Pete Rozelle agreed: "I think it was a tremendous show. It takes more than one game to evaluate the difference between the two leagues" (Starr, 1987, 152).

Lamar Hunt said, "I'd say anytime we lose a game by even one point it's damaging to a team's prestige, and in this case, a league's prestige. But one game such as this is not going to make or break the AFL."

In the locker room of the victors, Vince Lombardi was flushed with pride and excitement with the game victory, the trophy presentation, and the total package of that historic January 15, 1967. Cradling a football, holding it tenderly as one would caress a favorite pet, the emotional coach fielded questions from the assembled media.

Asked if the football he was holding was a National Football League one, Lombardi responded in a raised voice: "The game ball," he said proudly. "The players gave it to me. It's the NFL ball. It catches better and it kicks a little better than the AFL ball."

A reporter asked Lombardi if he thought his Packers were the best team in the world now that they had beaten Kansas City. "I don't know, we haven't played Alabama yet," he quipped.

Perhaps the postgame mood of the on-top-of-the-world Lombardi was best captured in the talented Milton Richman's nationally syndicated United Press International story, which appeared the day after the big game.

In Richman's story, a reporter asked Lombardi, "Was this your best game of the year?"

"I wouldn't say so" was Lombardi's terse response.

Lombardi was asked if Kansas City was a better team than Dallas. He responded, "I think Dallas is a better football team."

"How does Kansas City compare with the teams in the NFL?"

"It's a good team," the Green Bay coach answered. "It doesn't compare with teams in the NFL."

Richman reported that Lombardi later "amended that, saying he meant the Chiefs didn't compare with the top teams in the NFL."

BILL CURRY: Coach Lombardi kind of broke a sweat. He said he didn't want to answer that question. Then he blurted it out. "I think the Kansas City team is a real top football team, but doesn't compare with the National Football League teams. That's what you want me to say. I said it."

CHUCK LANE: The media was hounding Lombardi to try to get him to say something derogatory about the AFL or the KC Chiefs, and he would not give them that before the game. But after the game, he said, "Frankly, KC is a good football team, but not as good as Dallas, or the LA Rams, or the Baltimore Colts."

And that of course blew up in KC, and the media there went nuts on that. Lombardi really was saying all the proper things that entire week before that, and then afterward he let his hair down and was honest with people, and they crucified him for being honest.

MICHAEL MACCAMBRIDGE: It was a humbling experience for Hank Stram, that game. I know the comment Lombardi made afterward that the Chiefs were not as good as the best teams in the NFL punctured Stram's pride to a degree. He was sincerely hurt by that.

ED LOTHAMER: Here was the thing: We were real close in '66 to having the team that could have won that Super Bowl game. We had some things that went on during the season. I got hurt. I'm not saying that I was a big part of it, because I was just an average ballplayer. I played eight years, but I was about six feet, five inches, close to 300 pounds. The guy who took my place, Andy Rice, was a very small defensive tackle, weighed about 268 pounds and was about six feet, two inches. And so he was playing left defensive tackle.

Hurston, who was our normal defensive right end, had been plagued with stomach problems since the start of the playoffs, and he had lost quite a bit of weight. And he was small to begin with. Game day he only weighed in at 218 pounds, which was really awfully small for a defensive end. And then in the linebacker crew we had Bobby Bell, Sherrill Headrick, and E. J. Holub. You know, Bobby was a great linebacker, Sherrill had been an All-Pro several years in the AFL, and I think he played a pretty good game that day. E. J. Holub, his knees were so bad, and it affected him in that game. I think in his career he had 13 or 14 knee operations. His knees were just horrible.

It's my personal opinion that we went into the game confident, but, I mean, everybody knew how great the Packers were. We knew they were coming into their fourth world championship in the decade. And they had excellent people at every position. I really believe that somewhere deep down in the back of your mind or heart, we maybe knew that they were really, really, really great and that we were good.

I think when the bubble burst in the second half and they got the interception, I think then that the confidence on the Chiefs' side started to ebb a little bit.

LEN DAWSON: They had a heck of an offensive line. And we had Chuck Hurston, a defensive end, who was down to like 210 pounds. He had some kind of a bug or something. He couldn't provide much of any pass rush, and consequently Bart Starr had plenty of time back there. And as accurate as he is, he's going to do a lot of damage.

JERRY MAGEE: The Chiefs were a good team—size, strength, and a heck of a quarterback in Len Dawson. He had really fast hands. He could fake two or three times in a play just in the blink of an eye. He had a lot of skills. The Chiefs were a couple of players short in that game. They couldn't keep up.

DAVE ROBINSON: I knew a lot of those guys and they were all good football players, but the problem is that they were so good in the AFL. I say this guardedly: The AFL was so weak at that time that Kansas City just dominated. It was like men among boys. Buck Buchanan was a great football player, but in that game, when I saw him, his techniques weren't the best in the world because he didn't have to be good. He didn't have to do it the right way. He was good enough that he could dominate that league doing things the wrong way.

That was one of the big keys, the fact that our team was much, much better prepared to play a game, and our techniques were much, much better than theirs.

BILL MCNUTT III: Everybody was very dejected after the defeat, and Lamar Hunt and my father stayed up late that night. They replayed the game on television in Los Angeles. So Mr. Hunt and my father had a double bout of misery that day, not only being subjected to the defeat in person, but caring enough about it to stay up til midnight to watch the replay. I watched part of the replay, and then I just fell asleep.

It was not a happy flight back to Kansas City. The Chiefs may, however, have received somewhat of a pickup from cheering fans who greeted them, carrying signs that read, "No. 2—So What?"

HOWARD MCHENRY: A lot of people in Kansas City turned out to meet the Chiefs at the airport. The Chiefs lost the game, but they gave good effort and the people appreciated that.

SMOKEY STOVER: There was a turnout after we came back as losers in the first Super Bowl. Not a big one. Everybody likes a winner! There was not a scene like when we came back from the American Football League Championship Game, and our airplane had difficulty trying to land with the mob that was there. So many people there at that time that they had to clear the damn runway before we got down.

ED LOTHAMER: I flew back with the team on a somber flight. Not much talking. There were probably 300 to 350 people, maybe a little more, that were there when the plane landed. We had some really good fans, but everybody was what you would expect, disappointed, especially after all the negative and out of line comments that were being thrown around about the Chiefs—I'm telling you, guys really, really took that to heart.

The NFL felt like we were just some little gang of people that had got thrown together and we didn't have any tradition and we didn't have any NFL culture. And really, it was kind of like we were outlaws, cast off people that hadn't made it there in their league.

LU VAUGHN: When the weather cleared up, our chartered flight flew directly back to Kansas City from Burbank. We were disappointed because we thought we had a chance to win, but I wasn't nearly as disappointed as a lot of other people on the plane, talking about how many thousands of dollars they lost in Las Vegas. There was no parade in Kansas City for the Chiefs. Not then.

That game was talked about for a long time afterward, and there was so much publicity and it really was the start of a big, big thing. That's the only Super Bowl I've had the pleasure of going to, but I never miss them on TV.

TOM OLEJNICZAK: When my parents returned from the Super Bowl to Green Bay, their biggest feeling was relief. A lot of people thought the Packers would beat the Chiefs, 58–0. There was some worry, to be sure, when the game was so competitive. But it worked out well for those who were for the Packers.

KEN BOWMAN: It was "Titletown, USA," and those folks who supported us truly supported us. We never failed to come back from winning a championship game that they were not lined up at the airport, lined up in the streets, lined up on the airfield on the tarmac to meet the plane, to welcome us back.

BOB SCHNELKER: It was exciting coming back. Everybody in town was at the airport. Everybody was there, including all your relatives and friends. It was a very happy occasion. It was ice cold, especially after being in Santa Barbara for a week with that nice weather.

BART STARR: Arriving back in Green Bay by plane at night, we were serenaded by a brass band reception. It was just a marvelous moment for all of us to be treated that way. We had never ever seen so many fans welcoming us back after a ball game than there were that night. Well, sure, it was a little chilly! But the warmth and affection from those fans touched a lot of us.

BOYD DOWLER: Fuzzy Thurston and his wife, Herb Adderley and his wife, and myself and my wife stopped in Las Vegas for a couple of days. We went there the day after the game. Herb was a good friend of Bill Cosby, and Cosby was playing Vegas at the time. The six of us went over there and hung out for a couple of days, saw a couple of shows, and flew back on our own. We were able to do that; we were on our own as soon as the game ended, we could go do what we wanted to do. We didn't have to be on the plane back home with a lot of the guys on the team.

"Titletown, USA" knew how to celebrate victory. The team, the fans, the city, and the media had a lot of experience.

"Packers Conquer New World, 35–10," a Green Bay newspaper headline proclaimed.

The consensus was that Commissioner Pete Rozelle had done all he could with the new championship football game venture considering the circumstances. On the flight from Los Angeles to New York City he said, "I think it was a tremendous show. It takes more than one game to evaluate the difference between the two leagues. But never again will there be a championship game that is not a sellout."

MICKEY HERSKOWITZ: The next day after the game they had the National Football League owners meeting, and Vince Lombardi always represented the Green Bay ownership. He walked in, and the owners gave him a standing ovation. That was purely out of gratitude, but it was also out of relief because they had had that moment of fear at halftime.

Every top sportswriter in the country had been there. The game may have been slipped in under the radar. I realized it right then and there along with Pete that the game would be something special. The attendance didn't bother me. I thought it was a major triumph that we had two-thirds of the Coliseum filled given the time frame that we had, the matchup we had, the newness of the game.

I knew that it would be a very short time before one couldn't get tickets to the Super Bowl.

I stayed around the day after the game ended to finish up the business of loose ends—accounting, reporting, cars being returned and accounted for. We had tickets and were flying back to Houston. I went down to the desk of the Statler Hilton to check out. I was given an envelope. I looked inside. There was a parking stub.

I said, "I'm sorry, I do not know what this is."

The desk clerk said, "Mr. Barlow left it for you."

Jack was still there, so I called his room.

He said, "There's a brand new Chrysler Imperial LeBaron in the garage. No one drove it. It still has zero miles on it. It is yours for a year. Take it home, drive it, and pay for the gas. We will pay for everything else. At the end of the year if you want to buy it we will give it to you for 17 percent below the factory cost."

I cashed in the plane tickets. We drove back to Houston in the car. It was solid white with blue upholstery and opera glasses in the back seat. It was almost a limousine. It took us about three to four days to get home. I actually kept that car for about eight years.

That June, about six months after the game, Barlow called me in Houston and told me that some of the press had never returned cars after the game ended. He told me, "We found the last press car at the airport in Phoenix."

At the postgame party in Green Bay, a satisfied, jubilant, grinning Vince Lombardi joked with a confident and carefree Max McGee:

"I can't figure you out," Lombardi said.

"How's that coach?" McGee responded.

"I've been coaching you for eight years, and I've never seen anyone like you. You're a hell of a receiver, but you drive me nuts. You make a circus catch of a pass thrown three feet behind you, then you turn around and drop one that hits you right in the numbers."

The always garrulous Max McGee paused for a moment before putting his arm around the not so garrulous Bart Starr and smiling.

"Coach," he said, "It's easy to explain. I haven't had much practice catching ones thrown right at me" (Starr, 1987, 152).

"McGee was probably the most amazing hero of any Super Bowl that I remember," Edwin Pope said. "He was the shocker."

> BART STARR: After we were back in Green Bay for about three or four days, Max McGee and I made a lot of appearances before different groups. We were attending a father–son breakfast. We made our comments, and they opened it up for questions and answers.
>
> This gentleman in the back stood up and said, "Max, I don't understand you. I see you running down the field . . ."—and he's holding his hands up as if he were about to catch a ball on a post route. The gentleman continued, "and the ball's thrown right here, and you bobble it or drop it. I've seen you do that a lot. You bobbled it the other day, but at least you held onto it. Yet, in that same game I saw you do something that I don't understand: The ball's thrown about two feet behind you on a post route and you just reached back, plucked it up, pulled it into your chest, and ran and scored. Could you explain that to me please?"
>
> And Max turns and looks over at me. We're sitting there up on the stage. And then he puts his arms up like he is about to catch a post route. And he looks at this fan and he's like roaring, "But I never get a chance to practice this kind!"
>
> And the whole place came apart.
>
> Oh, Max, oh yeah, he had a real sense of humor. He was a character of characters, but a fabulous, fabulous player. Well, that was just his personality and the way he lived his life. That's very true that Lombardi tolerated it because he knew he had somebody good.
>
> Years later, Max made it clear that Coach Lombardi was never aware he stayed out the night before the big game. "Until he died, I never talked about it because I didn't want him to know," McGee said. "I wanted him to know that he always had control of his boys."

HANK STRAM: It was no accident that the Green Bay Packers, under Vince Lombardi, won the NFL championship three years in a row. They were a fine football team. They were a complete team with excellent kicking, good defense, solid offense, and excellent leadership. I don't consider it a great disgrace to have lost to them.

On the other hand, I don't consider it a great achievement to have played them even for part of the game. Some people who had expected us to get blown off the field right from the opening kickoff began to talk about the 35 to 10 score as being a moral victory for the Kansas City Chiefs. Maybe so, but I never noticed a category in the record book for so-called "moral victories."

I wanted to return to the Super Bowl and prove that the Kansas City Chiefs someday could also be called champions of the world.

BOYD DOWLER: Some guys were more than a little bit upset when the highlight film of the game came out. The way our team was portrayed in it was aggravating. It almost ignored us. I remember thinking as we watched it and wondering, if I didn't know better, I'd have thought Kansas City won the game.

They presented this film about how this young team from Kansas City, from the upstart league, and this and that.

I know one thing, it didn't go overboard in complimenting the Packers! It was more in that mood of, "Boy, these Chiefs have done a wonderful job getting to this game."

We had done a wonderful job. That era the Packers were like the Yankees of football, America's team of football. I always just shake my head a little when they mentioned the Dallas Cowboys in that way. Gee, I kind of always thought America's team was up in Wisconsin!

The Chicago Bears and Kansas City Chiefs were scheduled early on for a preseason exhibition game in Kansas City in 1967. The contest was on the calendar of every member of the Chiefs organization.

CLIFF CHRISTL: The game was scheduled to be played on August 23, 1967. I don't believe AFL and NFL teams had met in preseason games until that year.

ED LOTHAMER: The year we lost that first Super Bowl, we had so much pent up anger and anxiety we just wanted to prove to the world, "Hey, we can play football!" I knew about that date with the Bears, one of the real old guard teams of the National Football League.

DOUG KELLY: That may have been an exhibition game to the Bears; however, it was anything but an exhibition game to the Chiefs. That was comeuppance time.

Seething and steaming for some time after his team's loss to the Packers, and especially angered by Vince Lombardi's comments that several NFL teams were better than his Chiefs, Hank Stram sought payback. In his training camp office at William Jewell College in Liberty, Missouri, the afternoon before the game, Stram explained to some members of the local media in detail what he expected both teams would do in the game:

"Remember, this is not just another exhibition," he said, "but I haven't said too much about it to the players. They know it's the Bears. They know it's the National Football League they're playing. Sometimes words don't have any meaning, they're unimportant. This may be that time. We don't want to get so emotional that we won't play our game. If we do the job with the shoulder pads, all else will be taken care of.

"They'll probably take the same approach Green Bay did and run to the left side. And they'll try to set up a mismatch between Gale Sayers and a linebacker on one-and-one situations. But to me teams that win have solid quarterbacks, and the Bears don't have that established leader."

CHRIS BURFORD: The Chicago Bears. They were bigger, stronger, and faster than the Packers, quite frankly. We got matched up against the Bears with Gale Sayers, Dick Butkus, and Johnny Morris. Those were just of few of their many good players.

ED LOTHAMER: I was so depressed after that January 15th game because we heard Lombardi had said something like, "These guys need to go back to the wheat fields or wherever they're from. They could probably play with some of the weaker teams in the NFL."

LEN DAWSON: I figured that once we got them (the Bears) playing our type of game we could do everything we wanted. Then it got like any game that is out of hand—a little ridiculous.

DALE STRAM: All of Kansas City got behind that game. Instead of barbeques in the parking lot there were Bearbques.

BOBBY BELL: Hank Stram said, "Let's see if they can block this, let's see if they can see this." They were clueless. That's when they decided for themselves that we were for real.

CHRIS BURFORD: In the first quarter in that game, the Bears were actually ahead of us, 10–3, for a time. At halftime, we were ahead,

24–10. Around the third quarter we began to really start pummeling them pretty good.

I was just running back from a pass route, and Richie Petibon, one of the defensive backs for the Bears, says, "Hey Chris! When are you guys gonna lay off?"

And I said, "It won't be tonight, Richie!"

We ended up beating them, 66–24. I think that was just a little payback, mainly from the written abuse from the writers. You know, the writers back in those days from the major magazines and the major news sources were so pro-NFL. I think we got a little tired of all the nonsense, because they tried to make it like there was a big difference between the leagues.

CLIFF CHRISTL: The story of that game is a great story and one that was long forgotten. Clearly, by the score, the Chiefs were out for revenge or at least to prove themselves.

The game was depressing for the Bears but delicious for the Chiefs. Len Dawson played into the fourth quarter.

CHRIS BURFORD: "Warpaint," the Chiefs' mascot horse, almost had a heart attack because we scored so many touchdowns, and he had to run around the field. It seemed like one of those games where every time Lenny threw the ball up it was a touchdown.

Stram, with something to prove, had more than made his point. That trashing of the Bears made for the worst trouncing inflicted on an opponent by an AFL team to that point in time. It was also the worst defeat in the coaching career of George Halas, the third worst in the 830 games the Bears had played since his creation of the franchise as the Decatur Staleys in 1920.

LEN DAWSON: Since we had to live with that Super Bowl defeat for seven months, it was special putting 66 points on the board against Dick Butkus, Gale Sayers, and the Chicago Bears.

ED BUDDE: Beating up on the Bears, I tell you, I and some other guys didn't even play the fourth quarter. Oh yeah, you better believe it, Hank was very, very happy that day!

CHRIS BURFORD: Ever since we lost the Super Bowl we listened to a lot of nonsensical comments about the NFL and the Green Bay

Packers and Mr. Lombardi and how he said we aren't as good as the other top teams in the National Football League—like the Chicago Bears. Now I thought maybe everyone will get off our backs.

We got bad-mouthed very much, especially by Dick Butkus, who said he'd walk back to Chicago if they lost. After the win, Butkus got on the plane like everybody else.

MICHAEL MACCAMBRIDGE: There was an entire off-season of the Chiefs being told they were not good enough, that they were still a team from a Mickey Mouse league. That led to, what in many of the Chiefs' minds, is still their most memorable victory, the drubbing of the Bears.

That win was a kind of wake up call to the National Football League that the Chiefs and the American Football League were better than they wanted to admit.

DALE STRAM: There were four game balls given out after the Bears game, one to Dad, Lamar Hunt, Willie Mitchell, and Lenny Dawson. Each ball was given as payback for the Packers loss: Dad as the coach, Lamar for the league, Willie Mitchell for the defense, and Lenny Dawson for the offense.

LEN DAWSON: That victory over the Chicago Bears changed the perception many people had about the Kansas City Chiefs and also the American Football League. It would be a perception that would change even more as the years moved on.

It was that Super Bowl I and the merger that changed the game forever, providing the impetus for football to become the greatest sport in the world. That first game was the big game, the game changer. Look what has happened.

WILLIE DAVIS: I look back at my football career, including the 12 NFL years, being the first African American to own a beer distributorship in Los Angeles. Now I find myself in radio and I say, "Who could have ever thought it?"

I remember the talk about going to Green Bay—at that time it was called a "Siberia of football." And by the time I left there, we were recognized as a football team that was equal to any. So I couldn't have asked for a more wonderful career on and off the football field.

CLIFF CHRISTL: What I didn't really understand at the time was that it was more than just the dawn of a new era in pro football. The game kind of ushered in the era of African American dominance in the NFL that still prevails today, with almost 70 percent of the players being black.

The strength of the Packers' first Super Bowl team was its defense, and six of their 11 starters on defense were black. Vince Lombardi not only had no quotas, but also invested heavily in some of those players using first- and second-round draft picks. Willie Davis has said that Lombardi did more for diversity than anyone in the history of the NFL, and I'm not so sure that isn't true. Yet, unlike Branch Rickey in baseball, he has never gotten much credit for it.

When the Packers won their first two National Football League titles under Lombardi in 1961 and 1962, they had an outstanding defense but only two black starters. That was typical of the times and also true of their most formidable opponents during the early 1960s: Detroit, the Baltimore Colts, and Chicago Bears in their conference, and the New York Giants and Cleveland in the East.

By the 1966 season, when most of those teams still had one, two, or three black starters on defense, the Packers had six. That's what separated them from those other traditional powers. The Packers had lost some of their firepower on offense by the mid-60s, but they had one of the great defenses of all time. Four of their black starters on defense are in the Pro Football Hall of Fame: Willie Davis, Dave Robinson, Herb Adderley, and Willie Wood.

Following the first Super Bowl, all four of them started in the Pro Bowl, as well as Bob Jeter.

As for the Chiefs, they made it to Super Bowl I for the same reason. They had no quotas, either. That, in my mind, was the primary reason the best AFL teams caught up so quickly to the best in the NFL. They mined the black colleges, in particular, and no AFL team did it any better than the Chiefs.

Their defensive tackles were Buck Buchanan from Grambling and Andy Rice from Texas Southern. Willie Mitchell from Tennessee State was one of their starting cornerbacks, and Emmitt Thomas from Bishop was a rookie backup at corner. Their big-play threat on offense was Otis Taylor from Prairie View A&M. Plus they had three other key black players: Bobby Bell from Minnesota at linebacker, and their running backs, Mike Garrett from Southern California and Curtis McClinton from Kansas. Buchanan, Bell, and Thomas are in the Hall of Fame. Taylor probably should be.

There certainly was a sea change taking place in the game, and Green Bay and Kansas City were at the forefront of it. They weren't the only teams. Two weeks earlier, 15 blacks started in the NFL championship between Green Bay and Dallas. Ten started in the AFL championship between Kansas City and Buffalo. When Vince Lombardi won his first NFL title in 1961, a total of five black players started in that game. Teams had quotas. Some probably still had quotas in 1966, especially in the NFL, but not the Packers and Chiefs, and that's largely why those two teams were the last two standing.

The "Super Ball" that gave the "Super Bowl" its name, its glitter, its catchiness, its image was one and three-sixteenths inches in diameter and made of a material called Zectron. Its success ultimately led to its failure. The Wham-O Super Ball's "double-top secret" formula was emulated by competitors. And after just a few years, Super Ball sales slumped. By 1976, the lively bouncing ball was no longer being produced. In 1997, it staged somewhat of a comeback. A most interesting footnote to football history: The "Super Ball" is on display at the Pro Football Hall of Fame in Canton, Ohio.

Both Vincent Thomas Lombardi and Hank Louis Stram, much more than footnotes in football history, would be enshrined in the Pro Football Hall of Fame.

In 1969, just a couple of years after back-to-back Super Bowl wins, the Packer legend left Green Bay to become coach, general manager, and part owner of the Washington Redskins. Under Lombardi, the 'Skins had their first winning season in 14 years. On September 3, 1970, after battling colon cancer, Lombardi became the first from that Super Bowl I Packer team to die. He was just 57 years old.

Genial and brilliant, Hank Stram enjoyed great success for many years as an acclaimed football analyst on CBS network television and the radio broadcasts of *Monday Night Football*. There are many who can still recall turning off the sound of the television broadcast and listening to him and his partner, Jack Buck, on the radio calls and analyses of games. Stram died on July 4, 2005, from complications from diabetes. He was 82 years old.

"I've lived a charmed life," Stram said in 2003, the year he was inducted into the Pro Football Hall of Fame. "I married the only girl I ever loved and did the only job I ever loved."

In 1996, Pete Rozelle, the father of the Super Bowl, passed away at the age of 70 at his home in Rancho Santa Fe, California. He had been battling brain cancer. Commissioner of the NFL for 29 years, Rozelle had been in retirement since 1989.

"The most fun thing," the former commissioner said, "was watching the development of the Super Bowl because the game is what it's all about. I really felt a high at every Super Bowl, with all the glitz and the spectacular halftime shows."

According to the *1967 NFL Record Manual* and information made available by Green Bay Packer historian Chris Christl, 39 Packers took part in Super Bowl I. Paul Hornung was on the roster but did not play.

Packer players from Super Bowl I still living include Herb Adderley, Bill Anderson, Donny Anderson, Ken Bowman, Zeke Bratkowski, Tom Brown, Bill Curry, Carroll Dale, Willie Davis, Boyd Dowler, Marv Fleming, Jim Grabowski, Forrest Gregg, Doug Hart,

Dave Hathcock, Paul Hornung, Jerry Kramer, Bob Long, Red Mack, Dave Robinson, Bob Skoronski, Fuzzy Thurston, Bart Starr, Jim Taylor, Phil Vandersea, Jim Weatherwax, Steve Wright, and Willie Wood,

The Packer deceased include Lionel Aldridge, Bob Brown, Lee Roy Caffey, Don Chandler, Tommy Joe Crutcher, Gale Gillingham, Bob Jeter, Henry Jordan, Ron Kostelnik, Max McGee, Ray Nitschke, and Elijah Pitts.

Lionel Aldridge passed away on February 12, 1998. He was 56 years old. The former defensive star on the Packers had some good years as a NBC and Green Bay TV analyst, but he was haunted by mental problems and bouts of depression.

> **JERRY KRAMER: Lionel's death was not a surprise. He was having thyroid problems, and he was almost 400 pounds.**

Bob Brown played for 11 seasons in the NFL and was a rookie on the Super Bowl I team. A defensive tackle, he had a lifelong battle with maintaining his weight, often tipping the scales at more than 300 pounds. Brown died at the age of 58 in 1998.

Colon cancer claimed the life of Lee Roy Caffey in 1994, in Houston, Texas. The tough Packer linebacker is a member of the Texas A&M and Packer halls of fame. He was also on the Texas A&M All-Decade Team (1960s) and the Packer 75th Anniversary All-Time Team.

Don Chandler, one of the best placekickers and punters of his time, and a member of three championship teams with the Packers, died at the age of 76 in 2011, in Tulsa, Oklahoma. Cancer was the cause of death.

Tommy Joe Crutcher, former Packer linebacker, died in his sleep on February 16, 2002, in McAllen, Texas, at the age of 60. He was manager of a grain company in McCook, Texas.

A rookie in the first Super Bowl, Green Bay's Gale Gillingham died at his home in Minnesota on October 20, 2011. He was 67 years old. He worked in real estate after retiring from the NFL. Gillingham also traveled the world watching two of his sons compete in strongman and power-lifting contests.

A member of the Green Bay Packers Hall of Fame and two-time Pro Bowler, Bob Jeter, 71, died on November 20, 2008. The cause of death was reported as cardiac arrest.

> **DAVE ROBINSON: The first thing you think about with Bob Jeter was his speed. He had an awesome amount of it. People didn't say he was a speedster, but I remember one time Gale Sayers was running downfield, and it looked to me like it happened in four frames. Bob ran him down and stopped a touchdown.**

One of the youngest of the Super Bowl I Packers to pass, at just 42 years of age, Henry Jordan died of a heart attack on February 21, 1977. A member of the NFL Hall of Fame, after his career was over, Jordan created Summerfest, a highly successful music festival in Milwaukee. Number 74 was one of the great defensive tackles.

> **BART STARR:** Henry got better as he aged. He never slowed up. He could simply defeat that center, guard, or both, who were trying to block him.

Ron Kostelnik, 53, out of the coal mining town of Colver, Pennsylvania, died on January 29, 1993, from a heart attack that resulted in him losing control of his car while driving on Interstate 75 in Kentucky. The big-framed Packer put on a show in the first Super Bowl, with three tackles and a half sack of quarterback Len Dawson.

> **PAT PEPPLER:** Ron didn't get the credit he deserved playing alongside those Hall of Famers, but Vince respected him as a solid performer who did his job well.

> **JERRY KRAMER:** It wasn't glamorous work. There aren't statistics for steady dependable guys who plug up the middle and allow other guys to excel. But that's what Ron did.
> We called him the "Culligan Man" because he was always around the water bucket. Ron was easygoing and well-respected by his teammates. He never got too emotional.

The fun-loving Max McGee became a member of the Packer Hall of Fame in 1975. He found success as a member of the team's radio network. He was also a force in the Mexican restaurant chain Chi-Chi's and was involved in ownership of steak houses in the Midwest. On October 20, 2007, McGee died after falling off the roof of his home in Deephaven, Minnesota, while clearing leaves. He was 75 years old.

> **PAUL HORNUNG:** I lost my best friend. He shouldn't have been up there. He knew better than that.

> **BUD LEA:** McGee was the most uncomplicated athlete I ever covered in my whole career as a sportswriter. Always approachable. . . . What he said is what he meant. He stands out as one guy that I will never forget. There'll never be another Max McGee; just one of the guys that stands out, out of all the guys I've covered.

Raymond Ernest "Ray" Nitschke had a 15-year career as a ferocious linebacker for Green Bay. A Hall of Famer and member of the NFL 50th Anniversary All-Time Team and NFL 75th Anniversary All-Time Team, Nitschke died of a heart attack at the age of 61 in Venice, Florida, in 1998.

BART STARR: Nitschke had the strength to throw a ball 100 yards at times and 80 yards like it was nothing.

JERRY KRAMER: Ray Nitschke was a shock. Ray made me flinch. Ray hit close to home. He was in my rookie class. He and I played in the College All-Star Game together. We were months apart in age. We played together for 11 years, all of my career. We were friends. I had grown to really like Raymond and respect him and think highly of him. There are a lot of similarities between Ray and me. We both matured and had grown a lot as we traveled down the road. That one struck a lot closer to me.

Elijah Pitts, who ran for two touchdowns in the '67 Super Bowl for Green Bay, died from abdominal cancer on July 10, 1998, in Buffalo, New York. Pitts, 60, distinguished himself during a quarter-century in the NFL, from his time with the Packers in the 1960s through his coaching career with the Buffalo Bills in the 1990s.

Since his football days, Hall of Famer Herb Adderley, Green Bay's first African American first-round draft pick, has hosted a television show in Green Bay and authored the book *Lombardi's Left Side*, with Dave Robinson.

Bill Curry went on to become an educator and speaker, as well as head football coach (2008–2012) at Georgia State University. He is also a past president of the National Football League Players Association.

Carroll Dale is assistant vice chancellor for Athletic Development at the University of Virginia's College at Wise. He was inducted in the Packer Hall of Fame and the College Football Hall of Fame.

Boyd Dowler served for many years as an assistant coach in the NFL, with the Rams, Redskins, Eagles, Bengals, and Buccaneers.

Marv Fleming became the first player in NFL history to play in five Super Bowls.

The great Forrest Gregg is battling Parkinson's disease.

Paul Hornung gained success off the field as a real estate investor and businessman. He stays close to his "Golden Boy" roots on weekends, continuing to work with much skill as a television football analyst and public speaker. Hornung still lives in Louisville, Kentucky.

Jerry Kramer may be the best player in NFL history still not in the Hall of Fame. An illustrious offensive lineman for the Packers for 11 years and best-selling author of *Instant Replay*, the articulate Kramer is still in demand by the media as a speaker and consultant on football matters.

After his NFL career, Bob Long went full-time with Pizza Hut, a growing business in Wisconsin. He bought the franchise rights for northern Wisconsin and opened restaurants in major communities. He also purchased the real estate for the restaurants. In the mid-1970s, Long sold his Pizza Hut franchises to PepsiCo.

Dave Robinson was named to the NFL's All-Pro team of the 1960s. With Herb Adderley, the Hall of Famer authored *Lombardi's Left Side*. Robinson is a highly sought after keynote speaker.

Fuzzy Thurston made headlines in 2011, when his Super Bowl ring was auctioned off for $50,788 to pay off debts incurred in a federal suit concerning back taxes for his restaurant business. The former offensive lineman also wrote a memoir, *What a Wonderful World*.

Bart Starr was head coach of the Packers from 1975 to 1983. The decorated Hall of Famer is an ambassador for his old team. He remains active in many charities, including his longtime favorite, the Rawhide Boys Ranch, located 45 miles west of Green Bay.

> **BART STARR: It's a boys' home. It was so rewarding to help Rawhide get its start. We raffled off my MVP Super Bowl Corvette. In three days we sold more than 40,000 $1 dollar tickets. That Corvette is still owned by someone in the area.**

Another of the dozen players from the Vince Lombardi era in the Pro Football Hall of Fame is Jim Taylor, who, into his 50s, still participated in full marathons and charity golf tourneys. A bruiser of a runner, he played a season with the Saints in 1967. Afterward he signed a long-term contract with the Saints to work in the front office and as a radio color analyst.

> **JIM TAYLOR: I still push the envelope. I'm still active and long to have a high quality of life and maintain some fitness level. After my NFL career ended I didn't have to take a job. I had some other investments and things where I could give back with my time. I've been to thousands of different charity functions all over this country.**

In 1973, Willie Wood became head coach of the Philadelphia Bell of the World Football League, making him the first African American head coach in professional football of the modern era. Wood was also a head coach in the Canadian Football League. He made less than $20,000 as a rookie for the Packers in 1960 and never made more than $98,000 in a year during a career that ended after the '71 season.

"If I had it to do all over again," Wood said, "I'd do it the same way. Of course, I'd like to make more money."

The former Packer star has dementia and other assorted ailments. Two knees and one hip have been replaced. Doctors have performed four major surgeries on his back and fused two vertebrae in his neck. In 2014, Wood was diagnosed with Alzheimer's disease. He lives in an assisted living facility in Washington, D.C.

Kansas City Chiefs who played in Super Bowl I still living include Bud Abel, Fred Arbanas, Pete Beathard, Bobby Bell, Denny Biodrowski, Ed Budde, Chris Burford,

Tommy Brooker, Bert Coat, Walt Corey, Len Dawson, Mike Garrett, Dave Hill, E. J. Holub, Bobby Hunt, Chuck Hurston, Mike Mercer, Curt Merz, Willie Mitchell, Frank Pitts, Bobby Ply, Otis Taylor, Al Reynolds, Andy Rice, Smokey Stover, Fletcher Smith, Emmitt Thomas, Ed Lothamer, Curtis McClinton, Johnny Robinson, and Fred Williamson.

KC players who have passed include Aaron Brown, Buck Buchanan, Reg Carolan, Tony DiMidio, Wayne Frazier, Sherrill Headrick, Jerry Mays, Gene Thomas, Jim Tyrer, and Jerrel Wilson,

At just 51 years of age, "Big Buck" Buchanan passed away in Kansas City on July 16, 1992, after a battle with lung cancer. Doctors discovered the cancer in 1990.

Five years later, reserve defensive end Aaron Brown, 54, was struck by a car on a northeast Houston street. Brown, wearing his Super Bowl rings, and his wife were on their way to a party when their van broke down. The former Chief died on November 15, 1997, in Houston, Texas.

Reg Carolan was only 43 years old when he died in January 1983. The six-foot, six-inch tight end for the Chiefs was known as "Stretch."

Tony DiMidio passed away in 2014. He was 71 years old. Called "Biggie" because of his size, DiMidio played two seasons for the Chiefs.

Number 66, William Wayne "Cotton" Frazier, the first player introduced at Super Bowl I and the Chiefs' center, passed away in Alabama at the age of 73 on March 11, 2012, from brain cancer.

Former KC linebacker Sherrill Headrick died at the age of 71 on September 10, 2008, after an extended battle with cancer.

Cancer also claimed the life of Jerry Mays in Lake Lewisville, Texas, on July 17, 1994. He was 54 years old. A standout defensive end for the Chiefs for a decade, Mays was named to the AFL All-Time Team by the Pro Football Hall of Fame.

> BILL MCNUTT III: I was an usher at Jerry Mays's funeral. Hank gave everyone a little secret that day: He said that "Huzza" was Jerry Mays's nickname. He said that "Huzza" is a Yiddish word for "joy," and that was what Hank Stram explained Jerry was saying when he said "Huzza." He meant joy! Because to play football and to practice football was utter joy to Jerry Mays; it was his greatest and highest calling in life. Jerry had his greatest joy and satisfaction when he played football. Hank said that his joy at practice was as great as his joy in a game. Huzza, Huzza, Huzza—he just said it all the time.

> DALE STRAM: Jerry Mays's nickname, as I understood it, was derived from "Hustle." Jerry would always say "Huzza" to his teammates to encourage them to work harder.

Running back Gene Thomas, who came to the Chiefs out of Florida A&M in 1966 and had three seasons in pro football, died on August 27, 1993, in Independence, Missouri, at the age of 50.

Jim Tyrer had a tragic ending. The former KC offensive left tackle and father of four, beset by business setbacks, killed his wife and then committed suicide by shooting himself on September 15, 1980, at the age of 41.

Jerrel "Thunderfoot" Wilson, out of Southern Mississippi, passed away from cancer in 2005, at the age of 63, in Bronson, Texas. He had become involved in the hunting and fishing industry after retirement. Hank Stram said of him, "Jerrel Wilson made other people aware of how important the kicking game was at a time when special times were not given special consideration. I'm prejudiced, but he's the best punter I ever saw."

DALE STRAM: A good number of players from that first Super Bowl still reside in and around the Kansas City area. Dad stayed in touch though all the years. He had a list and would call and check in with all his guys. He was always available to write a recommendation letter or send money if a player needed it. He lived by that legacy that we are all a family.

BOB MOORE: By 1965, at least 16 Chiefs players and their families had made Kansas City their permanent home: Jerry Mays, Len Dawson, Curtis McClinton, Jim Tyrer, Buck Buchanan, Bobby Bell, Al Reynolds, Fred Arbanas, Ed Lothamer, just to name a few. Even with the passing of some of these men, their family members have stayed on.

Fred Arbanas was a legislator in Missouri for several decades. He was enshrined in the Kansas City and Missouri halls of fame.

Hall of Famer Bobby Bell became owner of Bobby Bell BBQ in the Kansas City area. As he said, he was in the business "to take more time to enjoy life and educate kids, players, and corporations about the generation of black Americans who worked so hard in order to provide opportunities for future generations of black Americans." Today Bell is an ambassador for the NFL. He is proud of maintaining his playing weight by water skiing, swimming, and dancing.

Ed Budde is a retired executive for Coca-Cola and lives in Overland Park, Kansas, with his wife Carolyn. He is active in the NFL Alumni group and Chiefs Ambassadors.

Chris Burford is retired and lives in Reno, Nevada. Even before he stopped playing football, the multitalented athlete was a sportscaster for WDAF-TV, a practicing attorney, and a licensed pilot.

Tommy Brooker went back to Tuscaloosa and was the kicking coach for the University of Alabama for many years before getting into the insurance business there.

Hall of Famer Len Dawson was on *Inside the NFL*" on HBO for quite a few years, game analyst for NBC, sports director at KMBC-TV (Channel 9), and analyst for Chiefs radio broadcasts since 1985.

Mike Garrett is athletic director at Langston University in Oklahoma.

Dave Hill ran his own auction company in Alabama and now owns the largest Toyota dealership in Panama City, Florida.

Bobby Hunt and Chuck Hurston went to work for Haggar Slacks in Dallas.

Curt Merz had a talk radio show in Kansas City for many years, a pioneer in that field.

Frank Pitts lives in Baton Rouge, Louisiana, and was a coach at Southern University for many years. He retired as sergeant of arms for the state legislature in Louisiana.

Otis Taylor worked for Blue Cross Blue Shield after football. He suffers from Parkinson's disease related to head trauma and has been bedridden for a number of years.

Emmitt Thomas has been an assistant coach on defense in the NFL for many years, with stops at Philadelphia, Washington, Atlanta, and Kansas City. A member of the Pro Football Hall of Fame, he is highly respected throughout the NFL.

In the mid-1970s, Ed Lothamer created a successful concrete-pumping business. Today he is owner of Concrete Placement Company, a concrete-pumping firm with offices in North Carolina, Oklahoma, Missouri, Arkansas, and Kansas.

> **DALE STRAM: Curtis McClinton lives in KC and is an investment banker. When Muhammad Ali decided to not go to the service back in the 60s, he had a meeting with the black leaders in the United States to see what their thoughts were. McClinton was one of those guys, along with Jim Brown.**

A former deputy mayor for economic development in Washington, D.C., and a graduate of Harvard University's Kennedy School of Government, McClinton holds a master's degree from Central Michigan University and a doctorate from Miles College. The former Chief, who sometimes sang to his teammates, still sings classical music at different venues.

Johnny Robinson had success as a stockbroker and then bought a club in northern Kansas City, partnered with Jimmy Moran, one of the great chefs.

Memories of those long ago glory days are still fresh in the minds of those who played in the Los Angeles Coliseum that summer-like day.

> **BOB LONG: In June of 1967, the mailman knocked on the door of my home in Wichita, Kansas. I knew right away it was "THE RING." I was very excited.**

That first Super Bowl ring was as influenced by Vince Lombardi's design ideas as his teams were influenced by his coaching dictums. Together with his two captains, tackle Bob

Skoronski and defensive end Willie Davis, Lombardi worked with the jewelry firm Jostens to create the look of the ring, signifying and celebrating the Packers' Super Bowl I triumph.

The ring is 10-karat yellow gold, 23 pennyweight, with a full-karat diamond on top, inserted into a white gold hemispheric globe, with the words "First World Championship Game" encircling the diamond. On one side, a detail from the Lombardi family coat of arms is combined into a pattern with emblems of the AFL and NFL. The opposite side features the scores of the 1966 NFL Championship Game against Dallas and Super Bowl I, along with the NFL and AFL crests. On the other side of the ring are the words "Harmony, Courage, Valor"; an image of the Packer helmet; and the name of the player the ring was presented to. Strangely, the lettering says, "World Champions 1966 Green Bay Packers," even though the game was played in 1967.

Steve Wright, an offensive tackle who played for the Green Bay Packers from 1964 to 1967, auctioned off his Super Bowl I ring a few years ago. The winning bid was an astounding $73,409 for a ring that was valued at $850 in 1967. Wright's ring is believed to be the first from that original Super Bowl to have been sold. Wright's ring and Fred Thurston's ring are the only two known to have been sold.

In 1981, Jerry Kramer was on a flight to New York City. In the washroom of the airplane, the Packer legend removed his Super Bowl I ring to wash his hands. A few minutes after he had returned to his seat, he realized he had left his ring behind. Returning to the washroom, Kramer discovered the ring was no longer there.

As the story goes, the flight attendant and pilot made announcements asking for the return of the ring. There was no response. A passenger, claiming to be a psychic, informed Kramer that she saw the ring inside a pocketbook wrapped in tissue. She said the pocketbook was being held by a little old lady. Moving up and down the aisle, Kramer was unable to find a little old lady with a pocketbook.

> **JERRY KRAMER:** I waited for several years to get a ransom note, but nothing ever happened. I bought a replacement.

In 2006, almost a quarter-century after its disappearance, the original ring showed up in an online auction. It was assumed that Kramer had put the ring up for sale, attempting to sell off a piece of history, for which he was criticized. The auction company came to the rescue, returning the ring to Kramer after learning it had been stolen. The former Green Bay player then auctioned off the replacement ring and used the proceeds to create Gridiron Greats, a charity focused on helping former NFL players.

> **WILLIE DAVIS:** Yeah, I sure do wear the Super Bowl I ring, mostly. I typically wear just one ring at a time. Jerry Kramer right now wears it every time I see him.

> **DALE STRAM:** I have dad's Super Bowl I and Super Bowl IV rings. I never would wear them. It would be sacrilegious.

JIM TAYLOR: I still wear my Super Bowl ring. I think it's a distinction that we certainly reached our pinnacle in playing the game of football.

DAVE ROBINSON: I wear a Super Bowl I ring because I call it *the Super Bowl*. The one, the only first *Super Bowl*.

How can anything be as exciting to a fan as Green Bay versus Kansas City, two teams that had dominated their divisions but had never played each other and had fans that thought each team was better?

It was the *Super Bowl*. The one and only. You couldn't be neutral with that first game.

BART STARR: I wear the ring every day. Absolutely. It is the most special Super Bowl ring of all, it truly is. It is one that makes you feel proud to wear it.

BOYD DOWLER: When I wear one, I actually wear the one from the 1967 game because it's a little smaller and not quite so gaudy. I don't wear my Super Bowl rings all the time; however, if I have some appearance to make or some such thing, I wear that first Super Bowl ring most of the time.

KEN BOWMAN: I wear the ring from that first Super Bowl every day. It is a beautiful ring, really well put together. It is not as gaudy as others that came later. When I wear it I think of some of the people who aren't here anymore. A lot of good people.

Today the NFL pays for as many as 150 rings for the winning Super Bowl team, at $5,000 each, plus adjustments for extra gold or diamonds. The league also provides 150 pieces of jewelry to the losing Super Bowl team at a cost of as much as half the price of the winner's ring.

SMOKEY STOVER: We knew it was a very important part in history, here, the first time that this has happened, merger, and that big game. In my mind I felt it was a very good thing. I didn't realize what it would actually turn out to be years down the line.

FRED ARBANAS: I don't think I've seen a Super Bowl game that wasn't in Spanish. I'd be sitting in some place in Mexico, and I've told people, "I played in the first Super Bowl." They look at you like you're Methuselah or something!

But, you know, I have a lot of pride to have played in that first game. Yeah, I do.

SMOKEY STOVER: Oh, I don't tell people I was in that first Super Bowl. Other people more or less tell them. Over the years I have gone through a lot of wear and tear. I played at 235 to 240. I was 6'1". I've shrunk a little bit. I've lost quite a bit of weight since then. They can't believe that I played ball. They look at me, and, you know, they can't believe it that I played in that first Super Bowl.

BOYD DOWLER: It was something special. And it becomes more so as the years go by. You don't realize at the time, you're pretty much caught up in the present. Most of us were in our 20s or early 30s. And that's what you've done for your life, basically you've been a player. And all of a sudden we're playing in a very important game, one that was never played before. We thought it was kind of funny they called it the Super Bowl. Every year that goes by, that first one becomes a little bit more part of history.

"I've never gotten sick of the Super Bowl," said former *Miami Herald* sports writer Edwin Pope, adding, "I have met and palled around with some great writers, and it's been a big thing in my life. It never crossed anybody's mind about covering 35, or 40, 50.

"Football is truly the national pastime. I thought even at the first Super Bowl that it would become the greatest sports show on earth. And it has become that. You can see the grip that football had on the American public. Baseball has a sentimental grip. Football is truly the national pastime now. It's a fever."

World
Championship
Game
AFLvs.NFL

chiefs vs
packers

AMERICAN FOOTBALL LEAGUE
CHAMPION
KANSAS CITY CHIEFS
VERSUS

NATIONAL FOOTBALL LEAGUE
CHAMPION
GREEN BAY PACKERS

SUNDAY, JANUARY 15, 1967
LOS ANGELES MEMORIAL COLISEUM
LOS ANGELES, CALIFORNIA

Title page of the official program, with the final score noted.
Courtesy of the NFL

Chapter
SEVEN

More Than Just
a Game

The Super Bowl is Americana at its most kitsch and fun.

—Sting

If it's the ultimate game, how come they play it again next year?

—Duane Thomas

MICHAEL MACCAMBRIDGE: The first Super Bowl announced the presence of this monolithic single-day sports event that was also going to raise the interest in the playoffs in both leagues. Every play-off game was a single-elimination contest leading into the ultimate Super Bowl.

That one-game, winner-take-all Super Bowl, that scarcity, is another thing that was, and is, and will continue to be the strength of television's focus and audience.

And all the time to market, to advertise, to build toward the Super Bowl is another element that sets the game apart from any other sports event.

What Rozelle was trying to do was create something very much like the Super Bowl is today. It has become America at its best and also America at its worst. It is America at its most: American culture, American fandom, American power, American marketing, all turned up at the same time for the same event.

All of that is the greatest strength and the greatest weakness of the Super Bowl. It is so much fun and glitz; however, it is also the game. Once the game is being played there is still the sense that the game is the thing.

Pete Rozelle would have liked a lot of what the game has become today because he helped bring it all about.

PLAYED IN the dead of winter in the United States in various time zones, the "Super Bowl," played on "Super Sunday," has become a de facto American holiday, right up there with Christmas, New Year's Eve, Thanksgiving, and the Fourth of July.

Of the top 10 most watched American television programs of all time, nine have been Super Bowls. The game has been broadcast live to almost 200 nations in more than 25 different languages. Many countries send television crews to the venue where the Super Bowl is being staged. Nations like Brazil, China, Denmark, France, Germany, Hungary, Japan, Mexico, Russia, and the United Kingdom have opted to do so for a more personal take on the big game.

With an audience that numbered about one-third of the population of the United States—an estimated viewership of 111.5 million—Super Bowl XLVIII, held at the Meadowlands in New Jersey, was the most watched U.S. telecast in history. And nearly 40 million conversations about the game took place on social media in real time. The Super Bowl produces more tweets than any other sporting event.

Super Bowl Sunday is the most important single-day event in the advertising industry. At the first Super Bowl in 1967, 30-second commercials cost about $40,000. In

2014, 43 advertisers purchased commercial time. A 30-second ad was sold for approximately $4 million. Many tune into the game simply to watch the inventive and alluring commercials, elaborate pregame and halftime entertainment, and stars on parade.

From the simpler entertainment featured at the first championship game in 1967, a cavalcade of "A list" personalities have lined up to perform during Super Bowls throughout the decades. Top-echelon entertainers are eager to become part of the extravaganza, because, as Paul McCartney observed, "There's nothing bigger than being asked to perform at the Super Bowl."

A sampling of past Super Bowl headliners includes Christina Aguilera, the Backstreet Boys, Beyoncé, Garth Brooks, James Brown, Cher, Carol Channing, the Dixie Chicks, Neil Diamond, Gloria Estefan, Faith Hill, Al Hirt, Whitney Houston, Michael Jackson, Billy Joel, Patti LaBelle, Madonna, Barry Manilow, Aaron Neville, the New Kids on the Block, *NSYNC, Prince, Diana Ross, Bruce Springsteen, the Rolling Stones, Shania Twain, U2, the Who, and Stevie Wonder.

The Super Bowl is big-time boom time for businesses. Several million large-screen televisions are purchased in the weeks leading up to the game. Super Bowl Sunday attracts the most NFL football betting action. All manner and type of "official" Super Bowl products are marketed.

Closed-door secret balloting by NFL owners and a supermajority of 75 percent has been the manner in which cities have been awarded the right to host a Super Bowl. Part of the requirement for a city to compete for the privilege of hosting the big game is that it provide a new environment for the contest.

Spirited and sometimes ruthless and cutthroat competition among municipalities for the right to accommodate the Super Bowl highlight the selection process. Massive financial rewards come to the host city. Millions of dollars are spent by visitors. Municipalities gain large amounts of publicity. Host cities partner with the NFL. Advertising and talent agencies, merchandisers, security personnel, and celebrity party planners prepare years in advance for the game of games. Myriad details need attention and fine-tuning. Decisions must be made to promote success and block out failures. No host city's team has ever won the Super Bowl.

The face value for a ticket to attend that first game in 1967 was between $6 and $12. The face value for Super Bowl tickets in 2014 ranged from between $500 and $2,600. According to *Forbes*, in 2014, the 32 NFL franchises were worth an average of $1.2 billion each. Pro football, overseen by the NFL, is a $9.5 billion industry, according to ESPN.

The Super Bowl economy provides added revenue to those who make it down that road of gold. Teams must pay their players within 15 days of the game. The winner's shares for the 2014 Super Bowl were $92,000 each. Losers were entitled to $46,000. Both are vastly different sums from the first Super Bowl payout of $15,000 and the winners of the first 11 Super Bowls. Taking into consideration that the playoffs last only four games at most, salary-wise "it's like having another season," noted Carl Francis, NFLPA director of communications.

Eating dominates the day. According to the USDA, only Thanksgiving Day surpasses Super Bowl Sunday as the highest calorie consumption day in the United States. On average, 79 million pounds of avocados, or 158 million, and 14,500 tons of chips are consumed. Approximately 50 million cases of beer are enjoyed. Frito-Lay, the nation's largest producer of potato and tortilla chips, increases its production by 10 million pounds for the event. Domino's Pizza delivers more pies on Super Sunday than any other day of the year. Restaurant sales plunge. Millions hunker down to drink, eat, socialize, and watch the game. And interestingly enough, after the game and Super Sunday pass into history, the following Monday features one of the highest workplace absentee rates of the year.

The Super Bowl has evolved into the grandest, grossest, gaudiest annual one-day spectacle in the annals of American sports and culture—incredibly spun off the game that was played on January 15, 1967, at Los Angeles Memorial Coliseum—a game that, for a time, lacked a name, a venue, and an identity, and a game that didn't even sell out.

Creating this book was like being cast back in a time machine to simpler times, a simpler game, a cast of characters who seem almost mythic, who laid the foundation for what the game is today.

The Super Bowl has been described by Professor Daniel T. Durbin of the University of Southern California's Annenberg School for Communications and Journalism as "One of the most profoundly effective media and public relations events that has ever been built in the United States."

"For every player who plays the game," said Carl Francis of the NFLPA, "it's the ultimate."

Mark Waller, chief marketing officer of the NFL, said, "Football is America's last great campfire. Imagine you were above the United States on a Sunday, you'd see these incredible glows of stadiums."

And the glow of the Super Bowl—much more than a game—outshines them all.

Super Bowl I Stats and Factoids

STATS

Table A.1. Team Rosters

STARTERS

Kansas City Chiefs   **Green Bay Packers**

OFFENSE

Frazier, Wayne	C		Curry, Bill	C
Budde, Ed	G		Kramer, Jerry	G
Merz, Curt	G		Thurston, Fuzzy	G
Hill, Dave H.	T		Gregg, Forrest	T
Tyrer, Jim	T		Skoronski, Bob	T
Arbanas, Fred	TE		Fleming, Marv	TE

Burford, Chris	WR		Dale, Carroll	WR
Taylor, Otis	WR		Dowler, Boyd	WR
Garrett, Mike L.	RB		Pitts, Elijah	RB
McClinton, Curtis	RB		Taylor, Jim	RB
Dawson, Len	QB		Starr, Bart	QB

DEFENSE

Buchanan, Buck	DT		Jordan, Henry	DT
Rice, Andy	DT		Kostelnik, Ron	DT
Hurston, Chuck	DE		Aldridge, Lionel	DE
Mays, Jerry	DE		Davis, Willie	DE
Bell, Bobby, Sr.	OLB		Caffey, Lee Roy	OLB
Holub, E. J.	OLB		Robinson, Dave	OLB
Headrick, Sherrill	MLB		Nitschke, Ray	MLB
Mitchell, Willie	CB		Adderley, Herb	CB
Williamson, Fred	CB		Jeter, Bob	CB
Robinson, Johnny	FS		Wood, Willie	FS
Hunt, Bobby	SS		Brown, Thomas W.	SS

SUBSTITUTES

Abell, Harry	Anderson, Donny
Beathard, Pete	Anderson, Bill
Biodrowski, Dennis	Bowman, Ken
Brown, Aaron L.	Bratkowski, Zeke
Carolan, Reggie	Brown, Robert Ed
Coan, Bert	Chandler, Don
Corey, Walter	Crutcher, Tommy
DiMidio, Tony	Gillingham, Gale
Gilliam, Jon	Grabowski, Jim
Mercer, Mike	Hart, Doug
Pitts, Frank	Hathcock, David
Ply, Bobby	Long, Bob A.
Reynolds, Al	Mack, Red
Smith, Fletcher	McGee, Max
Stover, Smokey	Vandersea, Phillip
Thomas, Emmitt	Weatherwax, James
Thomas, Eugene	Wright, Stephen
Wilson, Jerrel	

DID NOT PLAY

Hornung, Paul

Table A.2. Box Score

Quarter	Time	Team	Drive LENGTH	Scoring Information PLAYS	TIME	Score	KC	GB
1	6:04	GB	80	6	3:06	TD: Max McGee 37-yard pass from Bart Starr (Don Chandler kick)	0	7
2	10:40	KC	66	6	3:44	TD: Curtis McClinton seven-yard pass from Len Dawson (Mike Mercer kick)	7	7
2	4:37	GB	73	13	6:03	TD: Jim Taylor 14-yard run (Don Chandler kick)	7	14
2	0:54	KC	50	7	3:43	FG: Mike Mercer 31 yards	10	14
3	12:33	GB	5	1	0:09	TD: Elijah Pitts five-yard run (Don Chandler kick)	10	21
3	0:51	GB	56	10	5:25	TD: Max McGee 12-yard pass from Bart Starr (Don Chandler kick)	10	28
4	6:35	GB	80	8	4:13	TD: Elijah Pitts one-yard run (Don Chandler kick)	10	35

Table A.3. Final Statistics

	Green Bay Packers	Kansas City Chiefs
First downs	21	17
First downs rushing	10	4
First downs passing	11	12
First downs penalty	0	1
Third-down efficiency	11/15	3/13
Fourth-down efficiency	0/0	0/0
Net yards rushing	133	72
Rushing attempts	34	19
Yards per rush	3.9	3.8
Passing	16/24	17/32
Sacks/yards lost	3–22	6–61
Interceptions thrown	1	1
Net yards passing	228	167
Total net yards	361	239
Punt returns	4–23	3–19
Kickoff returns	3–65	6–130
Interceptions	1–50	1–0
Punts (average yards)	4–43.3	7–45.3
Fumbles-lost	1–0	1–0
Penalties (yards)	4–40	4–26
Time of possession	31:25	28:35
Turnovers	1	1

FACTOIDS

Coaches

KANSAS CITY

HEAD COACH: Hank Stram

OFFENSE: Pete Brewster (ends), Bill Walsh (offensive line), Chuck Mills (running backs)

DEFENSE: Tom Pratt (defensive line), Tom Bettis (defensive backs)

GREEN BAY

HEAD COACH: Vince Lombardi

OFFENSE: Bob Schnelker (ends), Ray Wietecha (offensive line), Red Cochran (backs)

DEFENSE: Phil Bengston (head defense), Dave Hanner (defensive line), Jerry Burns (defensive backs)

Officials

REFEREE: Norm Schachter (NFL)

UMPIRE: George Young (AFL)

HEAD LINESMAN: Bernie Ulman (NFL)

LINE JUDGE: Al Sabato (AFL)

FIELD JUDGE: Mike Lisetski (NFL)

BACK JUDGE: Jack Reader (AFL)

Hall of Famers from the 1967 AFL–NFL World Championship Game

PACKERS

Vince Lombardi (coach), Herb Adderley, Willie Davis, Forrest Gregg, Paul Hornung, Henry Jordan, Ray Nitschke, Dave Robinson, Bart Starr, Jim Taylor, Willie Wood

CHIEFS

Hank Stram (coach), Bobby Bell, Buck Buchanan, Len Dawson, Emmitt Thomas

Green Bay Packers linebacker Ray Nitschke.
Photofest

Green Bay Packers linebacker Dave Robinson.
Photofest

ROMAN NUMERALS

The first two championship games were known as the AFL–NFL World Championship Game. Staring with the third game, Roman numerals were put in place at the suggestion of Lamar Hunt, according to Robert B. Moore, official historian of the Kansas City Chiefs. It was said that the Roman numbers gave grandeur to the event. It was also said that it was for convenience since a football season spans two calendar years. Hunt also inspired the name "Super Bowl" and was instrumental in getting the championship trophy renamed the Lombardi Trophy.

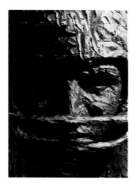

Bibliography

Angell, Roger. "The Sporting Scene." *New Yorker*, February 11, 1974, XLIX, pp. 51, 60.

Baker, L. H. *Football Facts and Figures*. New York: Farrar and Rinehart, 1945.

Carroll, Bob, Michael Gershman, David Neft, and John Thorn, eds. *Total Football*. New York: HarperCollins, 1997.

Claassen, Harold. *The History of Professional Football*. Englewood Cliffs, NJ: Prentice Hall, 1963.

Connor, Dick. *Kansas City Chiefs (Great Teams' Great Years)*. New York: Macmillan, 1974.

Daly, Dan, and Bob O'Donnell. *The Pro Football Chronicle*. New York: Macmillan, 1990.

Devaney, John. *Super Bowl*. New York: Random House, 1971.

Didinger, Ray. *The Super Bowl: Celebrating a Quarter-Century of America's Greatest Game*. New York: Simon & Schuster, 1990.

Ellenport, Crain, and Ken Leiker, eds. *The Super Bowl: An Official Retrospective*. New York: Ballantine, 2005.

Fortunato, John A. *Commissioner: The Legacy of Pete Rozelle*. Boulder, CO: Taylor, 2006.

Frommer, Harvey. *A Description of How Professional Football Employed the Medium of Television to Increase the Sport's Economic Growth and Cultural Impact*. Ph.D. dissertation, New York University, 1974.

Horrigan, Jack, and Mike Rathet. *The Other League*. Chicago: Follett, 1970.

Izenberg, Jerry. *The Rivals*. New York: Holt, Rinehart and Winston, 1968.

Johnson, William O., Jr. *Super Spectator and the Electric Lilliputians*. Boston: Little, Brown and Company, 1971.

Kramer, Jerry. *Instant Replay*. New York: New American Library, 1968.

Lombardi, Vince. *Run to Daylight*. Englewood Cliffs, NJ: Prentice Hall, 1963.

MacCambridge, Michael. *America's Game*. New York: Random House, 2004.

Maraniss, David. *When Pride Still Mattered*. New York: Simon & Schuster, 1999.

Maule, Tex. *The Game*. New York: Random House, 1964.

McGinn, Bob. *The Ultimate Super Bowl Book*. Minneapolis, MN: MVP Books, 2009.

Miller, Jeff. *Going Long: The Wild Ten-Year Saga of the Renegade American Football League in the Words of Those Who Lived It*. Chicago: Contemporary Books, 2003.

National Football League: *The First 50 Years: The Story of the National Football League, 1920– 1969*. New York: Simon & Schuster, 1969.

———. *The NFL's Official Encyclopedic History of Professional Football*. New York: Macmillan, 1973.

———. *The Official NFL 1992 Record and Fact Book*. New York: National Football League, 1992.

———. *The Official NFL Encyclopedia of Professional Football*. New York: New American Library, 1977, 1982.

Olderman, Murray. *Just Win, Baby: The Al Davis Story*. Chicago: Triumph, 2012.

Povletich, William. *Green Bay Packers: Trials, Triumphs, and Tradition*. Madison: Wisconsin Historical Society Press, 2012.

Pro Football Hall of Fame, http://www.profootballhof.com.

Rand, Jonathan. *The Year That Changed the Game*. Washington, DC: Potomac Books, 2008.

Rappaport, Ken. *The Little League That Could*. Boulder, CO: Taylor, 2010.

Ribowsky, Mark. *The Last Cowboy*. New York: Liveright, 2014.

Riger, Robert. *The Pros: A Documentary of Professional Football in America*. New York: Simon & Schuster, 1960.

Sandomir, Richard. "Rozelle's NFL Legacy: Television, Marketing, and Money." *New York Times*, December 8, 1996. Available online at http://www.nytimes.com/1996/12/08/sports/rozelle -s-nfl-legacy-television-marketing-and-money.html (accessed February 20, 2015).

Schachter, Norm. *Close Calls: The Confessions of a NFL Referee*. New York: Morrow, 1981.

Smith, Robert. *The Illustrated History of Pro Football*. New York: Madison Square Press, 1972.

St. John, Allen. *The Billion Dollar Game*. New York: Doubleday, 2009.

Starr, Bart, with Murray Olderman. *My Life in Football*. New York: Morrow, 1987.

Wallace, Bill. *Nelson's Encyclopedia of Pro Football*. New York: Thomas Nelson and Sons, 1964.

Weiss, Don. *The Making of the Super Bowl*. New York: Contemporary Books, 2003.

Books by Harvey Frommer

HARDBACK

When It Was Just a Game, Taylor, 2015.

It Happened in Miami, (with Myrna Katz Frommer), Taylor, 2015.

Remembering Fenway Park, STC/Abrams, 2011.

Remembering Yankee Stadium, STC/Abrams, 2008.

Five O'Clock Lightning, Wiley, 2007.

Where Have All Our Red Sox Gone? Taylor, 2006.

Sports Junkies' Book of Trivia, Terms, and Lingo, Taylor, 2006.

Red Sox vs. Yankees: The Great Rivalry, Sports Publishing, 2004, 2005.

A Yankee Century, Putnam/Berkley, 2002.

It Happened in Manhattan (with Myrna Katz Frommer), Putnam/Berkley, 2001.

Growing up Baseball (with Frederic J. Frommer), Taylor, 2001.

It Happened on Broadway (with Myrna Katz Frommer), Harcourt Brace, 1998.

The New York Yankee Encyclopedia, Macmillan, 1997.

Growing Up Jewish in America (with Myrna Katz Frommer), Harcourt Brace, 1995.

Big Apple Baseball, Taylor, 1995.

It Happened in Brooklyn (with Myrna Katz Frommer), Harcourt Brace, 1993.

Shoeless Joe and Ragtime Baseball, Taylor, 1992.

It Happened in the Catskills (with Myrna Katz Frommer), Harcourt Brace, 1991.

Holzman on Hoops (with Red Holzman), Taylor, 1991.

Behind the Lines: The Autobiography of Don Strock, Pharos, 1991.

Running Tough: The Autobiography of Tony Dorsett, Doubleday, 1989.

Growing Up at Bat: 50th Anniversary Book of Little League Baseball, Pharos, 1989.

Red on Red: The Autobiography of Red Holzman (with Red Holzman), Bantam, 1988.

Throwing Heat: The Autobiography of Nolan Ryan, Doubleday, 1988.

Primitive Baseball, Atheneum, 1988.

150th Anniversary Album of Baseball, Franklin Watts, 1988.

Olympic Controversies, Franklin Watts, 1985.

Baseball's Greatest Managers, Franklin Watts, 1985.

National Baseball Hall of Fame, Franklin Watts, 1985.

Games of the XXIIIrd Olympiad, International Sport Publications, 1984.

Jackie Robinson, Franklin Watts, 1984.

Baseball's Greatest Records, Streaks, and Feats, Atheneum, 1982.

Baseball's Greatest Rivalry, Atheneum, 1982.

Rickey and Robinson, Macmillan, 1982.

Basketball My Way: Nancy Lieberman (with Myrna Katz Frommer), Scribner's, 1982.

New York City Baseball, Macmillan, 1980.

The Great American Soccer Book, Atheneum, 1980.

Sports Roots, Atheneum, 1980.

Sports Lingo, Atheneum, 1979.

The Martial Arts: Judo and Karate, Atheneum, 1978.

A Sailing Primer (with Ron Weinmann), Atheneum, 1978.

A Baseball Century, Macmillan, 1976.

PAPERBACK

Shoeless Joe and Ragtime Baseball, Taylor, 2015.

Old Time Baseball, Taylor, 2015.

Five O'Clock Lightning, Taylor, 2015.

Rickey and Robinson, Taylor, 2015.

It Happened on Broadway, Taylor, 2014

Red Sox vs. Yankees: The Great Rivalry (with Frederic J. Frommer), Taylor, 2013.

Manhattan at Mid-Century (with Myrna Katz Frommer), Taylor, 2013.

New York City Baseball: The Golden Age, 1947–1957, Taylor, 2013.

It Happened in the Catskills (with Myrna Katz Frommer), SUNY Press, 2009.

It Happened in Brooklyn (with Myrna Katz Frommer), SUNY Press, 2009.

Shoeless Joe and Ragtime Baseball, Taylor, 1992; University of Nebraska Press, 2008.

Yankee Century and Beyond, Sourcebooks, 2007.

Red Sox vs. Yankees: The Great Rivalry, Sports Publishing, 2005.

A Yankee Century, Berkley, 2003.

Rickey and Robinson, Taylor, 2003.

Growing Up Jewish in America (with Myrna Katz Frommer), University of Nebraska Press, 1999.

It Happened in the Catskills (with Myrna Katz Frommer), Harcourt Brace, 1996.

It Happened in Brooklyn (with Myrna Katz Frommer), Harcourt Brace, 1995.

Shoeless Joe and Ragtime Baseball, Taylor, 1993.

New York City Baseball, Harcourt Brace, 1992.

Running Tough: The Autobiography of Tony Dorsett, Berkley, 1992.

Throwing Heat: The Autobiography of Nolan Ryan, Avon, 1989.

New York City Baseball, Atheneum, 1985.

Red on Red: The Autobiography of Red Holzman, Bantam, 1988.

Baseball's Greatest Rivalry, Atheneum, 1984.

Basketball My Way: Nancy Lieberman (with Myrna Katz Frommer), Scribner's, 1984.

Sports Lingo, Atheneum, 1983.

Sports Genes (with Myrna Katz Frommer), Ace, 1982.

The Sports Date Book (with Myrna Katz Frommer), Ace, 1981.

Acknowledgments

INTERVIEWING FOR, researching, and writing this book has proved to be one of the most gratifying experiences for me in a long publishing career, a merging of past and present. It all began long ago, when I was an undergraduate majoring in journalism at New York University. I was fortunate to get a job working as a sports assistant for United Press International. There I had the good fortune of being supervised by a man who became the first of my three mentors: Milt Richman, a man whose name is enshrined in the Writer's Wing of the Baseball Hall of Fame. To me, Milt was "the man."

I was a wannabe sportswriter/author. Night after night during my 5:00 p.m. to 2:00 a.m. shifts at UPI in the Daily News Building on 42nd Street in Manhattan, I would bang away on a sturdy IBM typewriter, hoping my story would magically end up on the teletype machine. Milt would stand behind me, watching as the words appeared on yellow paper, checking out my copy, pressing me to increase my pace and turn out more concise, carefully composed stories.

I stumbled a lot, but we both pressed on—the tyro and the tutor. A kind and brilliant coach, Milt was a sportswriter at the top of his game. From him I learned the art and craft of sports journalism, which has remained part of me all these years.

Years later, I was on the tenure track as a professor at the City University of New York when I enrolled in a Ph.D. program at New York University chaired by Neil Postman, famed communications guru and the second mentor of my life. Founder of a new academic field, media ecology, Neil swiftly became a confidante and role model whose engaging teaching style would greatly influence both my teaching and writing. It was, however, in his role as first reader of my thesis that he played the biggest part, convincing me to change my topic from the media's influence on Major League Baseball to its impact on professional football.

The result was *A Description of How Professional Football Employed the Medium of Television to Increase the Sport's Economic Growth and Cultural Impact*. It was labeled a "groundbreaking thesis" and would be the spark that would light the way for *When It Was Just a Game*.

After the publication of my thesis, I mailed copies to a wide array of publishers, hoping someone would offer me the contract to turn it into a book. There were no takers. But ironically, on the basis of my thesis, I received an offer from the media relations director for the National League to write what would become my first book: *A Baseball Century*.

Irv Kaze, a gentle and honest man who knew his way around the world of sports, would become my third mentor. He had a Super Bowl ring from his time with Al Davis and the Oakland Raiders. He sported a World Series ring earned while working for the George Steinbrenner Yankees. Through his contacts, I was introduced to a network of people in the world of professional sports who, in turn, smoothed my path as a sports author and historian.

Although my three mentors have passed on, their impact remains. It is felt each time I write a sports book or article. And I felt it throughout the process of researching, interviewing for, and writing this book. I will always be in their debt.

There are many others deserving of a "thank you" for helping to make this work possible, beginning with the 62 unique oral history "voices" who so generously gave of their time and memories to share stories and perceptions about the AFL–NFL World Championship Game of January 15, 1967, and football.

Represented in these pages are the Chiefs and Packers who I was able to reach. Relatives, media personnel, coaches, fans, and other witnesses also have their say. Their recollections, perceptions, and explanations bring back the vivid details of the time and place, and provide the action for *When It Was Just a Game*.

My son, Fred Frommer, is here, as he always is, for me. A sports author in his own right and prime-time journalist with a political focus, he was of great help in fact-checking and providing insightful commentary.

Two of my former (and outstanding) graduate students at Dartmouth College, Brian Mann, as editorial assistant for football language and terminology, and Jonathan Savage, as editorial assistant in transcribing interviews and organizing content, gave invaluable and significant assistance. Their intelligence and sensitivity helped a great deal.

At the top of the list at Taylor Trade is its director and the man in charge of Editorial Acquisitions: Rick Rinehart. A gentleman of great taste, he generously tolerated my "three e-mails a day" and has become a friend to the writing Frommers.

A sincere "thank you" goes to the rest of the "Book Team" at Taylor: Kalen Landow, Karie Simpson, Laura Reiter, Nicole McCullough, and Sharon Kunz.

Dale Stram, son of the late, great Kansas City coach Hank Stram, is a primary voice in this book, a supplier of many leads and contacts, reader of the manuscript, and multi-faceted "coach." In addition, Dale provided photos, as well as the invaluable unpublished manuscript of Hank Stram, who is also a "voice" in this book.

Official team historians without equal, Robert B. Moore of the Green Bay Packers and Chris Christl of the Kansas City Chiefs are not only "voices" in this tome, but also proved to be of great help in providing information and fact clarification.

Frank Gifford, one of the oral history voices, opens the book with his compelling and insightful introduction. A great football hero as both player and announcer, he was in the booth and on the field that January day in 1967.

Murray Olderman, who provided the fabulous artwork that graces the end pages of this book and is a fund of football backstory knowledge, was a wonderful asset.

Others who were of great assistance include Jessica Bedore of the Packers and the staff at Dartmouth's Baker-Berry Library and the Pro Football Hall of Fame.

A note of special thanks goes to the NFL's Joe Browne. I interviewed Joe many years ago for my Ph.D. dissertation and returned to him again for this book. His unique oral history voice enhances this volume.

Finally, my thanks go to each member of the team on the bench: Jennifer and Jeff, Fred and Michele, Ian and Laura, Arielle, Gabriel, Alexander, Sammy and Rafi, Ethan, Caroline Katz, and Marshall Mount.

My biggest debt is due my wife, partner, friend, coauthor, and constant spur throughout the years—Myrna Katz Frommer. Without her, none of this would have happened.

Special notes: The entries in oral history format from Hank Stram came from unpublished writing supplied by his son, Dale Stram. The "voices" of Howard Cosell, Curt Gowdy, Marty Glickman, William O. Johnson, Milt Richman, Pete Rozelle, and Paul Zimmerman are from my PhD thesis.

Index

About the Author

HARVEY FROMMER, dubbed "Dartmouth's own Mr. Baseball" by the *Dartmouth Alumni Magazine,* received his PhD from New York University. Professor emeritus, City University of New York, distinguished professor nominee, and recipient of the "Salute to Scholars Award" at CUNY, he was cited in the *Congressional Record* and by the New York State Legislature as a sports historian and journalist. Frommer's many sports books include autobiographies of sports legends Nolan Ryan, Red Holzman, and Tony Dorsett. His acclaimed oral and narrative histories *Remembering Yankee Stadium* and best seller *Remembering Fenway Park* broke new ground as examples of the genre.

When It Was Just a Game: Remembering the First Super Bowl was nominated for the Pen award in 2015 in the category of literary sports writing.

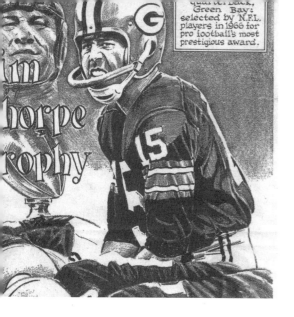

quarterback, Green Bay: selected by N.F.L. players in 1966 for pro football's most prestigious award.

31901056616347